World War II— Hometown and Home Front Heroes

World War II— Hometown and Home Front Heroes

Life-Experience Stories From the Carolinas' Piedmont

Edited by
Margaret G. Bigger

ABB   A. Borough Books

ISBN 1-893597-06-7

Library of Congress Control Number: 2003105701

Printed in the United States of America

COVER PHOTO: An AT-21 Gunner, built for the Army Air Corps at Fairchild Aircraft in Alamance County, North Carolina, on a test flight. 1943. Courtesy of Don Bolden, author of *Alamance: A County at War.*

ABB

A. Borough Books

Charlotte NC

Foreword

The rolling red clay hills of the Carolina Piedmont were half a world away from the battlefields of Europe and Japan, but World War II nonetheless changed our region forever.

The once-isolated South suddenly found itself engaged with the wider world. Carolinians went overseas, experiencing life beyond their own farms and mill villages, while young soldiers from elsewhere trained in the South. The Army constructed 60 of its 100 new training bases in Dixie, among them Camp Sutton at Monroe, NC, and what became Donaldson Air Force Base in Greenville, SC. Near some military bases, such as Columbia's Fort Jackson, local people still talk about seeing German prisoners-of-war laboring in the cotton fields.

Military installations represented just one way that Federal dollars rebuilt the region in the 1940s. Nearly every Southern city got a new airport, thanks to Uncle Sam. Defense contracts boosted local industry. Military work catapulted J.A. Jones, Inc., into the front ranks of US construction companies.

African-Americans began gathering the fierce resolve that would burst forth in the Civil Rights Movement. To even participate in the war required great persistence, because Southern military recruiters often refused to sign up black people. Once in, African Americans proved themselves as fighters and leaders—including in the renowned all-black Tuskegee Airmen. People who made such sacrifices would return home ready and willing to challenge Southern racial restrictions.

On the home front, much of the war burden fell on the shoulders of women. Mothers, sisters and sweethearts watched the mailbox for news of their young servicemen. To get salt, sugar, gasoline and other necessities, families had to make sense of a new system of rationing stamps. Women moved into jobs outside the home. The two Carolinas had long led the US in women in the work force, because textile labor was considered "fitting" for females. But now the war effort required that women go into all types of industries and office work.

The impact of World War II did not end with the joyous celebrations of V-J Day in 1945. We will never know how much the Carolinas lost in the soldiers who never returned, how much the Carolinas gained in the minds that opened to new opportunities. During the war years, Southern rural population dropped 20% while cities gained 30%. Sometime in the late 1940s, the South passed one of the major milestones in the history of civilization; the US census at the end of the decade showed that the majority of Southerners now lived in "urban places." That is the South we inhabit today.

Dr. Tom Hanchett, Historian
Levine Museum of the New South

Preface & Acknowledgements

Since 1992, the Special Collections Unit of the J. Murrey Atkins Library, University of North Carolina at Charlotte, and the Museum of the New South (now the Levine Museum of the New South) have collaborated with A. Borough Books to collect and record true stories from local people about historic events.

After our first trade paperback, *World War II: It Changed Us Forever* (1994) was published, we became aware that only five of the 33 authors originated from the Piedmont. Following the success of *The Great Depression—How We Coped, Worked and Played* (2001) concentrating on the Piedmont of the two Carolinas, we are returning to our first topic with more emphasis on the Piedmont of both Carolinas. As there are various definitions of "piedmont," we generally sought people from the central area of each state who left to serve their country, stayed there to do something significant for the war effort or trained in a local military facility to tell their stories for *World War II—Hometown and Home Front Heroes.*

Please note that the county listed beneath each author's name refers to the criteria just mentioned and is not necessarily the place where that person now resides.

In addition to all the authors and those who contributed to our compilations, we are especially grateful to Dr. Robin Brabham and Pat Ryckman of the University of North Carolina at Charlotte and to Dr. Tom Hanchett, Historian, Emily F. Zimmern, Executive Director, and the Board of Directors of the Levine Museum of the New South, without whom this book could not have been written.

And a hearty "thank you" to those who assisted us to gather facts and photos: Bet Ancrum, Don Bolden, author of *Alamance: A County at War;* Rev. Jacob D. DeShazer; Sis Dillon, Union County Heritage Room; Les Duggins, *Spartanburg Herald-Journal*; Bobby F. Edmonds, author of *McCormick County, Land of Cotton*; Hugh Harkey; Steve Haas; Dick Jensen, author of *Pearl Survivors*; Winston and Pelham Lyles, Fairfield County Historical Museum; John Mc-Farland; John Sherrer, Historic Columbia Foundation, as well as librarians from Piedmont public libraries: Rosemary Lands and Jane Johnson, Charlotte-Mecklenburg; Amy Rupard, High Point; Jake Lehrer, Carrboro (NC); Sarah Benson, Richland County; Susan H. Thoms, Spartanburg County, and Suzanne Case, Greenville County (SC)

Others helped us find the people with the best stories: Joe Barkley, Kathy Bridges, Dennis Carrigan, Agnes Corbett, Gordon Dillon, Ernest Dollar, Mardi Durham, Terry A. Edwards, Marie Harmon, Dusty Hoffman, Jane Hough, Leonard Hunter, Ola Jean Kelly, Betty Knox, Bob Lammey, John McFarland, Boyd McLean, Vicki Harris Proctor, Gen. C.W. Randall, Helen Snow, Tucker Taylor, Tony Teachey, Anita Weisner and Patty Wheeler.

We are grateful to many more, who gave us insights and tips.

Contents

Authors
Where to Find Their Stories and Comments

Authors
Where to Find Their Stories and Comments

Contributors
Where to Find Their Comments and Contributions

Introduction

"I'm no hero. The heroes didn't come home!" Ralph S. Ross, who made this statement, continued, "I was one of the lucky ones. I was wounded on Okinawa."

Ralph put into words the sentiments of many of the men and women who served in the Armed Services during World War II. People who remained on the home front have rejected even more strongly the notion that they might be considered heroes.

But history shows that the combined efforts of Americans and our Allies, whether on the battlefield, in ships, submarines or planes or behind the scenes in ordnance or at training bases overseas—strongly supported by the folks back home—kept our country from becoming a part of the Third Reich or the Japanese Empire. The unspeakable horrors that citizens of conquered countries experienced could have occurred in the United States, and thus, in the Piedmont of the two Carolinas.

American patriotism hit the highest peak from December 7, 1941 to September 2, 1945. Only during the month or so following September 11, 2001 have our young people seen or felt such fervor of dedication to our country, freedom and way of life similar to that era 60 years ago. Heaven forbid that there may be a World War III! But, if there is, will we rise to the occasion with the same willingness to sacrifice and do the hard work necessary like our grandparents did? Yes, if we can learn from our elders.

We should be sitting at the feet of these people, our own relatives and others, honoring them by listening to and reading their stories. Then we will realize that virtually *everyone*, even the children, did *something* for the war effort.

Old movies and more recent books show us what those in other communities did. This volume reveals what residents from the Carolinas' Piedmont did. These stories are told by the people who lived them, people who left the Piedmont to go to war, came to the Piedmont for military training or stayed at home and contributed as a paid worker or volunteer to the winning of the war.

After reading of their experiences, you will undoubtedly agree that every one of them is a hero.

Hollywood stars John Payne and Jane Wyman sell war bonds on Burlington's Front Street. Alamance County. September, 1944. Courtesy of Don Bolden, author of *Alamance: A County at War.*

The Shock of Pearl Harbor

Every adult—and many children—today remember where they were and what they were doing when the World Trade Center was attacked. Older adults called it "another Pearl Harbor." Both catastrophic events truly changed lives forever.

But for Bananas...
by
Charles Malvern Paty, Jr.
Mecklenburg County, NC

On the afternoon of Sunday, 7 December, 1941, I was listening to music in our living room in Charlotte's Plaza Midwood neighborhood, when the program was interrupted to announce, "The Japanese have bombed Pearl Harbor."

As a 17-year-old student at Central High, I had no idea where Pearl Harbor was located or its significance. As the bulletins continued to come in, my parents and I gathered around the radio and listened.

Shortly, I stated that I wanted to join up. This provoked a heated discussion between myself and my parents, who intensely resisted this idea. I was their only child. They gave me all the logical reasons for not joining. I was in no mood to listen to logic. The discussion continued on into the evening hours, but my case was getting stronger as news continued to come in. Japanese aggressions were taking place in other locations in the Pacific. By this time, I was arguing that I didn't want to fight the Japanese on the banks of the Catawba River in North Carolina. By 11 p.m., I had convinced them to approve my plan. Both were certain that I could not pass the requirements.

That night I lay in bed thinking of what I was about to do. Was I crazy—leaving this comfortable home and family situation to go into a totally unknown environment that could cost my life?

At 7:30 Monday morning, on his way to work, my father dropped me off in front of the Navy recruiting office. As I walked into the building, I thought I was going to look like a fool, because there would be no one there at that hour.

Well, much to my surprise, there were already about 100 guys waiting! The line had all kinds of people in it. There were young and old, well dressed and not so well dressed. The Navy recruiter culled out some who were in the Reserves or who had previous service and took them into another room. Then they pulled out the 17-year-olds, because we would require parental approval. All of this speeded up the process, but there were only two or three sailors in the recruiting office.

Finally, my name was called. My heart was pounding. My knees were weak. This was it!

Following a quick examination, I was informed that I did not weigh enough (I was 5'2, 105 pounds), and I did not have the written approval of my parents. The recruiter told me to go home, get that approval, eat a bunch of bananas and come back.

By the next morning, I had gotten the signatures. I stuffed myself with bananas as we drove to town and Dad again dropped me off. That morning there was an even longer line, but I was taken in ahead of the others. I presented my papers, was weighed and got an "o.k."

On the morning of 11 December, 1941, I said good-bye to Mother at the house, thinking I would see her again in two months. Little did we know that it would be two years and seven months before I would see my parents once more.

A War-Interrupted Romance
by
Mary Evelyn deNissoff
Moore County, NC

On Sunday, December 7, 1941, my fiancé and I were having lunch at the Pine Needles Hotel in Southern Pines. A reserve officer, Jim was temporarily stationed as an MP at Fort Bragg, on maneuvers with the Reserves with General Drum's First Army.

The son of a Navy test pilot, Jim had been raised in Hawaii, and when he heard Pearl Harbor had been bombed, he immediately volunteered for active duty.

I met James Martin Pratt through a friend who was stopped by him in Aberdeen and knew him from New York. He told her that he and a "shavetail" friend were looking for dates, so she sent them to my family's Pinehurst home.

14

He was the kind of man who overwhelms you—stocky, aggressive, dark haired and brown eyed like his French mother. My mother thought he was cute. My grandfather, with whom he shared controlling qualities, didn't, and threw Jim out after we became unofficially engaged following our third date.

Jim came to Pinehurst anyway most weekends, bringing a bottle of Bacardi rum and visiting my neighbors, two maiden ladies, one of whom broke a bed trying to seduce him.

I enjoyed being engaged and the showers and parties given for us on those weekends.

Mother kept fostering the romance between us, encouraging me to go to New York to pick out an engagement ring with Jim.

Right after Christmas, she and I went to the Sedgefield Inn for a get-away from her parents, and Jim phoned us, saying his mother, Aimee, wanted me to visit her at the Vanderbilt Hotel.

Leaving High Point in snow and ice, we slithered home at about 20 mph, getting to Southern Pines just in time for me to board the train north.

I took some of the trousseau I had bought at an exclusive boutique, including a waist-length skunk jacket called, for obvious reason, a "fanny freezer."

Jim and I went to dinner at the Officers Club on Governor's Island, where he was stationed. It was 12 degrees colder than New York City, so Aimee loaned me a full-length fur, but I wore pumps to trudge through the snow and developed frostbite in my left big toe (which still turns purple in the cold).

Wearing a one-karat diamond from Tiffany's, I returned home to Grandpa's wrath. He was always right, and in my heart, I knew he was probably right in thinking Jim was not good husband material. For instance, Jim insisted our children should bear his initials, JMP, so they could inherit the engraved luggage and silverware.

Ten days later, Jim wrote a seven-page letter insulting my grandfather, and I sent his ring back. He proceeded to get engaged to a Manhattan socialite.

Two years after that, while stationed at a port of embarkation en route to England, Jim came to Pinehurst for a weekend and gave me a Guatemalan poison ring, a great silver tombstone of a thing with imbroglio design, as an engagement token. I gave him my grandmother's platinum ring set with six tiny diamonds.

While entertaining a neighbor on her 16th birthday, Mother and I heard the news about the D-Day landings and were in turmoil, fearful that Jim may have been hurt or killed. He wrote, saying his outfit from the 29th Infantry landed on D-Day+6 to see their beloved Roman Catholic chaplain blown to bits by a land mine.

His twice-a-day letters were a history of the war. Before the guns had ceased firing, he was pressuring me to come to Belgium to get married.

Even the generals' wives couldn't go to the battle zone then, so I refused.

He sent my grandmother's ring back in a V-mail letter full of censorship holes. Then he married a Belgian girl, telling her she must give up her parents, her home and her religion to come to the United States.

I still have a photo of Jim in his military uniform on my wall. He's the spitting image of my Russian-born husband. Oh, and my children's names both have the same initials, BHD.

The Urge to be a Hero, Going Off to War
by
Floyd M. Simmons, Jr.
Mecklenburg County, NC

The Charlotte Clippers were playing the Norfolk Shamrocks in the Dixie Football League at Charlotte's Memorial Stadium on December 7, 1941, when the game was interrupted with the announcement that the Japanese had attacked and bombed the US naval base at Pearl Harbor.

There was, of course, excitement and much wonderment. I couldn't wait to see my high school sweetheart. So I ran all the way from the stadium to The Plaza, where she lived near the Charlotte Country Club, to tell her I was ready to enlist.

I was drafted August 12, 1943.

Shocking News?
by
Frances Pruette Falls
Mecklenburg County, NC

After graduating from Berryhill High School in 1941, I enrolled at Spencerian Business School. Early Sunday afternoon, December 7, I was upstairs in my bedroom at my desk doing school lessons with the radio on. I heard Charlotte's first news report of the attack on Pearl Harbor.

I hurried downstairs. Mom and Daddy were in the living room, reading the Sunday *Charlotte Observer*.

I told them, "Japan has just bombed Pearl Harbor!"

They didn't pay any attention, so I said, "Don't you understand? Pearl Harbor is our big Navy base in Hawaii, and this means *war!*"

Still no response.

I went over to the big radio console in the corner, turned it on and went back upstairs.

Even Sports Were Affected
by
Eugene B. Graeber, Jr.
Mecklenburg County, NC

After seeing the movie "Citizen Kane," starring Orson Welles, that Sunday afternoon, I returned to the NC State campus, where I was a freshman. Everyone there was talking about Japan bombing Pearl Harbor, an event that changed so many lives.

For me, it wasn't that sudden. I was still too young to be drafted. In October, 1940, the draft started at age 21. ("Goodbye, Dear. Back in a year!" they used to say.) Those guys got called back first. The draft age dropped to 20, then to 18.

But by December 7, 1941, I had already realized that I was at the wrong college, and I had talked my parents into letting me transfer to the University of North Carolina at Chapel Hill.

On January 1, 1942, my parents helped me move into my dorm at UNC and then took me to Durham.

Because of the events at Pearl Harbor, we were able to see the only Rose Bowl football game ever played away from Pasadena, California. If the Japs could secretly bomb Hawaii, why not California? No one wanted to take that chance.

And so, Dad, Mom and I cheered for UNC's biggest rival, Duke, when they played Oregon State at the Duke Stadium.

The score was Oregon State 20, Duke 17.

I really pulled for Duke, because they had lost their first Rose Bowl Game to the University of Southern California January 1, 1939, in the final minute.

They Were *There!*
A
Compilation

In the introduction to his book, ***Pearl Survivors***, Dick Jensen of Greenville County says: "Pearl Harbor was not about a romantic triangle involving two American fighter pilots in love with the same Navy nurse in Hawaii. That's a *reel* version. Pearl Harbor *was* about the 2,403 Americans who died violent deaths in a two-hour period on a day that 'will live in infamy.' That's the *real* version."

* * *

As the corporal in charge of the color guard on the USS St. Louis, P. John Fulton was on the fantail holding the flag, waiting for 0800, when he saw planes approaching. The first one, a Jap Betty, was no more than 50 yards away. "I could see the pilot and then the machine gunner sitting backwards grinning at us," he said, "and I saw a torpedo underneath the plane which was headed for the battle wagons."

The other two color guards had M-1 rifles but no bullets, so they didn't wait another minute. The three Marines raised the flag, tied the rope and headed for their mid-ship battle stations. Fulton was in his turret and had pushed the signal for the magazine to send ammunition before the HONK! HONK! HONK! of general quarters was sounded. Within eight minutes, his guns were loaded and firing at the very same plane he had seen before it had dropped its torpedo.

More Jap planes, after releasing bombs or torpedoes, were circling over the harbor seeking targets to strafe. "We started firing at them, too," said Fulton. He admitted sadly that, when guns from ships fired toward the Japs flying over the harbor, some shells were landing in Honolulu.

Some ships, however, were so badly damaged that their electricity was knocked out, which made it impossible to fire their guns.

As targets became available, the range finders on Fulton's ship sent info to main control, where someone would squeeze a trigger for a turret gun and BLAM! The sound of the gun going off in Fulton's closed turret was almost deafening. "And we didn't have earplugs. Nothing!" he said.

Both Marines manning the gun quickly opened the breech, got the brass powder casing out and then jammed another shell into it in time for another BLAM!

He was exhausted but there was another dilemma. "We fired so many shells in that hour and 55 minutes that we were waist deep in shell casings."

Meanwhile the St. Louis had left the harbor with guns blazing. A Japanese submarine was lying in wait at the mouth of the harbor. They sank it and sailed for Diamond Head, about ten miles away, searching for Japanese ships and a Naval task force which had not returned to port.

"But we found a nest of Japanese subs firing torpedoes at us," said Fulton, "We took evasive action and got away."

After the sub encounter, the captain sounded a "secure from general quarters," followed by the usual "smoking lamp is lit."

John Fulton got out of his turret, carefully climbing through the shell casings and joined other Marines on the main deck. "I was raised on a tobacco farm in Forsyth County but had never smoked. My father chewed and my brothers smoked, but I never did. That day I said to the guy next to me, 'Boy, give me one of those cigarettes.'"

* * *

At Schofield Barracks, Robert Whisnant was walking to breakfast when he heard some gun sounds and planes diving at a high rate of speed. "I thought they were maneuvers," he said. "P-39s would come in, roll over and flip, so I didn't think much about it. Then a plane came down over the top of the barracks, strafing. I saw a big orange rising sun and knew this was for real. It dropped a bomb at a water tank but missed."

In the wake of the strafing, Whisnant, who was 24 at the time, hit the ground behind a pile of lumber. Looking beside him, he saw a boy—dead. "I got up and moved," he said. "That wasn't the place for me."

He could then see them bombing Wheeler Field. After a quick breakfast, Whisnant, a member of the 34th Army Engineers, was sent to Hickman Field to fill up holes on the runway. "A couple of planes were out that had to come in," he explained. "We were frightened, but we were so busy, we could still carry our job out."

The men used wheelbarrows to run dirt out to the hard-surface runway, and within an hour or so, had packed it down the best they could to make landing safe.

"Except for a few officers, we were all greenhorns from Fort Belvoir," said the North Carolinian, who had been in Hawaii only since October. He told how recruits from Lincoln and Catawba Counties had ridden a bus together to Charlotte, where they were inducted, sent to the Virginia military base to be trained as engineers and sent on to Schofield.

The attack lasted about two hours, but Whisnant and many other Army men stayed on the ground in the bushes most of that day, awaiting more action. They spent that night repairing a bomb-damaged railroad track at Hickman, so that artillery guns could be brought out.

By then a realization had hit Robert Whisnant: "My time was half up, but I knew that this was going to be more than a one-year deal."

* * *

"I saw planes coming over the mountains, but when a bomb hit the hanger on Ford Island, I knew something was wrong," said Frank Davis of Randolph County. A Marine, Davis had been standing with a fellow private on the 1010 dock, waiting for a motor launch to Ford Island at the fateful hour. Both stood stunned for a moment before jumping into a ditch.

"The sounds were deafening, people were hollering, ships were blowing up, and lots of bodies were floating in the water," the scared Marine recalled.

Soon, he and others were racing for their barracks at the harbor to grab rifles and rush to the parade ground so they could fire at the strafing planes just tree-top high. "One probably wouldn't do any damage, but two or three hundred bullets hitting a plane could," he explained. "One went down that we thought the Marines hit. It fell close by."

By the time they could get out the .50 caliber machine guns and haul them to the top of an office building, the action was over. "We were sitting around the guns talking," said Davis, who had been at Pearl Harbor since May of 1940. "We knew that there went our trip home, and we'd all end up somewhere in Japan."

They were right on one count. None went home. But the closest Frank Davis got to Japan was Guam. His unit was waiting there to invade Japan on V-J Day.

* * *

While showering, Lindsay Wood heard explosions from about a mile away. A shipfitters helper with the Civil Service, Wood, who is from McCormick County, South Carolina, had been working in the shipyard at Pearl Harbor for a month. He stepped out of the shower and wondered aloud what all that air activity was. An Air Force sergeant from Hickman Field, who was housed in the same barracks, had the answer, "Just another mock drill."

ABOVE: The 1010 dock with the capsized USS Oglala (right fore-ground), USS Helena (left) and smoke columns from dock 1 (left) and the USS Shaw (right) the day after the attack. BELOW: A two-man midget Japanese sub, which ran aground and was abandoned outside Pearl Harbor. December 8, 1941. Military photos sold on a Honolulu street, purchased by Lindsay Wood in 1942.

"Why are there orange disks on the wings of the planes?" Wood wanted to know.

Lindsay Wood
Pearl Harbor
1943

"So those involved can distinguish between the two teams," the sergeant explained.

"Those engines have a high-pitched whine. They don't sound like American aircraft."

The Air Force guy took another look and listen. "They're NOT ours!" he shouted and ran off.

Wood never saw him alive again.

By the time he got outside, Japanese planes were strafing the airport road. "The planes were so close you could hit them with a rock," Wood recalled. A pilot grinned at him from over his head. When orders came over the p.a. system for everyone to report to their stations at the harbor, Wood piled in the back of a Chevy panel truck with all who could squeeze in. Before they could get to their destination, one man at the back of the truck was killed while on his knees, praying.

Wood reported to the shipfitters shop, where they were issued World War I helmets and 1903 Springfield rifles and was sent to Dry Dock #1, while the ships were still under attack. An ammo locker on the badly damaged destroyer, Cassin, blew up propelling a .30 caliber slug into Wood's chest. He pulled it out and kept going. A bomb hit nearby, killing his co-worker and sending debris into Wood's right thigh, but he stayed on the job.

After the raid was over, about 10 a.m., the wounded Wood was sent to the Oklahoma to help get men out of the upside down hull. "We first had burners cut holes in the 1 1/8" thick hull," he said. "When we got the plug out, we found that we had killed the men in that compartment, because they had cork insulation and those burned cork fumes were poison."

After that, they were instructed to honeycomb or drill half-inch holes next to each other until completing a circle. Then they sledge-hammered the plug out. Lindsay Wood estimates that he saw only 20 men come out alive. "They were tapping all over the bottom at first. The sound of those men begging to be rescued would wreck your mind—especially while their voices became weaker and weaker, as their air played out."

On December 7th, food was hard to get and it was rumored that the water was poisoned. "We bought up all the Cokes in the machines, being so thirsty," he admitted.

"The cafeteria was still closed, so I ate a partial bag of popcorn left over from a Saturday night trip to Honolulu. The next night, I ate the bag! Butter-soaked paper tastes pretty good when you haven't eaten in two days."

* * *

On the last day of their three-week at-home honeymoon, newlyweds Rebecca Suther Christenbury and her husband, Allen, were asleep in their apartment in a Honolulu home when one of their neighbors banged on the door. "Allen! Rebecca! Turn on your radio, because you won't believe me."

The young couple from Mecklenburg County obeyed. They had heard no shooting, but the announcer was saying that Pearl Harbor was under attack and for all military personnel to report to their duty stations. Soon, Allen was grabbing a piece of the cherry pie Rebecca had made the night before and rushing off to the USS Whitney, a destroyer tender, where he served as a first class metalsmith.

"It's a strange thing to admit," says Rebecca Christenbury, "but I wasn't afraid. I just couldn't believe it could happen."

She considered joining some of the other wives who headed for downtown, but choose to stay at home with the radio on. She heard the words: "The rising sun has been spotted on the wings of the planes," and thought: "Of course, there's sun on the wings!" Then she realized—the Rising Sun: Japan!

Throughout the day, she listened for more news. Periodically, the station featured a Japanese girl singing, "I don't want to set the world on fire..."

All four wives who lived in the house stayed that night in the apartment that had a screened porch, waiting. No lights were on anywhere, as there was a complete blackout. Suddenly, there was an explosion. A bomb? No, a transformer on a light pole outside!

The wait was a long one. "A week later, a couple of fellows from Allen's ship came and told me he was all right," said Rebecca. "But he didn't come home until a week after that."

He seemed unharmed and perfectly normal, but her new husband had lost his memory. He did not even recall getting married!

Allen picks up the story. "When I got to the base, I was

strafed at the gate. I headed for the fleet landing and passed a Marine firing a machine gun at a Jap plane. The pilot looked at me, eyeball to eyeball. Then I saw the holes popping into his plane. A motor launch picked me up, and while it was making a turn to go into the channel, I was strafed again."

Allen believes that is when the amnesia set in, even though he knows (from others) that he fulfilled his duties.

A half a century later, Allen Christenbury's memory clicked back on. "I saw on a TV news program a torpedo hanging on a crane," he said. In his mind, he was turning the corner to the welding shop on the Whitney.

"Five destroyers had been alongside, but the last one was backing out. It was firing a 5" gun off the stern. It seemed to be fir-ing at the USS Utah, which had already been sunk and was burning. But when I looked up, I saw it was firing at a Japanese torpedo plane coming straight at us. The plane exploded. Apparently, it had just dropped a torpedo, and the concussion pushed it into the mud."

Could that have been the torpedo found 50 years later? Probably.

When the Christenburys returned to Honolulu for the 50th Anniversary festivities, Rebecca made sure that they stopped by the First Christian Church, so Allen could see where they got married.

Rebecca smiled, "The lady who showed us around said her mother had played for our wedding."

Rebecca and Allen Christenbury
Honolulu, Hawaii
November 15, 1941

* * *

Stationed on the USS Honolulu, a light cruiser tied up to the dock next to the USS St. Louis and across from battleship row, William A. Boggs from Fountain Inn, South Carolina, was preparing for shore patrol duty in the city of Honolulu. At 8 a.m. on the quarterdeck, he heard general quarters sound and then the words,

"We are being attacked! This is no drill! This is no drill!"

"The first wave of planes—fighters and bombers—came over from the sea headed for Hickman Field," recalled Boggs. "They destroyed about all the planes there and then flew right over our ship to the battleships."

A Navy ordnance gunner's mate, Boggs raced to get the firing locks into the guns and ammunition on the decks for the anti-aircraft guns. He explained that, because it was peacetime, those were not on hand. There were no automatic guns. "Our 5" 25 caliber and 3" 50 caliber guns had to be armed and fired by hand."

As they were getting the guns in action, Boggs and his shipmates could see the Japanese pilots of the low-flying planes. "One was smiling and laughing at us as he headed for battleship row to drop his torpedoes."

He continued, "In a few seconds the whole harbor was on fire. The ships were rolling, rolling over. Men were jumping in the water, screaming."

Meanwhile, Bill Boggs was praying and trying to do his job, keeping a .50 caliber gun supplied with ammunition, while the gunners were shooting as fast as they could. Suddenly, another plane came over the bow and dropped a 500-pound bomb. "It missed us by two feet. But it popped the bow up out of the water and ruptured the seams of the ship and the magazine. Soon we were taking on oil and water in the bow and magazine. Everything was black and smoky."

Sailors on deck cut the St. Louis loose and she drifted out into the harbor, so the Honolulu could fire both port and starboard batteries.

The USS Honolulu was the first ship to get into drydock after the Cassin and Downes, destroyers which had been hit and turned over on their blocks, were removed. Once their vessel was seaworthy again, they took it to Hunter's Point, California, to be fitted with new automatic guns.

Bill Boggs then joined the crew of a ship named for the capital of his state, the USS Columbia.

* * *

A few minutes before 8 o'clock, Navy Yeoman Everette H. Mayes and two shipmates aboard the USS Pennsylvania, which was in drydock, were listening to records in their quarters. He had already had breakfast. Later on in the morning, he would have dressed in uniform to go to church in Honolulu. But through an open porthole, he saw planes diving.

25

"Wonder why they are practicing on Sunday morning," he said to the others. When he saw the diving Japanese planes with the rising sun emblem on their wings, he knew the truth. "This is the real thing!" he shouted. "Dog those port holes, and get to your battle stations!"

He tells what happened next: "All at once, on Ford Island at the air station, debris and flames began shooting what seemed like hundreds of feet high into the air. As soon as we had secured our part of the ship, we were on our way to battle stations before a voice on the sound system could alert us to 'Man your battle stations.' Some gun crews were actually at their stations and firing away before the alarm was sounded."

Mayes and his fellow sailors were hampered in the performance of their duties, because keys were not available to get to ammunition for the anti-aircraft batteries. Despite all the confusion, they were still credited with destroying two Japanese aircraft.

"With all the planes flying over, ships blowing up, anti-aircraft firing and explosions on Ford Island, we didn't even know we had been hit. A medium bomb went through the deck and exploded in the aviation department."

Everette Mayes, who was from Surry County, reflected, "The saddest part, along with the loss of our own men, was when we could see our fleet being sunk in Pearl Harbor with so many lives being lost."

* * *

The Pennsylvania lost 15 men; 23 were wounded. Of more than 2400 deaths at Pearl Harbor that day, 2008 were Navy personnel. The ships lost were the battleships Arizona and Oklahoma and a target ship, Utah. The battleships West Virginia, California and Nevada and minelayer Oglala, although sunk or beached, were salvaged. The destroyers Cassin and Downes were severely damaged but later restored. The battleships damaged were the Pennsylvania, Tennessee and Maryland. Other damaged ships: Helena, Honolulu, Raleigh, Shaw, Curtiss and Vestal. The Navy lost 92 planes, 31 more were damaged. But 96 Army planes were destroyed and 128 were damaged.

The Japanese lost 29 planes (of 353), one large submarine and five midget subs. Their casualties were also minimal in contrast: 55 airmen were killed plus nine seamen on the midget submarines and an unknown number on the large submarine.

It was, indeed, as President Roosevelt said: "A day which will live in infamy."

North African and Italian Fronts

When the Allies landed in North Africa, it was the first time in the war that American troops were on the offensive. The armies and navies of the US and British Empire surprised Hitler and Mussolini. Once conquered, it became a training area, a launching site for invasions of Italy and an "R & R" (rest and relaxation) location.

Charlotte's 38th Evac Hospital
by
Martha Pegram Mitchell
Mecklenburg County, NC

More than a year before Pearl Harbor, some Charlotte doctors, led by Dr. Paul Sanger, began organizing a military evacuation hospital unit to be staffed entirely by local personnel, both medical and administrative. Most of the physicians and staff would be from Charlotte Memorial Hospital, but rumors began flying at Presbyterian Hospital, and some of us nurses from there attended an organizational meeting. There was a lot of enthusiasm. Charlotte Memorial was the first hospital in the country not connected with a medical school to have its own military unit. It was designated Evacuation Hospital #38.

Those of us with nursing experience who wanted to join were sent to nearby Morris Field for physical exams. After we passed, we were duly sworn in as members of the Army Nurse Corps assigned to the "38th Evac." I became *2nd Lt.* Martha Pegram. It was not 100% patriotism on my part; there was a little romance involved, for I didn't want my boyfriend, who was training to be a fighter pilot, to have a war experience without me.

Dr. Preston T. White, who had served in World War I, was commissioned a lieutenant colonel; Dr. Sanger, a major. So that Memorial Hospital would not be depleted of physicians, Dr. Sanger recruited friends from nearby Southeastern hospitals. The Charlotte doctors were: Dick Query, Aubrey Hawes, Bill Pitts, John Montgomery, McChord Williams, William Leonard, Robert McCall, Hunter Jones (yes, an obstetrician), Charles Gay, Laurence Fleming and the Munroe brothers, Colin and Stokes. Others from the Piedmont: George Thomas Wood and Glenn Perry of High Point; Duncan Calder, Concord; William Cavanaugh, Cooleemee; William Matthews, Davidson; George Sotirion, Gastonia; and Robert Miller, Lincolnton. We had three dentists: Vaiden Kendrick, Milo Hoffman and Bernard Walker. Those on the administrative staff were all outstanding businessmen: Jim Felts, George Snyder, Stan Pickens, William Medearis and Lewis Burwell, officers; Sydney Murray and Clarence Kuester, enlisted personnel. A few others were added later. Col. Raymond Whittier of the Regular Army's Medical Corps had been sent to command our unit along with 108 enlisted personnel from the 41st Evac Hospital.

In late April, 1942, 30 of us nurses reported to Fort Bragg, North Carolina, where we received basic training in protocol and were immunized for diseases we had only read about in textbooks. We had to learn about the paperwork, be able to identify aircraft, do calisthenics, take five-mile hikes with backpacks and go through a gas chamber (with and without a mask).

By August 6, our troop ship HMS Andes nosed away from the 59th Street Pier out into New York Harbor and on the sea. Much of the day had been spent loading people and supplies for our 38th Evac Hospital, as well as engineers, communications specialists, a tank unit and other assorted personnel aboard this 33,000-ton vessel.

The next morning, we dropped anchor in Halifax, Nova Scotia. Later, as we left there, we joined one of the largest convoys of the war: destroyers, cruisers, a battleship and many more troop carriers began merging. As far as you could see—ships, ships, ships—an awe-inspiring armada!! But we knew that enemy subs were out there, too. They had been sinking our ships all up and down the East Coast.

We heard rumors that we were headed for England first, where, for about two months, we would practice "being military," before our tent hospital would begin moving, moving, moving somewhere, we knew not where.

The trip was uneventful except for one memorable general alarm. Since each ship was packed with soldiers, sailors, and other personnel, bathing was by quota and on schedule. My turn to take a bath came soon after lunch about five days out of Halifax. As I sat in a tub of glorious warm, soapy water, the siren went off.

This meant that we might be in danger of submarine attack, or it might be a practice drill. No matter. Everyone was to report immediately, fully dressed with helmet on and canteen full of water, to our designated lifeboat station.

My dilemma—do I enjoy this bath, possibly the only one for a very long time? Or do I obey orders? I decided that if we sank, I would at least be clean and sweet-smelling. So I disobeyed orders and sat on in the tub.

No one knew of this breach, as the general alarm created bedlam, and my cohorts answered roll call for me.

As time went on, and baths consisted of sponging with cold water from a helmet (without its lining), I thought my decision a wise one.

Tent Hospitals "Leap-Frogging"
by
Martha Pegram Mitchell
Mecklenburg County, NC

About 17 days after boarding the British ship Malta in Bristol Harbor, England, the 38th Evacuation Hospital Unit from Charlotte arrived in Arzew, Algeria, in North Africa on November 8, 1942. Ours would be the first field hospital ever set up in a landing operation in US Army history.

Just getting off the ship and into a landing craft was a challenge—clambering over the side of that rope ladder and dropping down into a dinghy that would take us to shore. Synchronizing one's legs with the sea swells to make a clean landing was downright tricky.

We landed in an area recently cleared by the infantry, so we knew it was land-mine-free. We had to stay within circumscribed areas. Once ashore, we marched up the streets to a building recently inhabited by Germans or the Vichy French, the most unclean and smelly place I've ever encountered. We dumped our bedrolls and our musette bags with food and personal items. Undaunted, several of us went out, turned a box upside down in the open space outside the door, took out a deck of cards and dealt a bridge hand. Very quickly, we were diving for cover, though, as snipers opened fire. No casualties, thank God. They were "taken care of" (by whom, I do not know), but we soon felt safe again.

The next few days were our first real introduction to C-rations, cold food and dirt. We slept uncomfortably on a cold cement floor.

PHOTO PAGE: Martha Pegram filling a basin from a Lister bag. St. Cloud, Algeria. December, 1942. Elva Wells, Martha Pegram, George Sotirion, Violet Burgess, Annette Heaton and Christine Wills in front of a nurses' tent with a hand-crafted paper flower garden. St. Cloud, Algeria. March, 1943. Tea time for Martha Pegram, Nelia Shields and Carolyn Haltiwanger while gathered on Martha's hand-built "stoop." St. Cloud, Algeria. March, 1943. Margie Bachoka, Margaret Mizell, Deborah Doskow, Elva Wells and Nelia Shields loading bedrolls and personal belongings onto a truck to leave Telergma, Algeria. June, 1943. Martha Pegram and Carolyn Haltiwanger with their corpsmen. Back row: "Muzzy." Front: "Moe" and "Trigger." Tunis, Tunisia. August, 1943.

At last we were granted the use of a wheat field at St. Cloud, Algeria, about 10 miles from Oran, which our forces entered earlier on the day we put in at Arzew. It was the first time in World War II that the United States had invaded anywhere. Within about 76 hours, the Allies had advanced on Oran, Casablanca and Algiers to surprise the Axis and take the North African Coast.

After arriving at St. Cloud in late afternoon, our inexperienced men set up a few tents. Here, we slept dormitory style on cots. During the night, a fierce wind called a sirocco blew the tents over on top of most of us. In complete disarray, we were scrambling around in the dark with our flashlights. The next day, they had to set everything back up. We nurses had to help unload cots off the transport trucks and set them in two rows inside each ward tent. In the center, a big packing box served as a nursing station, where we kept our records, basins, trays, dressings and medicines. A detail set up a big tank of water. Another detail set up a Lister bag with water we could drink.

That morning, we received the first five or six patients. By the end of the week, we had received about 300. In addition to war wounds, we treated medical diseases such as malaria, sore throats and even mumps. The soldiers would come in from the field very dirty, so we would have to clean them up.

Winter with its coldness and incessant rain came too quickly, adding to the discomfort of all. One fellow had pneumonia in this awful environment, but with penicillin available, he did recover.

Everything was different from Presbyterian Hospital, where I had trained. But, in North Africa, I learned about what I call "real nursing."

No room for frills. But no wastefulness either—of supplies, time or energy.

No polished floors. No neat mitred corners on beds. Our tents had dirt floors, thin mattresses on the cots, clean linen only on an irregular basis and rationed water supplies. Each tent had a pot-bellied stove. One scuttle of coal a day helped keep the chill off, but barely. Outside, during the rainy season, we were surrounded by mud.

For our patients, we were able to keep wounds cleaned and bandaged and give medicines for pain, antibiotics for infections or aspirin for minor discomforts. We had our own portable pharmacy, x-ray and lab. Three dentists maintained good tooth care.

We had a shock ward (now called triage) to determine needs. Each ward had a doctor, nurse and corpsman to treat the ill. The patients able to be up and about gave a hand to the ones who were bedfast. Those soldiers were very appreciative, but they didn't stay with us very long. We would get them stabilized to travel back to the States or to a hospital in the nearest city.

Early after arriving at St. Cloud, our colonel, one Rollin Bauchspies, Regular Army of some years (who had replaced our first commanding officer, Col. Whittier) called all us officers into the mess tent for a meeting. He announced his expectations, discussed protocol and firmly stated that no pregnancies would be tolerated in the 38th Evac. The nurses' tents were in a straight line, with an alleyway between ours and the male officers' tents. The colonel said that "a sperm can't crawl across the street by itself." He was warning everyone: "Nobody had better get pregnant." Col. Bauchspies had nothing but disdain for those soldiers who had contracted venereal diseases. In fact, he established a segregated area known as Casanova Park for those hapless victims. Their tents were behind barbed wire at the far end of the compound. "They should feel like heels," he declared.

As our infantry pushed forward and more territory was gained, we were ordered to strike our tent city, pack up supplies, evacuate patients to the rear and move up. We would "leap frog" with another evac unit, to follow the front lines.

From St. Cloud, we moved to Telergma, to Beja, and then on to a hillside outside of Tunis. The last two months of summer, 1943, we had no rain and so much heat that we had trouble getting rest and our patients with malaria grew worse. On September 8, we returned to Oran via cattle-car train and sailed to Paestum, Italy, landing north of there at "Blue Beach" on September 21.

The landing craft went to within wading distance from shore, where a British officer carried me to a small area cleared of land mines. Once again, we were warned to stay within marked lines for safety. We marched to a nearby pasture and set up pup tents. Quickly, we had a working hospital established. But two weeks later, we had to pack, load, and travel to Caserta, Italy.

There, we were actually in new buildings, complete with terrazzo floors. Our feet, used to dirt, soon became tired and aching amidst all that luxury!

Early November 1943 found us up in Riardo-Vairano, Italy—again in tents, with rain and mud a constant. Margaret Bourke-White, a *Life** magazine photographer, came to us about this time. Her assignment was to report the war firsthand. She flew a few missions to achieve this and wrote about our hospital in the February 21, 1944 issue.

On December 2, 1943, while on duty in one of our neuro-surgical wards, I received orders to return to the United States. What mixed emotions! I felt that my job was unfinished, but I looked forward to returning to home and family before my next assignment.

And yet, because of the hardships, I learned some life-long lessons through the 38th Evac: Self-sufficiency. Sensitivity. Good nursing can be practiced in primitive conditions. One can adapt taught procedures to the equipment and circumstances at hand without relaxing standards and goals. Things don't matter.

* Editor's note: Martha Pegram was the cover girl of *Life's* Christmas, 1943 issue—not in a photo by Margaret Bourke-White but in a symbolic painting by Fletcher Martin. The artist had sketched her when he was in North Africa.

Martha Pegram and Carolyn Haltiwanger near their pup tent in a field soon after landing at Paestum, Italy. September, 1943.

Five Little Rocks
by
Jim Geer
Rutherford County, NC

"Hang on to this," the officer said, as he handed to each of us what looked a lot like a Bull Durham Tobacco bag with a drawstring. "Keep it on you at all times. It just might save your life."

Inside were five little rocks, just pebbles.

I put mine in my pants pocket and checked every once in a while to see if I had it.

On November 8, 1942, the 2nd Armored Division under General Patton invaded French Northwest Africa. I was an Army tank mechanic, a staff sergeant. The Western Task Force's "Hell on Wheels" light and medium tanks went into action for the first time in what was considered the most difficult of military maneuvers, an amphibious landing on hostile shores. The mission was to capture Casablanca and French Morocco. The French later admitted that the threat of hordes of our tanks was the main factor in bringing about their surrender.

While the 1st Armored Division was fighting Rommel, we were sent to what we called "Cork Forest" to continue training and wait in reserve. During this stay in the Cork Forest, I was surprised one day when my brother, who was in Intelligence, came to spend the day with me. Was I ever so pleased, because I was homesick, and it sure helped me. (Later, he also visited me in Sicily.)

The 2nd Armored Division had as great firepower as any division—all mobile—including three tank regiments, the 66th, 67th and 68th and three artillery regiments, the 14th, 78th and 92nd. Also with us was the 17th Armored Engineers and the 14th Armored Infantry. The 82nd Reconnaissance Battalion was equipped with light tanks, half-tracks and scout cars. Our Maintenance Battalion was composed of three companies. I was a staff sergeant in Company A. My duty was to supervise inspections, repairs and maintenance of military vehicles. We had two wreckers strong enough to pull a damaged tank.

The 2nd Armored Division did not go into action until April 6, 1943, when officers and enlisted men were sent to reinforce the 1st Armored Division, which, we were told, suffered great losses at the Kasserine Pass. Men and equipment from our Maintenance Battalion were among the replacements.

It was, to us mechanics, a fight between "Blood and Guts"

34

(Patton) and "The Desert Fox." (Rommel). Both of these generals were tank men. But Patton out-foxed the "Desert Fox." Rommel thought we would have to go through the pass, and his men were dug in. Patton split us. Half of the 2nd Armored Division was sent to have sham battles (fight and withdraw) to keep Rommel busy. The other half would come by way of the Sahara Desert. No army would be expected to come from the desert.

Being tank mechanics, we would find ourselves in difficult situations when we were helping tanks cross a part of the Sahara Desert. That desert was very strange in that it changed appearance each day from the wind. A large sand dune that might have been in front of you when you sacked out for the night would be gone the next morning. Others formed in different locations. We had no markers to go by. During the daytime, it was very hot. At night, it would actually be cold. The sand scorpions would come out of their holes at night and give us problems, as they were very poisonous. Fortunately, no one was stung, but one night, one got in my crew leader's and my pup tent. When we awakened the next morning, this scorpion was on top of our blanket looking us straight in the face. I can see it now, with its tail curled up over its back.

William Tidwell and Jim Geer in their tent. North Africa, 1943

Slowly, without moving, I woke my crew leader, Joe Shields, and warned him, "Don't move!"

When I counted to three, both of us threw the blanket over it and scrambled out of that tent. We were fortunate, but it seemed that, while our men were fighting Rommel, we were fighting scorpions.

One afternoon, about 3 p.m., the sky took on an orange cast, and it began to get hotter and hotter. The sky turned to a dark orange, and the heat continued to increase at an alarming rate. We were in a heat storm! Our officer in charge said, "The first man who panics will be the first to die." We were instructed to dig out a trench under our vehicles and to lie perfectly still. No talking. No eating or drinking. Don't move. My trench was 12" deep, enough to get to a little moist sand.

Those five little pebbles in our mouths kept our tongues from sticking to our palates and kept our mouths moist so we could swallow in that high degree of heat.

Our breath burned, as we lay there the rest of that day and that night (trying to keep from panicking and wondering whether we would be spotted by the enemy). Thank God, the next morning, it began to cool down. It took us the rest of the day to slowly sip water, eat only a bite or two of food at a time and recuperate from that terrible heat.

It took us two days to go the rest of the way. We came by way of the Sahara Desert! Everyone said it couldn't be done. We did it.

Rommel was defeated, and the fight for North Africa was over. But to this day, I give those five pebbles a great credit for winning that war. Yes, with the help of those five little rocks, I am able today to talk about North Africa.

Voyages to a Dangerous Highway
by
James F. Shrum*
Lincoln County, NC

Did we ever get seasick! Our Combat Engineer Battalion left New York Harbor on a small troop ship for combat in Italy. We were overloaded, and it was still hot in September.

We landed in Oran, North Africa, September 17, 1943. We went inland by trucks and set up tents on the hot desert sand. Oh! It was hot! Flies, gnats, mosquitos everywhere! Then we had the Arabs and Ghourms to fear. They carried big Punjab type knives and swords. The tale got out that for every American soldier's ear they brought in, they would get great rewards. They would steal anything, especially food from our kitchens. They'd steal our toothpaste and eat it. One stole my shaving cream, and believe me, wasn't constipated any more.

Africa was a 30-day deal of rest and recreation (R & R) and a chance to get acquainted on foreign soil.

We left Africa to head for our first combat experience, the beaches of Salerno. At Sicily, we were put on landing ships. When we got off, it was amongst machine gunfire, artillery, tanks, everything you can imagine the German troops were throwing at us.

It was like our own beaches for looks—long, wide beautiful shoreline. The German troops were dug in. About a third of a mile back off the beach was a dense woods high up like a mountain.

The invasion had been going on about ten days when we got there. We were on the tail end of it. There were so many soldiers (Germans and Americans) killed that American bulldozers were making long trenches on the beach to bury the dead. We lost 29 killed and wounded out of our C.C. alone. It was gory, gruesome, awful—seeing 18-20-year-olds, Americans and Germans that God created, dying for the greed of a very few. It was a taste of war and Hell. I got my taste, but it was just the beginning. On to Naples, Caserta, Anzio, Cassino, Rome.

Naples is 100 miles or so from Salerno. We got to the outskirts of Naples in October. The port was busy with small boats to large cargo ships from all over the world.

There was very little fighting for the city, that is close combat. The Allied forces had bombed it. A lot of buildings were bombed out. Old people, young people and children were everywhere, and there was not much public transportation. The Germans had left the city in bad repair. They had taken most of the food and anything of value like autos, trucks for their own use.

We set up our Command Headquarters, kitchen on wheels and our regimental quarters just a few miles up the road from Naples in a little town. We were getting ready for the crossing of the Volturno River.

The Germans, as they retreated north up the boot, blew out all the bridges. To rebuild pontoon bridges, foot bridges and stationary bridges, we had all kinds of equipment: bulldozers, tramway lifts, front-end loaders. But we were pick-and-shovel men, too, digging out the mines and fixing bridge footings or bases. There was no end to picking and shoveling. Mud or no mud. Mines or no mines. The Germans set traps for us with the mines. A mine is about ten pounds of TNT encased in a shell about an inch thick. It would be booby-trapped. Whatever was within 30 feet of it would disintegrate.

We were foot soldiers. The Combat Engineers fought as infantry. We built bridges; we cleared the way for others. Big artillery, little tanks, big tanks, infantry—whatever was coming through —to drive Hitler's soldiers back.

To build a bridge for the Allied forces to get across the wide Volturno River was a big task for us. Waiting to forge ahead, there were British, Americans, Indians from the Western United States, Australians, French, and troops from Morocco, New Zealand and India. The Indians were quite interesting to see coming by with their equipment and their women (no children).

We crossed the Volturno with a minimum loss of heavy equipment. Several men, killed or wounded, had to continue with us. They would eventually be sent back to the US. Lucky fellows ("devils" we called them), but we mourned our buddies, too.

Germans were forever there, shelling us with heavy artillery. It seemed their men were expendable. Well, our equipment was, too. We lost a lot of it. Men, too.

We went back to our bivouac area. The next morning, when we awoke, there was ammo stacked everywhere. Truck after truck had been bringing it there for days. We just hadn't noticed it. Guards were everywhere. If you didn't know the password, you were in trouble, because the Germans wanted to blow it up.

Caserta was an old, beautiful town, a big town which had the king's summer palace. It's where the famous actress Sophia Loren was born. And it's where we got our first air raid. Bombs dropping everywhere!

We worked the main roads and highways, removing mines with another company (120th Engineers).

Our medic, whose name was O'Neil, went into a mine field. Three men had stepped on five mines. One lost his leg below his knee. The other two had bad shrapnel wounds, all up and down their bodies. The next day, O'Neil went back into the same mine field to help some more. He stepped on a mine and lost his leg at the knee.

The next morning, our platoon, 12 men, were going down a ravine led by Corporal Campbell. Suddenly, a loud explosion! Men were down. They'd hit a mine. Cpl. Campbell was hurt. Bad. Capt. Snyder went past us running and picked up Campbell. One leg was gone. He also suffered internal injuries. Pfc. Boyce, a medic, injected morphine to ease his pain. An ambulance happened to be passing. They put Cpl. Campbell in it. We heard the next morning that he died.

Mount Vesuvius was erupting about 25 miles away—had been for a couple of days. This is the same volcano that covered the ancient city, Pompeii. And while we were there, it was erupting and trying to cover it again.

On Thanksgiving Day, 1943, we celebrated. We had worked hard, especially with the Rangers and the 45th Division putting in a pontoon bridge and maintaining it, when there was heavy flooding, keeping it in place for the tanks and artillery crossing it. We requested a schoolhouse, had an Italian orchestra and were served by a group of pretty signorinas. Their menu was turkey, celery, olives, brown gravy, apples, nuts, and dressing, topped off with 20 gallons of vino (wine). Our commanding officer, Colonel Good-paster was there, pinning on some Good Conduct medals. That's when I got mine.

We began working on a railroad. The crossties had been ripped in two by a big railroad machine with a ripper and pushed aside. Thus, we began making the railroad Highway 48. For the rest of the time we were in Italy, we fixed and maintained this highway under intense enemy fire. It was a main supply route to the Front.

It was very slow going, keeping the Germans beaten back. There was always the screaming of the German 88 mm and mortars incoming. We were continually under their surveillance, artillery strafing and machine gun fire. We'd get pushed back at times. When we were advancing, we'd have more losses (men and equipment) than the enemy. One barrage lifted the Headquarters and Service (H & S) officers' tent into the trees and hit every office in the Command Post. Another plastered a company in the area from left to right. But, most of the time, it was one or two guys that got hit.

Those mountains, when you could see them through lots of fog, were really funny. All the artillery exploding on them reminded me of fireworks at Christmas.

There are three big hills in the valley: Trocchio, Lungo and Porchia, with Highway 48 winding through them. Three towns: Mignano, San Vittore and San Pistro. Miles of shell holes and stinking brown mud.

Every three or four weeks, the replacement truck would

drive up and 10 or 12 clean soldiers would get out and mingle nervously among the dirty ones.

Some of us got hit doing something big like bridging the Rapido River, which ran through Cassino. I got a bullet in my left hand in February, 1944, but most of the men got hurt by blasting rock or sweeping the roads for mines with mine detectors or filling some potholes with mud.

We needed a pass to Caserta, where people wore campaign ribbons with battle stars on them, and there were movies, signorinas and vino. But, instead, we would sit and listen to the guns and figure if the shells were coming in or going out.

* Editor's note: James F. Shrum died in 1999. His story is from a detailed handwritten account left for his family.

A "Big Shot," Big Polack and Bridge Player
by
Billy C. Coleman
Saluda County, SC

In July of 1943, as we invaded Sicily at Gela, I was an ensign in charge of three LCMs (Landing Craft Mechanized). Each one was 14 feet wide and 56 feet in length, big enough to carry a small tank or another vehicle like a weapons carrier or truck — or a group of 88 soldiers.

On one of our trips into Gela, we transported a "big shot" along with the GIs. He wore lots of stars, carried two big pearl-handled pistols, one on each hip, and was cussing and fussing the whole time. Frankly, I'd never heard tell of General Patton back then.

The third or fourth day we were in Sicily, I met someone far more memorable. Sliwa (pronounced Sleewa). This South Chicago street fighter was rather tall and blond and weighed about 215 pounds. He was one of my crew.

A line of pontoons had been set up out from the beach, where we were to pick up German prisoners, who marched out on the pontoons and were to jump into our boat. Each one jumped except a German officer with lots of ribbons and stuff on his chest and shoulders. "No! No! No!" he barked

"Get in the boat!" I ordered, motioning to him.

"No! No!" He obviously didn't want to jump down with the

enlisted men. He was ordered again and still refused to move.

Sliwa walked right up in front of that big guy with a balled up fist. "You get in that boat or I'll kill you!"

The German obeyed.

"Mr. Coleman," Sliwa, pointing to his balled up fist and arm muscles, said later, "that's universal language the world over."

He called me "Mr." because I wasn't much of a military man. Our crews were more like family, even though we had no place on an LCM to eat, take a bath or shave. In fact, every time we ate a meal, we had to pull up to a big ship and ask for food. We got either C-rations or K-rations.

On the next invasion, that changed. At Salerno, an LCI (Landing Craft Infantry) was assigned as a "mother ship," where we could get food.

Sliwa was constantly in trouble, doing a lot of things he shouldn't be doing, but I liked him. I'd sit down and talk with him, and he told me about a conflict he had with an officer named Moore, who had been a heavyweight boxer at the University of Kentucky.

While in a big convoy from America to North Africa, Sliwa was on a surface ship, where Moore was in charge of all surplus LCM boat crews. Moore had ordered drill after drill, and one of those times, Sliwa was in the head and showed up late for the drill. Moore ordered him to march carrying a full seapack for two hours. Sliwa emptied his sea bag and filled it with paper. After an hour, Sliwa took a break to get a cup of coffee.

Moore confronted him and made the remark, "If I didn't have on this uniform, it would be you and me."

Off went the uniforms, and Moore got the worst of it: two black eyes and some bruises.

Moore was in charge of all rations on the "mother ship." When I went there to pick up our rations, a sailor said, "Did you hear about Sliwa?"

"What?"

"He picked up a bucket of California peaches. Moore caught him and locked him in the head of the #1 hold."

"Where's Moore?" I asked.

"Ashore."

"Where's the key?"

"Moore has it."

"Where's a crowbar?" I broke the lock and got him out.

When I saw Moore later, he threatened to report me for doing that. "I could report *you*," I responded. "If we had an air raid, he'd be locked up and die."

When I asked Sliwa about picking up those peaches, he had a good answer: "Mr. Coleman, I don't call that stealing. Don't we belong to the Navy? Don't those peaches belong to the Navy?"

On my second trip to the beach during the invasion of Salerno, we were transporting a weapons carrier and troops. Among the soldiers was an Army lieutenant, a buddy I had played bridge with en route from Oran to Salerno. Every time we played, the guy, who frequently got seasick had said, "I'll sure be glad when I get on solid ground." When we got to the Salerno beach, the ramp was lowered, the weapons carrier with the enlisted men rode off the boat, then the lieutenant took a quick step and stomped both feet. "Man, I'm glad to be on solid ground," he said, as we shook hands.

Suddenly, four planes appeared overhead, strafing the beach. We went down together as the guns fired whoom-whoom-whoom-whoom and then were gone. I got up. He didn't.

The next day, all small boats got the order to rendezvous around a certain buoy. We wondered what was happening. There were ships to be unloaded. Dunkirk?

We looked up and saw two British battleships, the Lloyd George and Black Prince, line up with their starboard sides toward that beach. Soon they were firing 18 synchronized salvos that "shook the world." Then 60 German planes flew over, dropping bombs, hitting one of our ships and one of the British battleships, causing it to list but not sink. Another bomb fell into the water 20-30 feet in front of us, exploded and sent a geyser up 100 feet or more. Our bow stood straight up. Everyone was desperately hanging on until the LCM flopped back into position.

Months later, when we were preparing for an invasion that turned out to be on Utah Beach, I chose the men I wanted in my crews. In the battle, while we were delivering supplies to the beach, I was glad I had chosen Sliwa (not just because he was a good food procurer).

As one of my boatswains cranked up his motor to back up with the tide, something choked the motor. It was a body. I ordered a couple of guys to free up the propeller. One of the fellows started vomiting. We had a job to do and we had to do it and get out of firing range fast. Our lives were at stake.

I heard Sliwa shout, "Get outta my way!" With a machete, he freed us.

Observing Other Cultures
by
Alex R. Josephs
Mecklenburg County, NC

Like other Americans who had never left this country, I, during my Army experience, observed fascinating people from unfamiliar cultures.

The first were mill village fellows from Roanoke Rapids in my own state while I was assigned to a litter-bearing company of the 105th Medical Regiment, 30th Division of North Carolina. That experience was not too enjoyable. When they found out I was a lawyer, the top sergeant assigned me unending KP and latrine duties. Coming to my rescue, my commanding officer recommended me for Officer Candidate School.

After attending OCS, I was a medical administrative 2nd Lieutenant, assigned to the 34th Infantry Division, which shipped out in the first contingent of American troops to go overseas. Our destination was Northern Ireland for more training. My work was non-medical administrative. We moved from town to town over a ten-month period. My job as adjutant was not too heavy, so I became available for detached service to try cases and do other legal work as needed.

I found the folks in Northern Ireland to be wonderful people, but it was a very poor country. Proper nutrition was a problem. The joke around the camp was, whenever a guy would date one of the local gals, he'd be asked, "How many teeth did she have?"

A friend from Charlotte, Virginia Whitlock, had suggested that I contact a delightful family, the Gordons. I did, and they invited me to spend several weekends with them in Lisburn (Belfast). The father of the household was manager of a linen thread mill. Their product was used for the making of champagne in France. When their threads were dipped into champagne, sugar would crystalize on them like no other thread. However, during the war, the mill made camouflage nets.

Our division was soon involved in the invasion of North Africa at Oran, Algeria. The Vichy French gave little resistance, so we were not involved in heavy battles. Both in North Africa and Italy, we were usually close to the 38th Evac Hospital of Charlotte. Some of us would go there to spend the evening talking, eating and drinking (grain alcohol and grapefruit juice).

The Arabs there used to sell eggs to our guys for the equivalent of $1 an egg.

Some American soldiers got even by selling them GI mattress covers (worth about $1.25) for $25. The Arabs used them for clothing.

Alex Josephs
Northern Ireland
September, 1942

One day, I was in a jeep when I saw some Germans who had surrendered being marched down the road by Indian Gurkhas. I thought this might be a good time to get a German camera, so I got out and walked up to one of them and said, "Haben zie eine Leica camera?"

"I believe that's the worst German I ever heard!" said a prisoner. He said he was from Hoboken, New Jersey. He told me that he had gone to Germany to visit his grandmother. War was declared and Hitler drafted him.

West Point officers were not like us officers from civilian life. They had their eyes set on building an impressive military resume with ribbons, battle stars, promotions, acts of bravery, etc. In one instance, a recently assigned West Point captain in our outfit ordered a young corporal to drive him to where some Germans were waiting to surrender and be hauled away. The captain drew his revolver on one of the Germans, and the prisoner, who still had his gun, shot and killed him. Apparently, the captain was afraid the war would end before he could improve his military record.

Another thing I noticed about the military while in North Africa: the Free French officers snubbed the American and British officers. One French general would not accept invitations to have dinner with an American general. Never mind that we had supplied them with all their weapons, food, uniforms and money.

When we got to Italy, where we remained from July, 1943 to July of '45, it was obvious that the 442nd Battalion of Japanese-Americans were great fighters. At Veletri, an important military objective, after the Germans had beaten back one of our African-American divisions of 18,000 men, they came in with less than

3,000 men, took the town and routed the Germans. The difference was not ability but training. Back then, our Army didn't think blacks were very capable, so they put incompetent white officers in charge. The whites were often "rejects" themselves with little training.

After the 442nd Battalion had taken Veletri, General Mark Clark showed his true colors. He withdrew them, and then he paraded in by jeep, leading white troops through the town.

Probably 99% of the Italians liked Americans and hated Germans. When our outfit was in Piedimonte d'Alife, an Italian family invited a few of us fellows for Christmas dinner. Mama Perini and her son served spaghetti verde (bright green spaghetti) for the occasion. We thought we'd drunk too much vino!

Some of the legal work I did was helping soldiers with personal matters like understanding documents or getting a divorce. But most of the time, I was a prosecutor, a defense counsel or a law member of the court. We had an occasional murder or robbery, but the majority of court martial cases had to do with "misbehavior before the enemy," when the defendant had refused to fight. Those found guilty were sent back to a federal prison.

One rather unusual case involved a captain. Although I was the prosecutor, I went to the general who brought charges and convinced him to drop the case. The captain had been decorated four times for bravery. His men told of his courage, and yet he had "lost it." I got permission to send the captain to a hospital in the States for psychiatric care.

Because of that incident, General Eisenhower sent out a directive that in all such cases, where the defendant showed signs of psychiatric problems, he should first be sent to a psychiatrist.

One more observation I had about our civilian army: In our theater, we tried over 1900 general court martial cases involving cowardice, sometimes 30 to 40 a day. We never tried a single one who was a farm boy. The majority of the defendants were from big cities: Philadelphia, New York, Chicago, and San Francisco.

War is No Game!
by
Floyd M. Simmons, Jr.
Mecklenburg County, NC

I was fighting the war when I was 8 years old over in Charlotte's Dilworth neighborhood.

By way of explanation, it was not too long after World War I. Our fathers and other family members had brought back artifacts and helmets, so we began fighting Germans in games with lots of little boy aggressiveness. But I'd seen "All Quiet on the Western Front." That gave me the first slant on the war that it wasn't so keen.

Later, knowing that war was a possibility, I did not want to be in the air or on the sea. I wanted to be on land. With my love of nature, hiking, camping and sports, the 10th Mountain Division sounded really exciting: climbing mountains and skiing. The first mountain troops organized in this country, we trained in Colorado in the very cold high Rockies at 10,000 feet to condition us as mountain troops. Then we were sent to Texas (hot as Hell) for flatland training.

The average age of the whole division was 23 years old. Most of the volunteers were 19, 20 and 21, and there were lots of Europeans (many German-speaking). We had a Jewish Austrian ski instructor, for instance. We speculated where we might be going: Norway? Burma? No, Italy! That was logical. Italy had German mountain troops.

Just after Christmas, 1944, we were en route on the USS West Point, formerly the luxurious cruise ship SS America, now a military troop ship transporting more than 5,000 of us on rough high seas. Our emotions ranged from excitement to anxiety. G o i n g overseas with us for a USO tour, D'Artega's all-girl orchestra was quartered on the upper deck. We went out on our deck to spot them, and a few waved down to us. They were off-limits. Even so, it was very heady, just knowing they were there.

At Naples, we were put on landing craft. Would it be like Anzio? Not at all. The coast was beautiful, with peaceful blue waters. We went ashore at Livorno, then packed inland to some little villages in snow country, where we stayed about a month. We sent out patrols on skis and made some contact with the enemy, but it was still a secret that we were there.

Our assignment was to take Monte Belvedere, about 3,700 feet with a rock face on one side and a gradual incline on the other. Several infantry divisions had tried to secure it unsuccessfully.

On February 18, 1945, the 10th Mountain, now a part of the 5th Army, advanced and took it in about 48 hours, applying the skills of rock climbing using ropes, pitons and ice axes. One team went up the rock face and surprised the Germans from behind. My group took the gradual incline and ultimately suffered more

46

casualties than they did.

That was my first engagement in combat, seeing death on the battlefield. Remembering "All Quiet on the Western Front," I told my squad, "When we move up and get fired on, you've got to promise me, if you get hit, don't scream out." In the movie, when they got hit, they cried out. My men didn't. They might say "Help me!" or "Medic!" But they didn't scream.

We thought that was it. But we suffered a great artillery barrage and several counter attacks. When we moved out, we chased retreating Germans mountain to mountain, village to village.

As a budding artist, when I had the opportunity, I made sketches. It was beautiful. Spring was breaking, chestnut trees in blossom abounded—and no people. They had all been forced out of their farm villages. But then, every time we had a fire fight to take a

During flatland training in Texas, the 10th Mountain Division's main mode of transportation was pack animals. Pfcs of E Company had to break in Missouri mules.

Original drawing by "Chunk" Simmons. 1944.

village, German soldiers took out two or three or a dozen of our men. Our ranks were being depleted. Not all killed, thank God.

For me, if I were to get killed, I got killed. But enjoying athletics and living with nature, I thought to get wounded so that I couldn't continue to do sports would be worse.

When we were on our final position on Monte Della Spe, we had to dig in. The longer we stayed, the more we had to improve our positions. We started connecting bunkers and honeycombing underground (Back to Dilworth and our trenches!). Finally, after about two weeks, on April 14th, we were to move out. All of us were exposed, but we received no fire at all until we got to the base of the mountain. Then all Hell broke loose. Rifle firing. Cross-firing. Mines exploding. Mortars coming in.

Our orders, prearranged, had been to reorganize when we got to the bottom. We had to run across an open farmland. By that time, I was a platoon leader. I was to be the first man across the field ("Follow me!"). That suited me. When I ran across that field, I must have set a 100-yard world record. Even with all that metal coming in, I wasn't thinking war; I was thinking athletics.

When I got to the road where we were to reorganize, I jumped into a gun emplacement that the Germans had used. I had leaped over the heads of six German soldiers! I turned around and didn't see any of our other guys coming, but there these Germans were, unarmed—scared to death. I mean to the point of losing themselves in their pants. That gave me some comfort that I was in control, so I made them come out on the road. I got on the other side up against an embankment, thinking I was secure. Still I was waiting for some of our guys to come up the road.

Then, all of a sudden, something hit my hand like a baseball bat—my right hand that was holding a rifle on my knees. I thought someone had hit me with a stick or a rock. Shrapnel never occurred to me. Then the German corporal rushed at me, doing something with his belt. I thought the son-of-a-gun was attacking me. With my foot, I kicked him in the chest, knocking him across the road. And then I felt badly for an instant, because he had a medical packet in his hand. He was trying to help me. My finger was hanging; my arm was all bloody. He was saying in broken English, "I help, I help!"

I screamed out, "I don't need your help, you damn Kraut!"

About that time some of my guys came across the road. They had gotten pinned down. Someone in the outfit said, "You'd better get out of here and take these prisoners with you."

Floyd ("Chunk") Simmons, a "Pando Commando," in Pando Valley, Colorado, at Camp Hale, the highest military camp in the world. Spring, 1944.

    I took the six Germans up a little road that came in at an angle. We got pinned down by their own fire coming at us. It hit one of them. Then the other prisoners made a stretcher out of a coat. I walked on through them and soon saw GIs who could take over and medics who could get me to a field hospital.

* * *

    In the summer of 1948, I departed from New York on the SS America, no longer the troop ship West Point. The entire Olympic team (males, that is) was decked out in blue blazers, white duck pants, regimental stripe red-white-and-blue ties and boater straw hats, like they did in '32 and '36. The other gender wore cute white berets, skirts, and blazers.

    Before, when I was on this ship, I was just rabble. This time, I got to go to the upper deck.

    But there was no all-girl orchestra.

    Would my injury affect my performance in the decathlon?

I had lost all the joint in my ring finger. It was not a serious injury. Had it been the end of my index finger, I could not have thrown the discus or the shot put or held the pole vault or the javelin. The index finger is the one that initiates gripping the javelin and pushes off the discus and the shot put. The missing joint didn't affect my handling the football for Carolina in the Sugar Bowl. I was confident I could grasp the gold.

I was wrong. I got the bronze. Did I not win the gold because of my injury?

No, it was because of Bob Mathias.

Red Tail Angels
by
Wilson V. Eagleson
Durham County, NC

I got into flying when I was about 13 years old, when I got a chance to fly in a bi-plane at a state fair with barnstormers.

Although I lived with my mother, who was the registrar and an English teacher at the North Carolina College for Negroes (now NC Central) in Durham, I was graduated from Henderson Institute in Vance County before entering West Virginia State College, where my father was a chemistry professor

It was there that, in 1938, I took a Civilian Pilot Training Program. The intention was to have a pool of men familiar with aircraft, but there was one woman in our class, Rose Rose. They put our names on a list and said they would call us—if they decided to train black airmen.

After Pearl Harbor, I joined the Army and was sent to Camp Wolters in Texas and then to OCS at Fort Benning. When you wash out of OCS, they call you out of class at 9 a.m., and you're gone by noon. I got called out one morning and feared the worst. The Commander said, "Pack your bags, you're going to Tuskegee to learn how to fly."

That program was designed to fail. They said we didn't have the dexterity or the intelligence to operate complicated machinery. (Tell *that* to Michael Jordan!) They made two mistakes: we were all college men (some with doctorates) who had pilots licenses. We were determined not to fail.

The first class graduated in March, 1942. I graduated in the 13th class in April of '43. We had learned to fly a PT-13, BT-13 and T-6. After transitioning to P-40s and taking training in dive bombing and strafing at Selfridge Field, Michigan, I went overseas in September, 1943, where I joined the 99th Fighter Squadron of the 12th Air Force.

Ours was the only African-American squadron organized then, but later, the 100th, 301st and 302nd became the 332nd Fighter Group. They came over in the first part of 1944 to fly P-39s doing coastal patrols and sub spotting. We were dive bombing and strafing, while following Mark Clark's 5th Army in Africa, Sicily and the mainland of Italy. Then we supported Patton's 7th Army in Italy. Our job was to do fighter sweeps. Each squadron was operating independently. We would go out in twos or fours and shoot whatever enemy we saw: a railroad track, German convoy, bridge, whatever. We covered all of Italy and might have three missions in one day.

We were late getting to the target at Anzio one day, when we saw German FW-190s diving to strafe our positions and coming back up. We were coming down at a faster speed, so we were evenly matched. It was my 5th mission, and I got one; on my 10th mission, I destroyed another.

Our most extraordinary missions came after we got word from the Resistance that ranking officials were being transported in Red Cross ambulances. That red cross was an easy target.

On one occasion, we spotted a horse-drawn German convoy. Forty horse teams were drawing caissons. As we made two passes over them, the horses went crazy and destroyed the whole convoy.

Between missions in Italy, we would come back to our four-man tents, talk with our tent mates, eat and go to bed to rest for the next mission. We jumped from place to place to stay within ten miles of the front. Wherever we were, we rented a house in a nearby town, where we could take turns resting. We'd take our food and had our own cook, but we hired locals to do the menial labor. Enlisted men had their own rest camps.

Our only permanent camp was at a civilian field with a grass runway outside of Naples.

In Italy, there was abject poverty. I did not see a dog or a cat the whole time. One GI truck hit an ox. After ten minutes, you could not tell there had been anything there except for a little blood on the ground. The only animals they didn't kill for food were goats. They relied on those for milk for the children.

Kids, from 20 to as many as 50, would gather outside our

mess hall holding buckets or plates. A beautiful child, about 6 or 7, Anna Maria was out there every day. She never said a word, just stood there, waiting. They wanted the leftover food from our plates.

Our rest camp in Naples had a gorgeous view. Our house was on one side of the street, and a restaurant was on the other. Each of us got to spend seven days there every eight or nine weeks. During that time, three young teenage girls (two sisters and their friend) with the look of starvation came to us asking to work for food. We "adopted" them, and, when it came time to move, we took a trailer and put cots and the girls in it, locked the door and called it our "supplies." Those girls worked in the kitchen, waited on tables and made up our beds. They became nice looking after we fattened them up, and we called them "our girls." But nobody bothered our girls.

On July 4, 1944, we got new P-51s with Rolls Royce engines and dual stage superchargers. The first P-51s had camouflage paint. These were silver. They were supposed to have a red stripe on the tail. A lieutenant said, "That's not strong enough. Paint the whole damn thing!"

It was then that we joined the 332nd Fighter Group of the 15th Air Force. Our four squadrons were to fly protection for B-17s and B-24s on their bombing missions. They had been losing 20% of their planes per mission. Each member of their crews had to fly 25 missions before he could go home. Very few could win against those odds.

Generally, we sent four squadrons (24 planes plus 2 spares) to fly protection over, under and around those bombers. The Germans knew bombers couldn't take evasive action, so they tried to hit them at the target or coming off of it. We were there to stop them. Each time out, it was seven or eight hours of complete boredom and five minutes of complete bedlam.

At first, the reaction was disbelief. On one of our earliest missions, two P-51 pilots saw four German planes attacking a disabled B-17. They shot down the German aircraft, allowing the B-17 to return home. After we got back, a white captain and lieutenant, the pilot and co-pilot of that B-17, came to thank whoever had been flying those Red Tail fighters. When one of our officers introduced himself, the white pilot saw that he was black and said, "That's impossible! Where's the pilot?"

We had a lot to prove.

Two of my flights were over Berlin; 13 to oil fields over Romania. At all times, I was moving back and forth through the bombers. Most of the pilots knew we Red Tails were there. Sometimes, they called us the "Red Tail Angels." Actually, they began requesting us.

While we were doing long-range escorting, we never lost an escorted bomber to a German fighter. That was the "fault" of General Benjamin O. Davis. He told us, "If you leave those bombers and go off for personal glory, I'm going to court martial you or ground you."

The court martial didn't bother us a bit, but don't ground us and make us stop flying!

In that period, we lost five men from enemy aircraft. Sixty-six were shot down by ground fire. Of those, 39 pilots became POWs.

After 18 months, I was burned out. I had flown over 350 missions (186 with the 12th Air Force and 168 with the 15th). That's right, other pilots could earn points by flying a certain number of missions (usually 25) or doing combat duty for a certain period of time. But we didn't have reliefs. We were told that they didn't have facilities for training more blacks, so we had to keep going until we couldn't go anymore. It was two months before V-E Day, when I knew I had had it. In a couple of days, I had orders to return to Tuskegee Airfield.

Someone noticed that when we got back to the States, we went to the left and caught a bus or train and went home. The whites turned to the right and had a ticker tape parade down Broadway.

Over the years, people have asked me, "Why did you fight so hard for a country that didn't think you were capable?"

I tell them, "We're Africans by heritage, but Americans by birth. We have a right to fly and die for our country."

Editor's note: To learn more about Tuskegee Airmen, see "Unseen Angels" by John Archibald, page 88, "From a Plow to a Plane" by Ernest Henderson, Sr. page 191, and Wilson Eagleson's other story, "A Teacher? Not Me!" on page 297. Also, see the reference to the Tuskegee Airmen by Bert Connor on page 89.

The European Theater

America's involvement in the European Theater actually began in North Africa—or perhaps Ascension Island, neither of which are in Europe. But wherever our troops were, patriots from the Carolinas' Piedmont were among them.

Mid-Atlantic Filling Station
by
James J. Cardo, Sr.
Mecklenburg County, NC

Ascension Island was so strategic to the European Theater that it was a potential target for disaster. Only five by seven miles, it was 1400 miles east of Brazil and 1200 miles southwest of the Gold Coast of Africa, the ideal refueling stopover for a southern route to Sudan, Egypt, Italy, Persia and on to China, Burma and India (The CBI Theater). In winter, it would become the preferred route to Europe. A huge tank farm was set up in the center. One firebomb could take out the whole fuel supply.

Soon after Pearl Harbor, my artillery battery was assigned to an engineering regiment to form a task force to build an airstrip on Ascension Island. Other support units went with us: quartermaster, signal corps, finance, medical, etc., about 2000 troops on a transport ship. We assembled in Charleston, South Carolina, the port of embarkation, where freighters joined us loaded with bulldozers, dump trucks, construction materials, guns, ammo and drinking water.

Until we could get our distilleries running, we were limited to one canteen of water a day. There was no fresh water on that extinct volcanic isle. Just a lot of cones, ash, cinders and porous rock with one peak about 2800 feet, which normally had a cloud cover. And constant trade winds.

We built the airstrip on the flats. When the runway was completed, the engineers moved on, but the other units remained. A Citadel graduate and captain, I had 168 men in my battery to set up and man anti-aircraft guns around the island. Later, they sent in a seacoast battery with 155-mm long-range cannons.

In the Pacific, the Japs had a giant sub, which went to our West Coast, took out parts of a sea plane, assembled it at night in the water and loaded two 100-pound bombs on it. The plane dropped the bombs in the northwest area, setting forests ablaze, then returned to pick up firebombs to make more fires.

In the South Atlantic, the Germans had two subs with the same capability. One bomb from a sea plane would put us out of business.

On Ascension, we had a small air force of our own: six B-25s and 18 P-39 fighters. Daily, one B-25 and two P-39s would circle the island every morning and afternoon. During my time there, they spotted and sank twelve German subs.

We were put on full alert for three days, when two Vichy French battleships left the coast of Africa and headed for Ascension. The ships circled the island about ten miles out and returned to home port.

Capt. James Cardo
Ascension Island
1943

The potential of a submarine dropping off a rubber boat with two men who could make their way to the tank farm, cut into the barbed wire fence and set charges on some of the fuel tanks seemed so plausible that the brass sent in 500 troops to ring the tank farm with a human fence, one man about every ten feet.

During the two years I was there, not a shot was fired from the island or onto it. The disaster never happened.

Two Panics and a Promise
by
Jim Geer
Rutherford County, NC

Patton had an experiment in his plan to invade Sicily. A platoon of tanks would come in first to establish a beachhead, then the infantry would secure it. It was the opposite of all that had ever been done. Those of us from the 2nd Armored Division were all volunteers.

We landed east of Gela at midnight July 10, 1943. The seas were rough, so, even though our medium tanks were waterproofed, we could get only 18 ashore. The moon was shining as we pulled them up on a big sand dune, where we could see a valley and woods beyond. We dug in and waited until morning.

But we were awakened by the sound of tanks, 45 German Panzers rumbling out of the woods and getting into battle formation. There we were with them in front of us and nothing but the Mediterranean Sea behind us. As those tanks rolled toward us, our commanding officer hastily called us together and said, "Men, I'll leave it up to you. We can surrender or die fighting."

Every man voted to die fighting.

I was a tank mechanic, but we were given M-1 rifles and rifle grenades.and told to dig a foxhole and not to fire until we were told to. I did some earnest praying in that foxhole. I told the Lord, "It looks like this is as far as I am going. This is the end. Just be with us."

Just then, we heard a noise on the Mediterranean: a small craft from the Navy revved up on shore, and a little sailor in a white uniform ran up the dune and rushed between two of our tanks. With a spool on his back unwinding some wire, he ran halfway between us and the Panzer tanks and dropped to the ground. No one fired a shot.

Overhead came what sounded like huge shells coming from a ship so far out in the Mediterranean we could not see it from our position on the sand dune. That first shell hit in the woods behind the Panzers. The next hit between the woods and the tanks. The third one was on target, thanks to that sailor directing the fire. He must have then said, "Fire at will," for the next shells rained down on those Panzer tanks. What a glorious sight it was! Every one of those German tanks was either put out of commission or turned tail and retreated back into the woods. On land, not a shot was fired from either side.

Two of our guys who were closest to the sailor made a seat out of their arms and hands to carry him back to his boat.

Patton's Army entered on the west coast of Sicily; Montgomery came in on the east side. It was a race to meet at Palermo. We arrived two days ahead of the British. When they came in, we held signs that said "Welcome! We have this town secured."

From there, our division headed to Tidworth Barracks in Salisbury Plain, England, where we trained for the French invasion. Our training was over when they starting putting our tanks on LSTs and the men with them. There were so many ships in the English Channel that we had to stay on board three or four days before we could move. We landed D+9. (We were supposed to be there D+5.) It really got next to me to see how many of our guys gave their lives on that beach.

We moved 30 miles on land to take the town of Carentan and secure it. Next, we found ourselves on farmland in Normandy, among the hedgerows, which were as high as 10 to 12 feet, usually with sunken roads, which made them almost impassable. If a tank hit one and its nose went down, it was stuck. Bulldozer blades were attached to the front of some tanks, and those tank-dozers could knock down the hedge, cover the hole up and cross right on over. Germans were thick in those hedgerows, but a tank could go parallel to the row and, with the .50 caliber machine gun going full blast, could take care of the situation. A new barrel had to be installed after each occurrence, as excessive heat would melt and warp the barrel.

After the Battle of St. Lô, Patton stopped for nothing. Our tanks were rolling so fast that gas and supplies had to be dropped to us by parachute. Our maintenance battalion was working day and night repairing disabled tanks and vehicles and trying to keep up with the division.

One night, I lay in my foxhole, tired and really sick of it all. German planes were dropping personnel bombs everywhere, and our artillery was shooting over our heads. I didn't know how much longer I could go on. Thousands of miles from home, I wondered if I ever would get back. Right then, I made a covenant with God. I prayed, "God, I'm a thousand miles from home. But if I get home, I'll do anything you ask me."

He got me through that, but I had another scare during the Battle of the Bulge. Our outfit was 25 miles inside Germany when Von Rundstedt made the break through our lines. Our division was called back to halt this breakthrough.

At the time, my company was working on three disabled tanks. I was left with orders to repair the tanks and return to Belgium and find my company. A 2nd lieutenant with a jeep was left with me to lead us back. On the second day, he chickened with the excuse that he must find our division and come back for us. To this day, I have not seen that 2nd lieutenant.

We protected ourselves by commandeering a house, placing

.50 caliber machine guns from the disabled tanks at three windows and .30 caliber guns around the house and having someone man the 78 mm turret gun.

Early one morning in late December, we left Germany. We had eaten our last food the day before. Soon we came upon some engineers who were waiting for us to cross their pontoon bridge, so they could take it up and move back themselves. I asked their officers, "Do you have any food to share with my men?"

He called the man in charge of their rations, who reported, "All I've got is a roll of bologna and one loaf of round homemade bread that we've been saving for Christmas dinner."

And so, on Christmas Day, 1944, they took a vote and divided their food up equally. The 25 of us laughed about wishing we could do what Jesus did to feed the 5,000, but, after a devotional, we were glad to get the thin slice of bread with a very thin piece of bologna.

Bastogne was so depressing. The weather was so cold. The snow was almost knee deep and crusted on top. In walking, you would break through. If someone was wounded and couldn't get up on his own, he died there. Many of the German soldiers were youth, 14 and 15 years old. No one was taken prisoner.

By early April, 1945, we had gotten to the Elbe River and I was working on a disabled tank when my commanding officer said, "Sgt. Geer, if you could leave, where would you go?"

"To Gilkey, North Carolina."

"You have more points than anyone else in the company," he said. "Pack your bags. You're leaving in the morning."

After hitching a ride on a hospital ship, I arrived home on June 8. On my first Sunday home, I went to church. After the assembly, the Sunday school superintendent walked up to me. "Soldier, would you teach a class of intermediate boys? They don't have a teacher."

"I've never taught a class," I told him. "I never studied the Bible much."

"I'm sorry to hear that," he said as he turned and headed for the door.

Suddenly something hit me. A voice sounded in my head. "What did you promise me in that foxhole in France?"

I caught up with the superintendent. "Show me that class of boys," I said.

And I've been teaching Sunday School ever since.

Defying the Odds
by
Edgar D. Talbert
Stanly County, NC

As far as I know, only one enlisted man out of our platoon of 50 got to Berlin without ever having been wounded. That's excluding the motor pool who drove the half tracks. Of the approximately 500 in our regiment, 525 were killed, including replacements, of course.

H Company of the Army's 41st Infantry, 2nd Armored Division ("Hell on Wheels") landed in North Africa, moved on to Sicily, then to England to train for the Normandy invasion, and off to France, Holland (the Siegfried Line) and Germany.

In Sicily, the first day was not too bad. The Germans had left Italians to fight, and they gave up, wanting to go to the US! On another beach below us, our ships lit up the sky shooting at paratroopers dropping on the shore. They were our own paratroopers, although we didn't know it at the time.

Our outfit landed on Omaha Beach D-Day +3, June 9, 1944. We saw no Germans on the beach, so we drove up into a field to clean off our half-tracks. I saw a German plane way off, coming in real slow, so I began shooting a .50 caliber machine gun. If I didn't hit it, the tracer bullets scared him off. When I got through, not one of my men was in sight. I found all of them down in a ditch and had to get an axe off a half-track to cut them out of the briars.

By then I was a staff sergeant, so on the first day of fighting (June 13), I put five of my men behind one tank while the rest of us followed behind another. We passed through Carentan that morning with little trouble, but when we hit the hedgerows, things got tough. Germans surrounded us as we waited to move up. One of our tanks came out between two hedgerows and trapped three of my men against a bank of dirt by the road. If I had not whistled really loud, the tank would have run over me. It did hit the heel of my shoe Those three men who were trapped were not killed, but never returned to my unit. Of the first two to die, my best friend Etters was one.

When we left Carentan, we and the Germans were consolidating our line, so there was little fighting until we got just outside St. Lô.

In late June, we were on a patrol when I saw a GI running beside the tank I was riding on. His rifle had been shot in two. His face was bleeding from the splinters, but he looked at his left hand with half a gun, turned to the right half, then threw the whole thing down and kept running.

Before the breakthrough at St. Lô, the Germans would shell us and then we'd shell them. One night, we made a deep foxhole with dugouts on each side for sleeping quarters. We piled logs on top, leaving a small hole for us to get in and out. All night long we could hear enemy soldiers just 250 yards away. We heard a wagon drive up and the rattling of pots and pans as they cooked. I thought how much better that was than those canned C-rations we ate 90% of the time.

In July or early August, we were were still in the hedgerows, when I was moving from one to another with my squad. I looked up and saw one of our tanks firing at some Americans over on a hill. I jumped up out of the ditch and onto the tank to tell him to stop shooting. Just then, German artillery shells hit some trees, killing and wounding the squad members I had left behind.

Edgar Talbert (right) receiving the Bronze Star. France. Summer, 1944.

When our platoon of 48 regrouped, only 13 were left. Earl Woodruff of Selma, North Carolina, was wounded, but he went to the aid station and came back to help me.

That same day, we saw a lone German calling in artillery. A shell exploded near us, spreading hot fragments which hit Woodruff. He was so mad, he took off after the German boy, causing him to run. I stopped them and made the boy lie down with his hands over his head. He would be a prisoner, not a casualty. Woodruff thanked me later.

Once, when we relieved some other troops at the front lines, we saw the most ragged, unshaven guys we'd ever seen come out of foxholes. Before it was our turn to be relieved, Woodruff, a tech sergeant, made us crawl back to get water to shave and clean up. When we left that place, we looked like soldiers.

Another day in August: a squad near us lost all the men but a Pfc named Breedlove. I told my captain to make him a staff sergeant

"I can't do that!" Captain Carrothers of Chester, South Carolina, said. "Heck, he has to be a squad leader, and I'm not going to do that."

I guess it was because Breedlove was 5'4" and weighed only 120 pounds, but the Captain finally did made him a staff sergeant, although he put him under me.

On October 6th, we were on the front at the Siegfried Line, where the Germans were holding. The day before, some of our tanks had started across the field and had gotten knocked out. The tanks had been left in the field. On the 6th, we prepared to attack. They were shelling us, but I told the lieutenant that we were going to move either forward or back. "Go ahead," he said.

I was crawling in a ditch until I could see some Germans in a foxhole. As I got closer to them, I'd crawl and shoot, crawl and shoot—until I got shot. The bullet must have hit the receiver on my gun and knocked fragments into my face and eyes. I looked around, and all but four of my men were not there. The lieutenant had left us, too.

When I got back to the group, I starting kicking boys to go help the ones I'd left behind. About that time, I heard some bullets and took a dive, but I didn't make it. I got shot in my femur before I hit the ground.

They kept moving me from one hospital to another: Holland, Belgium, Paris, England. On Christmas Day, they put me, along with 10,000 others on the SS Queen Elizabeth, which was dodging submarines. Eventually, I got to a hospital in Oklahoma, where I was surprised to be awarded the Silver Star—something about being instrumental in capturing a town the day before our troops crossed the Siegfrield Line out of Maastricht, Holland.

Obviously, I was not the one who made it to Berlin. Breedlove was.

Comrades in Combat
by
Paul Preston Hinkle
Rowan County, NC

When I joined the Army, I didn't know a private from a general, but after awhile, I could see that a little Pfc (one level above a private) controlled his men better than a general. What was most inspirational was knowing comrades willing to die to save one another, fellow soldiers actually closer than brothers. That was comforting, for I was in Europe for two years and in combat most of that time.

I got overseas June 13, 1943, in Africa, first Casablanca then Algiers, and was in combat from that point on. During the winter of '43-'44 and the spring of '44, we were under fire every day at Cassino, Italy.

A member of General Mark Clark's 5th Army, I was a lieutenant in the 59th Army Field Artillery, which was operating from a valley below. The Germans had established a stronghold that seemed impossible to penetrate. They were spying on us from a monastery on the hill, but we respected that sanctuary. Although we shelled all around it, we were told not to hit the monastery.

We had 105 mm Howitzers, but the Germans had 88 mm guns, that I believe were the best weapon used during World War II. They could shoot direct fire one way, turn to another side and use indirect fire and then point up and have an anti-aircraft gun.

Our unit had tents, but I slept more often in my jeep or sometimes in the shell of a building. We had to stay alert, but one or more of us would drop off while others would keep guard duty. In winter, when the snow was up to the top of our jeep tires, we were supplied with Army coats and hot food. At Christmas, we exchanged gunfire not gifts. Spring brought better weather but no letup on the front.

Sometimes I found time to write to my new wife, Becky, who was expecting our first child.

Finally, in May 1944, with help from numerous Allies, especially the Air Forces, we took and held Cassino, so that our unit could move on to liberate Rome. We met almost no resistance. Once inside, we were assigned to guard certain bridges, but the city was left pretty much intact. And as we moved through that ancient city, the people were very friendly, happy to be liberated. Some of our American boys were using the little Italian they knew, but we were surprised that many Italians could speak English.

At Spencer High School and Wake Forest College, we were encouraged to take French. No one took Italian! However, I was lucky to have an interpreter with me much of the time. My jeep driver was a Jew, who was born in Germany but was an American citizen. He could speak German and knew some Italian and French, too.

Our time in Rome was too short. Soon we were loaded onto ships in Naples to go to France, entering at Marseilles. At that point, we joined the infantry of the 7th Army, and I became a forward observer. That is, when we met resistance, I had to stick my head up to see where the enemy fire was coming from, then I would radio the gunners which direction they should shoot. At times, I used a cub plane for observation. That was not too effective, for a strong wind would blow us backward.

Sometimes, we couldn't tell the source of the resistance, so we would circle the guns and fire in all directions.

No matter where we were, even as we moved through France, we found it remarkable that food, weapons and supplies had been produced in America so fast and then transported to keep us supplied on schedule.

I did make some interesting observations. One thing about the British, no matter what was going on, at 3 o'clock, they would stop for their tea. The Germans were so methodical that they would shell a road at the same time every day.

Throughout our movement, the comradeship of our unit kept up our spirits. It hurt to see fellow GIs fall. One boy from Pottstown, Pennsylvania, who always wore his helmet and dug his foxhole immediately whenever we stopped, was shot before we could settle in. We had come so far together and had almost gotten into Germany, but he didn't make it home.

Soon after that, on November 27, 1944, I was walking along a street in Strasbourg, France, when shells exploded and shrapnel began falling all around. As I was knocked to the ground, I saw my leg bleeding, but my arm was hurting. Medics got me to a nearby field hospital, where they found that I had been wounded in the left leg, hip and arm. Doctors were able to remove the shrapnel, but I got an infection and had to stay nearly a month.

When I was able to get around some, I saw other guys much worse off than I, strung up in traction. But a lot of those left the hospital before I did. Some were so anxious to get back with their unit that they left on their own before being released.

I didn't want to go with a strange unit either. I hurried back to be with my buddies.

The shock was that, while I was in the hospital, my whole crew of forward observers had been wiped out. The replacement crew got captured.

By the grace of God, three of us Rowan County boys, Ellis Leslie, Bill Barrow and I, from the 59th Army Field Artillery Regiment got back safely.

A Nice Reception
by
Ed Thomas
Abbeville County, SC

My fighting war was spent with the US-Canadian 1st Special Service Force. We saw six months of combat in Italy then changed arenas to lead the invasion of Southern France on August 15, 1944. After the landing, we joined the 1st Airborne Task Force, which had the mission of driving the enemy eastward out of Southern France. At the time, I was a battalion commander.

By August 26, we had driven the Germans from Cagnes-sur-Mer, and their withdrawal was so swift that we were no longer in contact. I was ordered to bivouac my battalion east of Cagnes to await orders. About five miles east and still in enemy territory was Nice, the principal city of the Riviera.

I found that our designated bivouac area was in a small forest containing a clear, inviting stream, so I located our campsite along its bank. In the two weeks we'd been in France and for some days before, we'd had no chance for a shower. After the companies settled into their assigned areas, many of us stripped naked, jumped into that cold, clear stream and removed a deep accumulation of grime. That was the most enjoyable bath of my life.

At this time, our artillery support was furnished by the 602nd Field Artillery Battalion, and the next morning, the commander of the battery supporting my battalion jeeped up.

Having heard on his radio that the enemy had evacuated Nice (artillery unit radios being far superior to those of the infantry), he was planning to check out the city and invited me to join him. I accepted the invitation, ignoring the small technicality of requesting permission. From experience, I knew full well the response such a request would bring from my regimental commander.

So off we went on this "reconnaissance," I somewhat AWOL. Besides the jeep drivers, the party consisted of the battery commander, the forward observer assigned to my battalion, Captain Adna Underhill of my 2nd Company and myself.

We went to the coast road, headed east, and soon reached the Var River, which at that time of year, fit the description of some of our Western streams ("a mile wide and an inch deep"). But whatever its width and depth, it was impassable to our vehicles. Our Army Air Force had accurately zeroed in on the road bridge, and it lay before us, a mass of twisted girders.

While we stood contemplating this obstacle and debating our next move, a Frenchman rode up on his bicycle. By sign language and a few words of common comprehension, he communicated that he was going to cross the river and volunteered to lead us across. Leaving our jeeps and drivers behind, we followed him. And lead he did, as he somehow navigated the twisted girders with his bicycle held above his head, a balancing act fit for a circus performance. We scrambled unsteadily along behind.

When we four reached the far bank, we were still a long way from the city center, and again, we debated our next move.

The problem was soon solved. An ancient flatbed truck fitted with the ubiquitous charcoal stove for fueling roared up with three members of the Free French Forces of the Interior (FFI) aboard. When we identified ourselves to them as US Army and desiring to visit Nice, they became greatly excited, loaded us onto the bed of their truck and headed for town. Whenever we passed the few pedestrians on the way, they pointed at us and yelled, "Americain, Americain!"

We went into Nice by what I now know is Avenue Victor Hugo, a major inland road paralleling the coast road, the latter blocked to inland access by concrete barricades, a German invasion defense.

The truck reached a point in the downtown area very near today's location of the Hotel Splendide that was the site of the FFI headquarters. A parade seemed to be forming in the street, but when our arrival was announced, the fledgling parade broke up, and we were carried onward to the Place Messina, an open area in the city center.

Place Messina was filled with joyous citizens celebrating the end of an era of suffering under the heel of a very cruel oppressor. Their ecstasy of liberation was palpable.

Just being present in this throng expressing joy and relief was exhilarating!

We were pulled from the truck, and a woman pressed a small doll made of twisted pipe cleaners into my hand, saying, "Souvenir of Nice." Soon, we were escorted by a citizen to the Hôtel de Ville, a few blocks away.

There, our group (the two artillerymen, Underhill and I) was led up several flights of stairs to the council chamber, where a celebratory lunch was beginning. Along one end of the chamber was a raised platform. On the front side of this was a long table with chairs behind, obviously where the council members sat while in session. With a number of local officials, we were seated here as guests of honor, and lunch was served.

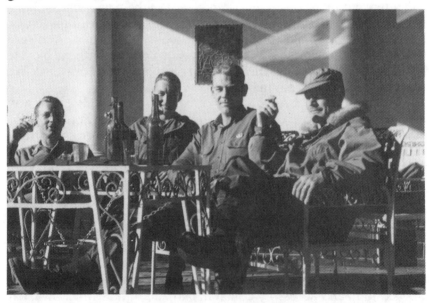

Officers of the 2nd Regiment, US-Canadian 1st Special Service Force: Maj. Stanley Waters, Maj. Ed Thomas, Capt. Adna Underhill and Capt. Bill Bennett on the terrace of a house of Averill Harriman. Menton, France. October, 1944.

Wine flowed freely and I, a major, as senior in our party, was called on to speak. My comments had to do with being glad to be included in their celebration and that the Germans had left Nice without a battle.

During the meal, one of my seatmates, a city official, asked me when I could supply Nice with food. As diplomatically as I could, I conveyed to him that this was not in my line of work, but help would be coming soon (I fervently hoped). I did not confide in him that for me to help would be difficult in light of my current AWOL status.

As the luncheon slowly drew to a close with much exuberant conviviality, I decided I had pushed my luck far enough, and I'd better get back to my command. Captain Underhill and I said our thanks and farewells. A ride was provided us to the Var. Then, despite our wine consumption, we crossed the blown bridge successfully and returned to our bivouac, leaving behind the artillerymen. Fortunately, we did not immediately need artillery support.

A couple of days later, we were ordered forward to again engage the enemy and continue the drive eastward. We loaded onto 6x6's and were trucked through Nice to the High Corniche and onward, an ignominious way to pass through a city where a few days before, we'd been treated as conquering heroes.

* * *

In August, 2001, I was lucky to be one of three 1st Special Service Force veterans to participate in liberation ceremonies still being held by towns in Southern France that were liberated by our unit.

The climax of that week was on August 28 in Nice. We participated in the wreath laying at the magnificent war memorial, then were invited to a reception in the Hôtel de Ville.

We ascended several flights of stairs and were ushered into the reception room.

As the guests gathered and wine was served, I did some exploring. Next door was the council chamber, the room I'd been in 57 years before, to the day, and, I think, the hour!

I asked for and was granted permission to say a few words before the formal program and then recounted my visit to the same place on another great day.

On this day, I was not AWOL!

An Excess Officer Spills His Guts
by
Charles A. Wetzell
Gaston County, NC

I was sent up to the front lines on a truck with food and ammo, protected by a tank. The tank made so much noise that it brought in artillery, and I almost became a casualty before joining a unit.

A part of what was called an "Excess Officers Company," my friend Jim Wilson and I were among the last to be assigned, as we were sent out alphabetically. In November, 1944, I became commander of the 3rd Platoon, F Company, 378th Regiment, 95th Division in Patton's 3rd Army, joining them just after the Metz campaign.

The few officers in the company were glad to see me, but they surely thought, "Oh my, another lieutenant, another one we will have to bury!" I was the second replacement they had had as a platoon leader, so they already had it figured that I would not last long.

As we approached the German border at the Saar River, we ran into the Siegfried Line (a series of forts they had built as a defensive position). Our objective was Saarlauten, whose name later changed to Saarlouis. Germans had knocked out one span of the bridge across the Saar.

My platoon was sent out on December 9 (my 23rd birthday) to see if it might be possible for foot troops to cross it, even though it was below water. I got out on it and was almost swept away by swift water. I told the company commander there was no way we could cross. The Saar River was at a flood stage due to weeks of incessant rain.

We knew the Siegfried Line forts were on the far side of the river, so a daylight crossing was not possible. On the early morning of December 10, our engineers took many of the assault boats (room for eight men, one behind the other) to the river's edge. We arrived at about 4 a.m. and pushed off, one squad per boat.

For me, having taught rowing and canoeing at Piedmont Scout Camp, paddling a small boat like this was easy. But very few others had my experience.

Almost immediately, Germans shells started falling around us. This, plus incompetent paddlers and surging waters, almost spelled our doom. Somehow, we got to the other side only losing three men. So we were down to 25—half of the 50 maximum that should be in our infantry platoon.

We ran for cover in the nearest building in Ensdorf to wait for daylight. For the next week, we had to fight from house to house. We were in one house and Germans were in another when one of my men tried to charge across the street. He was shot and fell wounded in the middle of the street. He was only ten feet from the doorway where we were, but the Germans had a machine gun at the end of the street, covering anyone who tried to cross. He lay there bleeding and groaning but could not crawl back to us.

The medic decided to try to rescue him. He stuck his Red Cross arm band out to tell the enemy gunman who he was. (That should mean not to fire on a non-combatant.) But when he crawled out to the soldier, he was shot.

As I watched both die, I concluded that there must be a better way for men to settle their differences than by killing each other in such a senseless fashion. How did I manage to keep my courage and not run away under such conditions? From the time I was a Boy Scout, I was trained to do anything to preserve and protect this country of ours. It's called patriotism. This is what our country was built on. This is what will guarantee our survival.

On a cold and wet December 14, we reached another fort camouflaged as a house and lost several men trying to take it by daylight. Our commanding officer, Lt. Gerald Macy, kept sending us messages to move on. He said, "You are holding up the war!"

Finally, that night, all was quiet, and I decided to rush it. I instructed my "bazooka man" to shoot the door off at my signal. I led Sgt. Elroy Rautman and seven other men from my platoon up an alley to the target house. I had my carbine slung over my shoulder and a grenade ready to throw inside after the bazooka had knocked the door down.

The bazooka blasted, and light from a burning house nearby showed that the door was indeed blown away. Just as I stepped into the doorway with my finger ready to pull the pin on my grenade —BANG! A flash came from inside. Something hit me in the chest, spinning me around and knocking me down as if a mule had kicked me. My carbine flew in one direction, and the grenade fell under me. Thank God I had not pulled the pin!

I was conscious enough to know that all the shooter had to do was pump a few more rounds to finish me off.

I started crawling toward the door when Sgt. Rautman fired his M-3 submachine gun beyond me. I heard a thump of the fallen

German soldier and voices shouting, "Kamerade, Kamerade!"—meaning they wanted to give up.

Lt. J.S. Wilson and Lt. C.A. Wetzell
Warminster Barracks, England.
August, 1944.

Strong arms gathered me up and dragged me back to the house across the street. Sgt. Rautman called for our medic.

Fully conscious, I was aware that I had been hit in the upper left part of my body, but the pain had not started. In the dark, I reached my right hand into my field jacket and felt warm gooshy stuff! Something had blown my guts out! I reached for my left arm and couldn't find it. So when the medic came, I told him he was wasting his time. "My guts are blown out and my arm is blown off!"

He examined me and pulled out a ripped C-ration can. Those "guts" were meat and beans! The bullet that would have hit my heart was deflected by the can. Rolling me over, he pulled my left arm out from under me. Though shattered, it was still attached, and he assured me that it could probably be saved. He gave me a shot of penicillin and a shot of morphine, bandaged my chest and put a splint on my arm.

As they placed me on the stretcher to take me to a field hospital, Sgt. Rautman brought in three German prisoners. He placed something on the stretcher beside me, saying, "You might want to keep this as a souvenir."

The pistol that shot me, given to me by the man who saved my life, is now one of the most prized possessions of Gastonia's American Military Museum.

A Day in the Woods
by
Robert Brownlee Welsh
Author of *Two Foes to Fight*
Mecklenburg County, NC

Supposedly, we were to be pushing the Germans in the Saar Valley on the French-German border. Our tanks were running out of gas, and all forces had slowed to a stop and taken defensive positions. On December 15, 1944, my company from the 3rd Battalion, 347th Regiment, 87th Infantry Division, Patton's 3rd Army entered Nazi territory for the first time.

Captain Kidd had told me to take the company up in the woods behind Walsheim into some previously prepared foxholes topped with earthen covered logs. I told my runner, Jack, to tell the platoon sergeants the plan. He and I would be in the center on the phone, communicating with the platoons with hand signals.

It was a bright, lazy, still but cold day, and hot chow would be brought up. The guys went into the holes and just sat there, resting up, after a hard week of having lost half our company.

Suddenly, here came a familiar whooshing of a shell. We scrambled for cover, and I got on the phone reporting the situation. The shelling became incessant. The Krauts had something more in mind than harassment. It was preparation for a counter attack.

Yelling into the phone demanding counter battery fire, I was lying on my back looking between my legs through the opening of the foxhole on the forward side of the hill. A burst in the tree above me came crashing into the hole. "I've been hit in the knee!" I hollered into the phone. "Send the meat wagon!"

Then I looked right next to my leg. A steaming slab of shrapnel was imbedded on the side of the foxhole, one inch from my thigh. Like a chain saw, it had severed the log that hit my knee

About that time the shelling ceased, and Sergeant Twibill was coming up with one of his squad. They weren't in my platoon, and I was only a lowly 2nd lieutenant, but since I was the acting company commander and the only officer present, they were reporting to me.

"Lieutenant," Twibill began hesitantly, "Stenhouse here is scared. Just look at him shake. He's driving the guy in his hole nuts. He wants to ask you if he can go to the rear...to the hospital."

I looked from one to the other momentarily, trying to guess what Captain Kidd would say. Stenhouse was kind of vibrating, as if from the cold. We had never even had lessons in German, let alone in shell shock. No one expected to see soldiers crack up. If we had been on the offensive, rather than just sitting on our butts, we wouldn't have had time to get in this shape. I thought of Sergeant Lane in the foxhole next to us, who had just frozen in place sitting on a stump: KIA, then I scanned Stenhouse to see if there was a zombie look in the private's eyeballs. I wouldn't know the difference. No one had ever described battle fatigue to us at OCS.

"Stenhouse," I finally said in the firmest, most authoritative voice I could muster, "we are all scared. If you leave this area, you will regret it the rest of your life."

With that, they both turned around and went back to their positions.Then the shelling resumed. Again, I was on the phone, telling the operator to get Captain Kidd. The line went dead. I turned to my runner. "Jack, the line has been severed. Get ready to trace this wire to the break and splice it. Then go tell the captain to do something. We are getting murdered!"

"Look at that woods across the field, " he said.

A reinforced patrol of Germans had materialized, getting ready to come across to our positions. We had left the radio back at HQ and had no communication at all!

As soon as the shelling stopped again, I shoved Jack out of the hole. He started running back toward the town of Walsheim, with the wire sliding through his fingers.

I held the phone to my ear, desperately hoping to get a connection. "K company to CP," I kept repeating.

"This is Cannon Company," a voice said.

"Cannon Company," I shouted in relief. "I need you!" What type of Divine Intervention had taken place to connect me to them rather than Company Headquarters? I wondered. "I need some artillery in the field in front of this position. There are a bunch of Krauts in the woods opposite us. We've been pummeled for about an hour. They may think they can attack a company-sized position." I told him I'd give the coordinates, so they could put a round of phosphorous in the field, "so I can see it's your gun and not one of theirs."

"On the way," the calm voice replied.

The round landed exactly as ordered, the contrails of pluming phosphorous streaking in jagged angles from the smoke cloud of the exploding shell. Now I could "fire for effect."

The Krauts, on seeing that, simply disappeared. The shelling ceased.

Surrounded
by
Robert Brownlee Welsh
Author of *Two Foes to Fight*
Mecklenburg County, NC

As the newly appointed leader of the Tiger Patrol, I was stunned when Major Chapman took about 30 minutes after organizing us to send us out without a dry run or rehearsal.

An infantryman in Patton's 3rd Army, I would have liked to have simply sat listening to the crackling fire in the grate at the Battalion Headquarters, a house in Bonnerue, Belgium, but Chapman already had an assignment for us.

Previously, I had been replaced as platoon leader in K Company after Major Chapman had ordered me to retrieve two men from I Company's positions on our defensive ridge in the Saar. When our company pulled out without us, we had to hitchhike 125 miles up to the Ardennes.

Now, despite the GIs' cardinal rule against it, I was "volunteered" for the Tiger Patrol. The other dozen of the patrol, I assumed, had volunteered rather than go to the stockade for some misdemeanor. Nevertheless, I had to follow through.

During what is now known as the Battle of the Bulge, in late December, 1944, our mission was to make contact with the Germans who had surrounded Bastogne and the 101st Airborne.

I just arbitrarily selected Private Gilbert Rea, to be second behind me as my "back up." This proved to be a significant choice on my part, for we became a team for the duration of the patrol's existence.

Following orientation by Lt. Guest, who was in charge of intelligence, we left at about 10 p.m., I sent Sergeant Wejan with four men to move up the right flank of the battalion sector. I would take four more up the left flank. Wejan and I were to meet at about 3:30 a.m. to consolidate information to be presented to our regimental commander, Colonel Tupper.

I had the map of the itinerary in my head as we went forward. After wading a little creek and crossing some cattle wire, we proceeded along the edge of a wood for a while in snow that varied from two inches to two feet. Generally, there was a several-inch powder thickness over a nice crunchy base, so we could walk silently except for a slight squeak. Soon, we noticed there were empty foxhole emplacements behind the brambles on the left of a trail toward a forest.

Does that tell us something? Well, I guessed so, and it later proved that the Krauts abandoned their foxholes of the day to retreat to farm buildings at night in the bitter cold. We could tell they were there because of the smell of their tobacco.

When we returned to Regimental Headquarters, I suggested to Col. Tupper that the battalion take the same route by the empty foxholes at night. If we were quiet enough, the Krauts in the five Tiger tanks off to the right 500 yards away across the L'Ourthe River would not be alerted to fire on us.

He took my advice. The next night, I Company and K Company took that route in single file. The trouble was, I wasn't with them to keep them going on through the forest to the fields on the other side. As they reached the dense woods, they were not unobserved. A German patrol came in from the side and snatched one of the men. No one knew what happened. There was little noise. No scuffle. Not a shout and not a shot. He just turned up missing.

I was at headquarters, where I later learned that other tanks were covering that field beyond the woods we had reconnoitered in addition to those covering the woods where our troops ended up. This was the German Army surrounding Bastogne, which was still ten kilometers away. Like the 101st Airborne, our companies, too, became surrounded.

"Lieutenant," Major Chapman ordered all of a sudden, "Go round up all the cooks, jeep drivers, clerks and anyone else not on emergency duty." We both knew this was a desperate situation. Our battalion could not retreat. There was no reserve to relieve them. We had to resupply those men. Enemy patrols were harassing them and the tanks in the fields were firing high explosives into the trees with shrapnel flying like buckshot.

Chapman looked straight at me. "The only people to carry the food, ammo and batteries is your patrol and the extra personnel. You get the people and I'll make up a list of supplies."

Yes, it was true. I had recommended the strategy of possible annihilation and capture of the whole battalion. I had to atone.

The first night, our patrol made it without incident. The next night, a German shepherd was staked out near the empty foxholes to bark the alarm for the tanks to open fire. Startled, I took a short breath and walked boldly to the dog, as if I were going to feed him. Without hesitation, I put the point of my trench knife to his jugular. Talking to him in low tones, I jerked my head to the patrol, motioning to them to go on by. I'd grown up with dogs, and I guess I had a way with them, for this one did nothing. Didn't whine or wag his tail, just kept eye contact. After they passed by, I moved up to the front of the file.

When we got to the stream, we filled five-gallon water tanks. Some kind of thaw was happening, maybe nature's signal that aircraft could soon fly. Patton, we heard, had ordered his chaplain to make up a prayer asking God for better weather. (The story that got down to us was "Patton ordered God to clear the skies.")

That night, we found that German patrols had been throwing grenades into the foxholes, which were open on both ends. The wounded were loaded on stretchers for us to take out, and our guys were reticent about having to take wounded prisoners out.

The third night, they wanted M Company's heavy machine guns to put on one of the corners of the battalion square. We took the same route, but as we approached the battalion area, we were stopped by heavy firing. A German patrol was slicing through the area. "Put that gun on its tripod and load up," I ordered.

We didn't need it. After ten minutes, we proceeded. On the other nights, I had simply called out to the guards that we were coming in and not to shoot. This night, we needed a password. GIs who didn't know the password would be suspected of being another German patrol trying to infiltrate. No one could radio in the password without some Kraut on the same frequency picking it up. This was going to be tough.

Then we got the idea to yell, in our accents from Brooklyn to Georgia, words that the besieged battalion would recognize: "Betty Grable! Benny Goodman! Joe DiMaggio! It's us, bringing in supplies."

In other words, "Don't shoot!"

It worked!

Overlord, Market Garden, Battle of the Bulge
by
Steven Epps
York County, SC

At 1:55 a.m. on June 6, 1944, the 82nd and 101st Airborne Divisions were over Normandy, preparing to jump. Those of us from the 505th Parachute Infantry Regiment of the 82nd had been trained, when the red light comes on, to stand up, hook up our main parachute to the static line and check the equipment of the paratrooper in front of us. When the green light goes on, out we go.

Our Company F had been briefed about the terrain and landmarks around our target. Our mission was to drop five miles inland, take a town and then hold two bridges to keep the Germans from sending reinforcements.

We had been told that, on approach, the planes would go up to 2,500 feet momentarily, where there was not so much light artillery (we called it " ack-ack"), and then descend to between 800 and 600 feet, so that we could jump. Our chutes would have just time enough to open before we hit.

As we got to 2500 feet, the red light went on, then the green—and out we went. I found out years later that, when the pilots were aware of artillery popping, they flipped on the green lights and turned back to England.

For me, it seemed that French ground was lower than the English, where we'd trained. Other parachutes were floating all around me. Those who hit water with 110 pounds of equipment (rifle, ammunition, rations, emergency parachute, blanket and half a tent) drowned.

I hit an open field a mile or so from Sainte Mère Eglise. I reached for the trench knife to cut my leg straps and chest straps. It was missing. We were supposed to quickly cut those straps, roll up the parachute, hide it, and get out of sight. I was wrestling with my straps when I heard someone coming my way. I froze to make myself think I was invisible. In the moonlight, I saw the stalker— the prettiest cow I'd ever seen.

Some of our guys came by. "Want some help?" one asked, and cut off the chute. Soon others had gathered, and we started toward our target. All around were small fields surrounded by hedgerows. Some of the hedges were above our heads. If we heard something, we would click our cricket (a child's toy that made a click). If we got a double click back, we knew it was one of us. If not, we shot the enemy.

At Sainte Mère Eglise, we had heavy casualties. Several paratroopers had floated over the town. I recognized three who had been in the plane with me. One was hanging in a tree, his guts spilling out. Another, who was on the side of the road, looked as if he'd been trying to get out of his parachute. The third, about 19, was lying on the ground, parachute on, probably dead when he hit. Three buddies that I had just talked to while loading the plane—*all dead!* That matures a 19-year-old real quickly.

John Steele, whom I knew personally, was hanging on the steeple of the church playing dead. I didn't recognize him at the time.

Although it had been heavily guarded, we had taken the town by 6 a.m. The Germans were in disarray, but they began regrouping. It was not fully daylight when I saw a couple of gliders come in. The German Field Marshal Rommel had planted what we called "asparagus" (railroad ties or telephone poles) in large fields to disintegrate those light gliders. I don't know how anyone could walk away, but I saw members of both crews alive.

That afternoon, we heard a rumble as a tank rolled up. Then we saw an American star on it. Still, we had sleepless nights there awaiting rescuers. When more came, we started driving inland toward St. Lô. Thirty-three days later, we went back to our tent city in England, where we had trained. Of the 12,000 from the 82nd Airborne who jumped in Operation Overlord, 5,900 returned.

Soon, we were training for Operation Market Garden in Holland. On a sunny Sunday afternoon, 2 o'clock September 17, we jumped 22 miles behind enemy lines at Groesbeek, where we'd be attached to the British. The 82nd and 101st Airborne Divisions were to link with the British Red Devils. Our spy network told us that the Germans would concentrate on one division. It was the Red Devils. We made our way from Groesbeek to Nijmegen to take a Waal River bridge so that approaching British tanks could cross it. We stayed on a hill overlooking the bridge in a park that we took over. When two tanks were crossing the bridge, the Germans knocked them out. We were supposed to relieve the Red Devils, but, with our way blocked, we and the British armored division had to sit there while they were slaughtered. Of 10,000, as many as 8,000 were killed.

Meanwhile, our troops were infiltrated by Hitler Youth dressed as Americans. German snipers were shooting from nearby apartment buildings. We lost quite a few on that hill.

Finally, we got to France for some R & R. Immediately on our return, we were put on a flatbed truck and driven to Bastogne, Belgium. Field Marshal Von Rundstedt was amassing troops on what would be a suicide mission to break through near St. Vith in Belgium. They had equipped 24 to 26 divisions (including two armored Panzer divisions) into three armies for this final push known as the Battle of the Bulge.

The 505th was the first to leave for the front. We passed through Bastogne and moved north to Werbomont, where we would

77

form a wedge for our troops to come back through. Snow was up to our knees and sometimes to our waists, but we had no snow equipment, not even waterproof snowpack shoes. Some men got frostbite as we marched in a column at night. At daylight, three of us would dig a foxhole and wrap up in our frozen blankets. Two would try to sleep, while one would watch.

We had been in Belgium two months when several of us got a chance to ride on a tank. We were warming our hands on the exhaust as we met another tank. Neither crew recognized the others as enemies at first. The tanks were nose-to-nose and got to firing. That's when I bailed out and was rolling in the snow, trying to protect myself. I got a flesh wound in my thigh, bad enough to get sutured, but it didn't take me out of action. In fact, I crossed the Siegfried Line with the 505th.

The German offensive came to an end, and the 505th participated in a counteroffensive that drove them back to the Siegfried Line. We continued fighting through the Huertgen Forest. In February of '45, we returned to our base in France to be re-equipped and receive replacements before being sent to the Elbe River.

As we waited for the Russians to join us, German soldiers began surrendering in droves. We took a break from processing them one day when our commanding officer called us together. "I forgot to tell you," he began. "The war in Europe was over yesterday."

D-Day: Utah Beach
by
Billy C. Coleman
Saluda County, SC

With all those thousands and thousands of men and millions of tons of equipment in England in May, 1944, it's a wonder that island didn't sink!

I was stationed at the Dartmouth Royal Naval College, which the US Navy had taken over. We officers stayed in the college, and the enlisted men had quonset huts outside. A lieutenant junior grade, I was put in charge of 67 LCMs, and we were sent to Poole near Bournemouth on the southern coast of England, where we spent two weeks, eating, sleeping, listening to radio music with German propaganda and waiting.

On June 3, the captain of the base called me in. "At ease, Coleman," he said. "I am going to let you in on one of the world's greatest secrets: D-Day is June 5th. H-Hour is 6 a.m. Go back and call your officers together. Tomorrow, your boats will rendezvous at a certain buoy at 1300 (1 p.m.), where a British MTB boat will pick you up and lead you where you need to be." He told me that, at 5 a.m. on June 5, we were supposed to get abreast to go in and hit the beach.

That afternoon, D-Day was postponed for 24 hours. Some of our boys celebrated, they believed, for the last time. But the next day, they were back on their feet ready for business.

As our 67 boats headed down the river toward the English Channel, they looked like a big long snake, but when the MTB showed up at the buoy, we fell in four abreast. We were not allowed to strike a match to light a cigarette in the darkness. I told everyone to keep a man on the ramp to watch for the boat ahead. At 5 a.m., we lined up in front of the beach as ordered. We didn't know that it was Utah nor that it was Normandy. It was still black dark.

At 5:30, all the world went off! Thousands of ships that we did not know were out there all turned loose, shelling the beach and inland, especially the fortified "pill boxes." The shells were flying over us, but the whole boat shook. Our LCM carried five Army guys with something that looked like a big fire hose, 5-6" in diameter. When they hit the beach, they wound that around the big crosses of railroad irons, which were wrapped with barbed wire to protect the beach. Other men were winding their hoses on other crosses, and then they lit a fuse and destroyed them with explosives. Immediately, the Army boys were cleaning up a certain area and marked it with a red flag on the port and green on the starboard side. We were to unload between those flags and go to whatever ship to get another load of supplies. As we headed back from taking our second load, day was breaking. On our third trip, they were still cleaning up the beach while under intermittent fire. By the next one, all the debris was out of the way.

Behind the sand was a wall 2-3' in thickness with German pill boxes along the coast. On the third day, one of my men, Sliwa, ventured up to a pill box and found three Germans burned to death. He "liberated" a German Lugar and a long sword for a souvenir.

The enemy was still firing long-range to the beach. Every time we went in, we did not know whether we would come out.

Our crew's only weapon was my .45, which I quit carrying because it was too heavy and got in the way.

Only one man from all 67 LCMs was killed during the Utah invasion. The rest of us were just lucky.

Red Ball Express
by
Leroy ("Pop") Miller
Rowan County, NC

As we came onto Omaha Beach around D-Day+5, I already felt nauseated from bobbing up and down on the LST in the English Channel and then trying to wade our way onto the beach, dropping into bomb craters and having to swim out of them. Then I saw the bodies floating upside down and all around.

That afternoon, soon after we entered Sainte Mère Eglise, we were strafed. Around 9 p.m., I was giving a boy from Philadelphia, Lloyd Martin, a light. His lighter had gotten wet coming in. I had aviation gas in mine, so I was holding my cigarette against his when a sniper hit him. The bullet caught Lloyd above his left eye and blew the back of his head off. I jumped as his brains spilled out. The only thing we could do was cover his body with a blanket and affix his bayonet onto his M-1 rifle. Then we stuck the rifle into the ground and placed his helmet on top of it.

When we landed, we were the 846th Anti-Aircraft Battalion, but while we were dug in after St. Lô fell, orders came down that made almost every black outfit a trucking company. Our B Battery became B Company of the 4252 Trucking Company with 42 trucks. Our commanding officer, Zebedee Chaney, had been with the 369th National Guard out of New York. (Black officers were almost always from the North, because there were no blacks in the National Guard in the South.)

We called ourselves "Top Hatters" since Chaney was from New York, and New Yorkers knew everything, had been everywhere and done everything. We had cut a stencil and were putting top hats on our trucks, when orders came from battery headquarters that all trucking companies would be the Red Ball Express. A red ball was painted on our trucks.

Tanks and artillery had to be serviced with gas and ammunition, and our first job was to supply the 2nd Armored Division of General Patton's 3rd Army. When Patton broke out from St. Lô, it was hard to keep up with him; he was moving so fast. About that time, General Eisenhower authorized battlefield promotions. I went from buck sergeant to staff sergeant and Chaney made captain.

I tried to have two drivers for each truck. A couple of our outfit didn't know how to drive, but they got on-the-job training. At first, a jeep with a 2nd lieutenant and staff sergeant would lead the convoy. Later, an officer would ride "shotgun" or bring up the rear.

Two things I didn't like to haul: gasoline and personnel. They'd shift when you'd go around a curve.

Several times, we had to carry POWs. The first ones were Italian, and they stayed with our group and worked in the motor pool area, changing tires, and whatever the mechanics had them do.

When the 101st Airborne Division got surrounded at Bastogne, 18 of our trucks took a large group of the 320th Field Artillery of the 82nd Airborne around on the left flank and then had to wait about a week for further orders. It was cold as the devil, and the white snow was red with the blood of soldiers.

I had an M-1 and a .45, and we had .50 caliber machine guns in the turret on some of our trucks, but we didn't have to use them there. We just tried to stay warm and do whatever they asked us to do.

We did have some close calls.

Once, while in Germany, 16 trucks were on a mountainous road when Lorenza, a guy from Chicago, lost his brakes. He was passing everybody when he lost his gears. I saw him throw his gear shift out the window while going 60 miles an hour. I ordered our truck to pull in front of him.

Fortunately, it did more damage to his vehicle than ours.

Near the Bay of Biscay, we got caught in the cross fire between our Navy and the Germans.

Another time, we had a load of gas and had to go through a town that was on fire, trying to catch up with Patton.

General George Patton, with his pearl-handled revolver,

Leroy Miller
Bolbec, France
Fall, 1945

81

was the most colorful officer I've ever seen. After one of our runs, he told his orderly, "Give each driver a bottle of Ancient Age." Then he told our lieutenant, "Let them have some fun."

Along with rations, we usually got cigarettes (a carton for two men) and a bottle of schnapps or cognac. Schnapps tasted like white lightning, and cognac was not for me, so we'd usually sell it.

"Spot," B Company's mascot, France. Late summer, 1944

In Bolbec, a French doctor, who pulled a tooth, gave me some cognac. I stayed drunk for a week. Every time I'd take a drink of water, I got drunk all over again.

After the fall of Paris but before DeGaulle came in, some of us went in to see the Arch of Triumph and the Eiffel Tower. We parked our trucks, leaving a guard with them, and began walking around.

It was the only time I saw some black girls in Europe. They were Senegalese out of French West Africa.

One of our buck sergeants named Thorne got real tight with a French girl. The next time I saw him, he was crying. While he was with her, he met a bunch of white guys who worked him over and made him do a "buck dance" (tap dance).

Another light-skinned GI we knew decided to stay in France to marry a girl he met on a bicycle.

Our first day in Paris, I saw an old black fellow. We stopped to talk with him. From Georgia, he spoke fluent English and French. "I ain't never going back there," he said.

We told him how things had changed.

"Naw." He shook his head. "I can't go back."

On V-E Day, we were in Hagenow, Germany. One Sunday shortly after that, we were making a delivery in Charleroi, Belgium where I saw the darndest thing I've ever seen: girls who had been fraternizing with the Germans, had had their heads shaved. They were being chased out of town naked.

From the English Channel to the North Sea, I served my country. People praise the Red Ball Express now, but we certainly didn't get any accolades then. We were just doing our job.

They made a movie about the Red Ball Express some years ago. It had a few white guys in it, but I never saw a white soldier in a trucking company.

Just Getting There
by
Chad Efird
Stanly County, NC

As a B-17 pilot, I flew 36 missions, but one of my most dangerous flights was not over Axis territory. It was taking a new plane from Nebraska via the Great Northern Circle route to England in August, 1944.

The Army Air Corps was losing a lot of planes on the ice cap of Greenland. Some, I have been told, are still in excellent condition, buried in deep snow.

A lot of those pilots got lost and ran out of fuel trying to get oriented. I know how that felt.

At Goose Bay Air Base in Labrador, we got a briefing, at which we were told to fly at 13,000 feet to get over the mountains of Greenland.

Normally above 10,000 feet, we had to go on oxygen. We had no oxygen.

At 13,000 feet, my co-pilot, Bruce Miracle of Palo Alto, and I could see nothing but clouds, and our propellers were icing. With no de-icer, those props get very inefficient. The speed slows down. We had to increase power to maintain altitude.

As our timing was off, I asked our navigator Chris Tack to check to see if we had crossed Greenland, so I could go down and get out of the ice.

"Oh yeah!" he said.

Immediately, we headed down to 10,000 feet.

A few minutes later, Tack was screaming "bloody murder." "NO! I miscalculated! Greenland's ahead!"

I pulled back up to 13,000 feet. More ice on the props. I increased the prop speed by lowering the pitch. It took more rpm's, but the ice began sliding off. That threw us out of balance and set the whole plane to vibrating.

Lost! We all knew that if we ended up on an ice cap, there would be no search-and-rescue. If we went down in the North Atlantic, we would freeze to death. Had we survived for even a few minutes, we knew there were not many air-sea rescues then.

At last, Tack assured me that we had cleared Greenland and could go back down. The only time I saw water was through a cloud break as we were approaching Iceland. All I could see was white caps until something seemed to extend out of them: Meeks Field!

Iceland was gloomy, but we were elated.

"Thank you, God!"

Our Bombs, Their Suicide Bombers
by
Chad Efird
Stanly County, NC

"We might have to get out!" I called out to my crew.

Only one month into combat duty, and I was ready to ditch my B-17 and take my chances.

As members of the 8th Air Force, 452nd Bomb Group, 730th Squadron, we were approaching Ludwigshafen, Germany, to bomb a railroad bridge/autobahn complex, some chemical works and industrial areas.

The pins were not out of our bombs when, at 25,000 feet, 88 mm anti-aircraft fire hit our #3 engine.

I needed to feather the prop, but I couldn't, because we had lost oil pressure. Had I been able to feather it, we could have made it back to England with three engines.

The nose section of the #3 engine was getting extremely hot. Flames broke out. Bruce Miracle, my co-pilot, hit the red button to feather the prop and kill the engine, but that didn't work. He had dropped off his oxygen mask and was yelling, "What do we do now?" He was getting woozy, and I was getting more scared by the minute.

Turning back toward Belgium, I alerted the crew. Miracle, who was holding his mask in place, and I made eye contact. We knew what we had to do.

An ex-football player from Stanford, Miracle had wanted to be a fighter pilot, but he was too big. He had to settle for co-pilot, until he could get checked out to pilot a B-17. *If* he lived to do that.

Once over Belgium, I gave the order, "Get out!"

Our crew had discussed such a possibility before and had learned from reports about the fate of those who had hesitated or debated. Now, without a word, everybody got out—except Miracle and me.

We tried another nose dive with more speed to attempt to put out the fire. It didn't work. It was our turn to bail out.

"Get out!" I said to him. Miracle dropped between our seats into the navigator's compartment. I left my seat to check the rest of the plane to be certain everyone else was out. They were.

As I was moving down, Miracle popped back up, still woozy. "How in the Hell does that door stay open with the wind blowing against it?"

"The door is gone! Get out!" I screamed. My mask was off by then.

Miracle weighed 220 pounds, and all we had were small chest-type chutes. When his opened, one panel ripped from top to bottom. He could see me through the hole. The suspension lines held it together until he landed safely in a field.

I looked at my watch on the way down and it was 10 a.m. Wham! I hit a fence, going backward, and ended up flat on my back in a cow pasture, bruised and banged up.

Within a few hours, we had all been rescued by the Free French (the Underground). I thought they were Germans at first, but that area of Belgium had just been liberated.

Two of the guys carried me until I regained my senses. Then the leader came over and said in perfect English, "Are you hurt?"

"Banged up a little bit."

"I grew up in Chicago, lived there 13 years," he said. "We're going to take care of you."

He was true to his word. They took us into a little village nearby. The top of the hotel was blown off, but we stayed in the basement. The next day, they linked us with a unit from the Canadian Army, who took us to Lille. The Canadians got in touch with the British who sent a DC-3 type cargo plane to get us back to London. From there, we called our base in Attleboro, north of London, and our commanding officer came to pick us up in a B-17.

After that, I went through cycles. On some rough days, I would think: "There's no way I can make it." On others, I would say to myself: "This is not too bad. I'm going to make it."

By April, 1945, it seemed that there were not as many German fighters opposing us. The flak was not as intense as before.

On April 7th, we headed out on our 29th mission. That day, the weather in England was better than usual. We left Attleboro's Depham Green Field and headed out in formation, three V-shaped squadrons of 12 planes each. Slightly behind the lead squadron to the left and below was one set. We were to the right and above.

Our target was a tactically important airfield at Kaltenkirchen, Germany. If we were successful, we could not only ground a sizeable force of jet-propelled fighters and reduce the effectiveness of Hitler's aerial harassment of Allied ground forces, but we could knock out the buildings where jet technology was being tested.

On our approach, four German planes came at us head-on. "What in the Hell was that?" yelled our co-pilot Wilford Foeste.

I called out, "A-20." That was a medium bomber with larger engines than ours.

"A-20s can't fly that fast!" said Foeste.

He was right. Those were jets. They could fly much faster than our B-17G, the latest model. Ours had a total of 13 .50 caliber guns, with a new chin turret under the nose, but our maximum speed was about 200 miles per hour. Their jets could fly at 450 to 500 mph. Their rate of closure was so fast they were a blur.They made a sharp turn and headed away from us. But more jets were coming at us. Propeller driven planes were all around us, too.

1 St. Lt. Chad Efird

Chad Efird in his B-17 "Hi Blower" on which he flew 30 missions. Depham Green Field, Attleboro, England. Spring, 1945.

"Oxygen okay?" I called out. "Y'all okay?"

"Yep." came from all nine other positions.

Then someone yelled, "That SOB's right up under me!" Seconds and a round of gunshots later, the same voice added, "I got the SOB!"

Suddenly, it felt like our plane was going to shake apart. The chin gun, operated by our bombardier, was in front of us pilots; the upper turret right above us. Both were firing repeatedly. We had on headphones which really didn't keep out the noise of those workhorse cyclone engines. That, with the fuselage shaking and the gunfire, were deafening.

Then we saw what we know now were young "greenhorn" pilots on suicide missions, heading for our planes and firing at the same time. Their purpose: to knock down B-17s and B-24s. They might be above and dive down on our group, clipping off a tail, or they'd hit head on, nose-to-nose. I was looking below, watching our commander in the lead squadron, when his deputy got hit on the windshield. It burst into a ball of fire. There went another one!

A German fighter was coming at us, chased by a P-51. The German plane blew up. Its engine fell off right in front of our plane. The pilot's body flipped end over end, end over end, like a rag doll right before our eyes. Then the P-51 blew up, probably from friendly fire.

We got one big lick as a jet fighter came by and hit our left wing tip with a large projectile, most likely a 20 mm cannon.

Apparently, the Luftwaffe knew that we were about to win. Their plan was to wipe out a whole bomber group, to buy time so they could do more work on jet technology and the atomic bomb.

They followed us to our target. Even with their interference, most of our squadron's bombs got within the target area.

All but four of our 36 planes got back to base, although there was lots of battle damage. Ours had a trench from that 20 mm hit.

Whew! Eight hours and 20 minutes of flying, with 45 minutes of pure Hell. Could we rest now?

No way! The next day it was Pfauen, eight hours and 40 minutes. The next: Munich, nine hours, 25 minutes. Then Zerbst, eight hours. Donauwörth, eight hours, 5 minutes. In all, 36 before April 15th.

Sometimes, between missions, we didn't get any sleep at all. We could not eat on the flights, because we couldn't remove our oxygen masks, so we'd arrive weak and hungry. I would be so exhausted that, at 22 years old, I couldn't climb up onto the back of a GI truck. Someone would have to boost me up so I could get back to the briefing room.

Right after the wheels touched down from that 36th mission, I knew I was home free. All I had to do was taxi that monster to the other side of the field and get out. I raced to the communications area of base headquarters to send a telegram to my brand new wife whom I hadn't seen in nearly nine months. That was the happiest day of my life.

Unseen Angels
by
John Archibald
Rockingham County, NC

When the 8th Air Force in England reduced crew sizes from ten to nine, I was dropped and given an office job. I complained.

My commanding officer thought I was crazy. "You've got a monthly trip to London, a new Jeep and a desk job, and you want to fly combat?!"

"Yes, sir. That's what I trained to do," I said confidently. For me, a B-24 combat crew member at age 19, dying was an abstract notion.

He told me that the 18th Air Force 559th Bomb Group was taking tremendous casualties—about 50%—and I could volunteer for that.

I did and in October, 1944 was transferred to Italy to serve in a pool of bombardiers. Never on a specific crew, I flew whenever the need for a bombardier arose. My first mission was to support the Russians in northeast Poland, and I was needed on 26 more missions, mainly going through Hitler's back door to the Hungarian oil fields and oil refineries, which were heavily guarded by anti-aircraft artillery.

Sometimes, we dropped bombs on railroad bridges or on marshalling yards, where multiple tracks converged and war materiel was transferred and transported out. We knew that if we could stop the fuel and supplies from getting to the front, we could win the war.

Think of it: 27 missions with a 50% rate of casualties! That's why I read my Bible every night. I am not ungrateful to God.

But until 1990, I never knew who His angels were. Only when I watched an HBO movie, did I hear of the Tuskegee Airmen, who flew above our formation, guarding us on all our missions. That's why I never saw any German fighters. The Tuskegees became decoys, engaging them in battle while we did our jobs.

I knew there were blacks in the Army, but not on flight status. All the ones I saw were filling the menial jobs (quartermaster, motor pool, cooking). Yet, these brave men never lost a single bomber to enemy fighters, although some of them were killed or taken prisoner.

The Airmen proved our government wrong. The prevalent thought then was that blacks were incompetent. Before Pearl Harbor, government powers-that-be did not consider an air attack from Japan imminent. They thought that Japanese couldn't see well enough to fly with those slanted eyes.

Now, I am grateful to those Tuskegee Airmen. They were willing to die for freedoms they couldn't enjoy.

John Archibald
Arignola, Italy.
April, 1945.

Another Kind of Guest
by
Bert Connor
Lexington County, SC

We called ourselves "dinner guests," because, after flying four hours from Foggia, Italy, to our targets in Germany, we'd be dropping our bombs around the noon dinner time. In anticipation of anti-aircraft fire, we'd open the windows and throw out 15 to 20 bushels of tinfoil like what we hung on Christmas trees, singing "Jingle Bells," while the foil was messing up the Germans' radar. Although accompanied by Tuskegee Airmen fighter escorts, but with 500 88 mm guns pointed in our direction, a large percentage of our B-24s were likely to be hit.

As a ball turret gunner with the 456th Bomb Group in the 15th Air Force, I could see 360° around, when our target was the synthetic oil fields on the Oder River near the German-Czechoslovakian border. At midday on December 2, 1944, I saw that the storage tanks looked like a forest. Trees had been tied on the tops.

Our formation had three layers (Able, Baker and Charlie) of six planes each. We were flying Able #5 that day. Our bomb bay doors were open when I saw Able #2 explode. Then Able #4 got hit and fell out of formation. I looked to my left to see our #1 engine get shot clean off. With loss of hydraulics, our pilot, Lee Warren had no control, and we went into a slow, flat spin. I had to climb out of the turret to get my parachute, hook it on my harness and bail out. Lee was waiting for me, and we jumped together.

Bert Connor (right) greeting his Navy friend, W.B. McDowell, who was also on furlough in Cayce, SC. April, 1944.

I delayed opening my chute as long as I could so I would not be a target as we floated over Czechoslovakia's white Capathian Mountains with trees like spikes with no limbs. In that whole area, there was only one clearing, a garden with goats, and I landed in it.

Lee came down within 30 feet, but wind caught up his parachute and flung him into a big boulder, busting his mouth and knocking him "out of his head."

Through the falling snow, I saw a little boy, wearing a green felt hat, hiding behind a goat house. He was probably scared, having seen two strange-looking men fall from the sky through a snow cloud. But he soon came over, pointed to my oxygen mask and handed me his hat.

I took off my mask and gave it to him. I didn't wear his hat long: it smelled like those goats!

Lee was talking junk, making no sense, but I got him up, and we searched for the rest of our crew. Within three hours, we had found all but Olly, our waist-gunner, who had jumped first. Then the boy led us down a log road to a community of six or seven houses. His mother served us tea and bread, which we ate sitting on the floor, because her home did not have nine chairs. I gave the boy and his mother some chewing gum, which they happily chewed and swallowed.

As we were trying to talk with our hands, I heard a old man's voice at the door. "Where did you guys come from?"

We asked him the same question.

"I'm the grandfather," said the 85-year-old. He explained that he had worked in a clothing store in Pittsburgh, Pennsylvania, and had come back to visit when the war started. He told us that we would have to get out by 7 p.m., because that's when the German patrol came through. A relative would try to get us to the underground.

The relative was a 16-year-old, who told us to stay close together, as we crossed the road and started up a mountainside. Just then, a truck with eight Germans drove up and began looking around the houses, bushes and trees. In a hushed voice, the boy said, "Follow this trail. Don't look back." Then he rushed up another mountain and was soon firing from the woods to divert the Germans.

After 18 or 20 miles, it was midnight and snowing. We were exhausted. I suggested we make a fire behind a boulder and showed the others how to build a lean-to. "Where did you learn this? " our tail gunner wanted to know. "At survival school?"

"No, Boy Scouts," I said.

We had opened our Army-issued escape kits (with a silk map of the region, compass, $48 in American money marked with a gold seal, vitamins, and matches). From the map, we determined that we needed to go southeast, so that next morning we headed toward Yugoslavia.

Later, we came to a clearing in a valley near a church. As it was Sunday, we watched until we thought all the villagers had entered the church before crossing the field. A couple, arriving late, spied us. We kept going.

On Monday morning, we were in the woods on the next mountain, when two men in their 70s or 80s, approached us. I went out to meet them, and one handed me a note with Olly's Polish name on it.

Assuming Olly was trying to make contact, we followed the men to a country store.

On the counter was a parachute and some GI shoes that looked like they had been through a meat grinder. The mayor of the town, in broken English, told us that they had found Olly's body and had buried it. Their description indicated that his body looked like a bean bag. His chute was sticky with hydraulic fluid and had never opened. We thanked him for burying our friend and turned to our silk map on the table where we were seated.

As we studied the map, a man in a German uniform with a satchel in his hand appeared at the back door. I lunged for my gun, but an old man grabbed my arm. The visitor was a local resident conscripted into the German Army who was on furlough. A doctor, he came to treat Lee.

When it got dark, the mayor and his 13-year-old son took us in an old, old touring car along a narrow mountain road to the next underground stop. He wanted to talk, but I begged him to keep his eyes on the snow-covered road with long precipices below. About 25 miles later, we were relieved to arrive at another village.

We airmen were taken into the back door of a house which had a big room with a heater in the middle of the floor. That's where we ate our first real meal, a bountiful stew with vegetables and some kind of meat, followed by entertainment, a guy playing a guitar and singing. I was thinking, "Gee, this is a lot better than taking the chance of being shot down every day!"

After a good night's sleep, I woke up to see a German sergeant in the middle of our room. All of our clothes were in the hall. Our hosts were gone. Shot? Taken prisoner? We never knew. But we were ordered out, one at a time, to get our clothes so they could take us to gestapo headquarters in Zelenec.

From that day until the end of the war, we experienced no more warm hospitality. From Zelenec, Czechoslovakia, to Luftwaffe Headquarters in Vienna, Austria, to an interrogation center near Frankfurt, on to Berlin and then Stalag Luft #1 near Barth, Germany, we were pelted with rocks by civilians, locked in boxcars (while everyone else hid from the British "block busters" in bomb shelters) and were kept in isolation between interrogations.

Even when we were liberated, the Russians, at first, would not let the 10,000 prisoners fly out of a nearby airfield. But they *did* bring us food—and plenty of vodka.

Our 11th Mission: 1100 Guns Against Us!
by
James Basinger, Jr.
Mecklenburg County, NC

On our 11th mission, our target was Merseburg, known as the oil capital of Germany. It was those synthetic oil fields that kept the machinery going that ran their Wehrmacht. As members of the 34th Bomb Group, 8th Air Force, our B-17s were flying out of Mendlesham, England. I was the radio operator and a gunner of the lead crew. We were called the Pathfinder Group, because we were to hit the target first.

This was about the time of the Battle of the Bulge, and we could fly over and observe those men who were encircled by German troops, cut off from everything in the snow and ice. It was awesome to see those guys survive and come through as American heros. Meanwhile, I was sure glad I was in the air.

Our pilot was John Livingston from Fort Worth, Texas. He never would waver one degree from the target. We would get zeroed in on one in the blackness of the flak from those heavy guns the Germans trained on us, and he never flinched. John's intestinal fortitude and his ability to take a job and do it and never look back were inspirational to me.

My friend from Charlotte, Cadwallader Coles (Cad) Bruns, the tail-gunner, was a real character. I was a boxer in high school. He thought that I could just about whip Joe Louis, and on occasion, he would get me over matched. Cad had more nerve than fighting ability and very poor judgment about picking my opponents. On more than one confrontation, I was the one who got a black eye.

One night in England, Cad "borrowed" a jeep (without anyone's permission, of course) and took us all for a ride to Stowmarket, where the pubs were—and also (more important) the girls. The handles of the jeep hood came loose, and the whole hood turned back in front of us. We ran off the road in a ditch and had to hitchhike back to the base. They never did find out who did it, thank goodness.

As we were proceeding on our 11th mission, a bomb got caught up in the bomb bay with the detonator coming open. Cad was our armorer. He knew all about weapons. While we were over the oil fields, he was hit by flak over his left eye and had a piece of plexiglas from the tail-gunner's position blown through his left eyelid. Cad was a scary sight indeed! He came out of the tail gun section with blood coming from his forehead and the plexiglas still in his eyelid, ran past the waist gun and moved all the way up to the bomb bay. Cad had to take off his parachute and flak vest to hook his arm around the struts. Then he kicked that bomb out and saved the crew—and the airplane!

That day in December, 1944, Merseburg had 1100 guns defending those fields. It was the most important mission, I believe, for our bomb group, because the fields at Merseburg supplied most of the oil that kept Hitler's Wehrmacht in action. We knew that our mission was critical! We were caught in a black barrage of flak we could not see through. There truly was no escape: we had to go through that totally black blanket of destruction and death to accomplish our mission. I made a chapel our of the radio room that day. There was a terrible loss of life among all the crews of that mission. We considered ourselves fortunate. Well, most of us were.

Eddie Ostrowski was operating the right waist gun when a piece of flak struck the opening between the sides of his flak vest. He was killed standing right beside me about six feet away. The other waist gunner, Vern Parker from Goodland, Kansas, rushed to aid him, but it was too late. There was nothing anyone could do for him. At that age, you believe you're invincible until someone next to you dies.

After that, we tried our best to get Livingston to take us to Switzerland, so we could spend the rest of the war over there, but instead, our never-waver pilot put down in Mendlesham.

When we vacated the plane, our crew began counting holes. There were 503 holes in our aircraft. Incredible!

A month or so later, when we went to bomb Berlin, Hitler was hanging out there. They had 500 guns defending the capital city. We hit Berlin twice and never got a scratch, not one hole in the plane!

And yet, you never knew what was right around the next cloud.

First Hit
by
Wallace S. Osborne
Mecklenburg County, NC

Flak! The first time I saw a cone of flak, I was 21 years old and I thought: "Take your gold bars, your silver wings and let me out of here!" When you fly through a wall of flak, it ain't skill, Baby, it's pure luck! I've seen them blow up right next to me. People I knew.

In December, 1944, we were on our first mission to Vienna. I was piloting a Liberator (B-24) with the 716th Squadron, 449th Bomb Group, 15th Air Force. Sixteen planes were in a squadron, four squadrons in a group. We were to bomb the marshalling yards, a crossroads and one of the principal railroad freight yards in Europe for Hitler. They had 300 105 mm anti-aircraft guns and hence, the cone. Three miles ahead we could see the wall of black flak and planes blowing up. Then when we were into it, the plane began to bounce around from the concussions from the flak.

WOOF-WOOF sounds competed with engine noises. The worst thing was seeing the red flashes. Those shells (4 inches in diameter, 10 to 12 inches long) were filled with explosives and shards of metal. The flashes of red were the gunpowder exploding. I wondered when one would go through my head. We couldn't dodge it, because we were following the lead plane. That time, we got home safely.

A number of missions later in February of 1945, we had just gone through another wall of flak and were over a heavily-fortified Innsbruck, Austria, when a burst of flak exploded between our #3 and #4 engines on the right. They both quit.

When you're at an altitude of 25,000 feet, the air is quite thin, and you have superchargers to make those engines work. The flak knocked out our supercharger! We dropped from 25,000 down to 8,000 feet just like a rock! At that point, our navigator/ bombardier, Warren Ames, salvoed our bombs. Our top and bottom ball turret gunners, our waist gunners and even our engineer, Jack Hamilton, threw out all our guns, ammunition and everything else we could get rid of.

We were north of the Alps, which are 13,000 feet high, and we had to get over the Alps to get back to our base in Grottaglie, Italy. At least, when our B-24 got down to 8,000 feet, we didn't need the superchargers. So we "crawled" over the Alps, never knowing when another engine would quit.

It was 40 ° below zero, inside the airplane and outside. We knew if we disconnected our electrically heated jackets, we would freeze to death if we bailed out on top of the Alps. We were so close to those mountains, you could almost reach out and grab a snowball.

In the meantime, Warren Ames was blinded by plexiglas.

The former first-year Harvard law student couldn't see temporarily.

I asked, "Warren, what we gotta do?"

"Just head south over the Adriatic," he replied.

I called the emergency radio station (known by the code name Bigfence) to ask where we were. They could get a fix on us and tell us where to go. Other pilots were calling them, too, but I finally got through. I was told to give them a long count. I said, "Ten, nine, eight, seven, six, five, four, three, two, one..."

I knew to look for Zadar, the emergency landing field, actually a scraped corn field on the western coast of Yugoslavia, but had no idea how to spot it. Just then, the Bigfence controller said, "Look over your left wing."

I swear to God, it was right down there! Truly Providential!

We took a vote on the intercom, "Do you want to bail out or try to land in that corn field?" I asked. We were a family. Everyone had an equal vote.

The crew voted unanimously to go for the landing. We knew that we had only one pass. We didn't have enough power to get around, and we were about out of gas. Otherwise, we feared we might drown. The hydraulic system was disabled, and we had no brakes!

So—we landed safely but went off the end of the field through a barbed wire fence. The whole crew jumped out of the airplane as fast as we could. There was a serious danger of fire. One of the crew helped Warren get to safety.

An officer's jeep came out and picked us up. An American Air Corps major assigned to that emergency landing field took us back to his wall tent. Only three miles from the German front, we could hear artillery and worried that we might end up in a POW camp.

After we had gotten hit, I smoked two packs of cigarettes in two hours, and I was shaking like a leaf by the time I was on the ground. I said to the major, "You wouldn't have a drink, would you?"

The dark-haired Yankee answered sympathetically, "I got a brand new fifth of scotch."

"I'll give you $100 for it," I said. That was a lot of money back then.

He wouldn't take it.

Every Sunday, when I go to church, we have silent confessional prayer, and I thank God for getting me out of that mess. I was glad to do it, but I sure was glad to get back.

An Angel Flies Along on Our 17th Mission!
by
R. Mack Jones
Author of *Detours Along Life's Highway*
Guilford County, NC

The red "alerted" sign over the bar of the Grafton Underwood Airfield Base Officer's Club the night before had notified us
of a mission. Red meant "no booze."

This would be my 17th combat mission as a B-17 pilot
attached to the 384th Bomb Group, 545th Bomb Squadron, Army
Air Corps flying out of England. Our crew of three officers and six
enlisted men anxiously watched as the briefing officer pulled the
cover off the briefing board, showing the map of Germany with the
long red lines indicating the path to and from our target. Berlin—an
extremely long, dangerous mission!

It was February 26, 1945, two days before payday, and I
was practically broke. I had two English pounds of currency in my
wallet, the equivalent of about $8 American.

We had never flown to Berlin before. I had been to Munich
five times. Those were long flights, but this one to the heart of
Germany would be exceptionally tough. We expected a lot of flak
and possibly fighters. The forecast called for a front over the
Channel, which meant we would have to get above the front at
whatever altitude that might be. Usually, we flew at about 25,000
feet, and the service ceiling for a B-17 was about 30,000 feet. We
would be above that, which would mean more fuel consumption.
We would be cutting it close to get to our target and return on our
fuel supply.

Sure enough, we stabilized our altitude at 32,000 feet. Boy,
it was cold up there! I looked at the outside temperature gauge; it
read minus 60 degrees centigrade! We had frost all over the
instrument panel, and our heated gloves were melting the frost on
the throttle controls. The water was dripping down the throttle
control panel and icing up on the floor of the pilot's compartment.

We got well into Germany without incident. No flak. No
fighters. As we approached the target area, bomb bay doors were
open on all the B-17s.

At the most critical stage of our bomb run, the #3 engine,
which was on our starboard side, developed a runaway propeller!
We had no control over it at all, and it created a terrific drag on the
airplane. I tried repeatedly to feather the prop, but it wouldn't

feather. The oil in the prop had frozen and wouldn't allow the control to function. Our air speed was down to 110 mph, just above stall speed!

About this time Jack Barnett, my co-pilot, and I were fighting to maintain altitude, when one of our gunners, Mario Cassagrande, called out on the intercom: "We have a leak in the oxygen supply. We're losing oxygen fast."

The lead plane released its bombs, and, as we staggered over the target smoke markers, Prebble, the toggelier, dropped our bombs.

This helped some, since we had less weight and could close the bomb bay doors, and thus maybe pick up a little airspeed. We still couldn't feather the engine and were losing oxygen. Then our navigator, John Foreman, announced that we would have a 100-knot head wind if we headed back to England.

Our alternatives were Switzerland, where we would be interned for the duration of the war, or to head west across enemy territory and hope we could get to Allied occupied territory or go east. The crew opted to head due east and try to get to Poland or Russia. But Foreman advised us over the intercom: "We have no maps of that area!"

Flying entirely on instruments, we set about getting to a lower altitude. We had no choice. The oxygen was getting low.

Near twilight, we kept on letting down. Our group leader knew of our troubles, but we were no longer in radio contact. Our group was long gone. Having flown for several hours, we figured we must be over Poland. I sure wished my good buddy "Shorty" Slatchetka, who used to be our bombardier, was with us. He could speak Polish.

At about 500 feet, someone called out on the intercom, "Look! Look down there, about four o'clock, a railroad track!"

A ray of hope, finally! A railroad track had to lead to a town. Right. We started circling the town. That's when they began shooting at us with 20 mm cannons. I told our engineer, John Cunningham, to shoot red flares, a distress signal.

We couldn't find an airfield. It was getting darker by the minute and it had started snowing. We picked a plowed field as a good prospect for a landing site. After debating, Jack and I decided we would have a better chance of survival on the unknown snowy terrain if we came in wheels up and skidded on the belly of the plane. Our generally easy-going co-pilot shouted frantically, "Take your crash-landing positions!"

We had to clear some wires at one end of the field, but we made the smoothest landing you ever saw! As soon as we started skidding, I cut off all the switches, so that there would be no chance of an explosion or fire.

As we came to a stop, Jack and I looked at each other, with the realization that an angel had flown with us that day. No one had a scratch on them!

Our radio operator, Donald Hilliard, detonated certain classified equipment before we got out of the airplane. Cassagrande and the other gunners, Edwin Holmes and Ralph Hughes, scrambled out. Just as Jack and I were climbing down, there came a contingent of Russian soldiers in Dodge trucks to welcome us.

Well, we were *hoping* they were coming to welcome us!

Suspicious Allies
by
R. Mack Jones
Author of *Detours Along Life's Highway*
Guilford County, NC

Prior to take-off on our bombing mission to Berlin, shoulder patches with the words "Americanski" had been applied to our flight clothing. During our briefing, we had been told of the possibility of our meeting Russian forces if we had to land.

Now our Army Air Corps crew, having belly-landed in a Polish field, were facing Russian troops who had shot at us until we set off red distress flares. They seemed friendly enough as they loaded the nine of us and our gear onto their trucks and took us to their headquarters in a nearby town, but none could speak English.

After trying to talk with the officer in charge, a Russian major, without much luck, we spread the map of our mission out on a little table next to a kerosene lantern. Several enlisted men watched as we pointed to England. Tracing our route to Berlin, we said "BOOM! BOOM!" Then we made signals to indicate that we had engine troubles and had to land somewhere other than enemy territory. They got the message. We indicated that we were lost. They produced a map to show us that we were in Rawa Ruska (pronounced Rahva Rooska).

Several of us rubbed our stomachs. They understood and produced fried eggs, Russian black bread and lots of vodka. After that, we felt quite a bit better about our situation.

Front row: John Cunningham, Mario Cassagrande, Ralph Hughes, Ed Holmes; back row: Mack Jones, Jack Barnett, John Foreman. England, 1944.

Later, we were taken to the major's quarters, a house about a half-mile away. Our "beds" were pieces of cloth stuffed with straw, very thin and lumpy. At bedtime, the short, rather stout major came to each of us and made us take off our flight suits, indicating that we were to sleep in our longjohns. Even though he had a fire in the fireplace, it was cold.

Figuring he couldn't speak English, I said, "Okay, you SOB, but when you leave, I'm going to put my clothes back on."

That's exactly what we did.

Throughout our stay, we weren't sure whether we were being protected or guarded. When any of us even went to the "bathroom" (a one-holer outside privy), we were escorted by a Russian soldier carrying a sub-machine gun.

They sent us an interpreter, a rather plain woman about 35 years old who had learned English in Canada. Reluctant to speak to us about anything except translations from Russian soldiers, she seemed scared (of the Russians, not us).

We were there only two days, but that last night, the major threw us a party, probably more for his benefit than for ours. When all the vodka was gone, he sent a corporal out for some Russian spirits. He poured that potent liquid into a small vial for each of us. Every time we toasted Stalin, Roosevelt or Churchill, I'd hold up my vial and then pour it under the table. It smelled like they had drained it out of a truck!

The next day, we were trucked to a larger town, Lwow (pronounced La Wuuf), known as Lemburg when it was still in Poland. By then it was part of Russia.

We were taken to military headquarters, where we officers were separated from the enlisted men of our crew and interrogated.

Despite our arm patches, they seemed unsure that we were Americans. We asked the colonel, who spoke English, to contact our commanding officer at Grafton Underwood in England and see that our families were notified. He told us that a plane would come the next day to take us to Moscow.

They sent us to Hotel George, a four-story building, with a "john" more memorable than the privy. In a closet down the hall was a seat with a hole in it and a big bucket beneath. Nothing else, not even a window. You didn't go to the bathroom unless you really had to. When you did, you took a deep breath before entering and held it as long as you could. To take a bath, we called a German maid who brought hot water and poured it into a tub located in another closet.

A Russian civilian who could speak English was assigned to us. Every day, we asked him when the plane was coming. His answer was always the same: "Tomorrow."

We got two meals a day: breakfast (usually black bread and cheese) and dinner (more of the same with a soup known as borscht, plus sausage and vodka). No sweets. We pooled what little money we had and traded it on the black market for rubles, then headed for the Polish bakery.

They told us not to go out after dark for our own protection. We resented the curfew, assuming it was so they could keep an eye on us. But occasionally, we could hear artillery and rifle fire in the distance and figured we weren't too far from some of the action. Then one night, we heard gunfire right below our window! Our room was on the second floor in the front of the hotel. Someone screamed. We all rushed to the window, but it was too dark to see anything. We heard some scurrying around and some shouts in Russian, then all was quiet. Did someone from the town get caught breaking curfew? We never found out.

Of Italian descent, our waist gunner, Mario Cassagrande met a pretty Italian girl with long black hair who worked at the hotel. They conversed in their native language. Through her, we found out that the military had assigned a civilian woman, a member of the Russian NKVD (similar to the Cold-War KGB) to keep track of us. I didn't recall noticing her before, but it became obvious that the tall, 45-year-old woman with dark-rimmed glasses who hung around us was listening to every word.

After that revelation, I told the fellows that we should talk "pig Latin" any time she was around. As boys in Greensboro, my cousin Harry, Jr. and I used to speak it in our neighborhood. Some of our crew picked up on it and got a big kick out of saying things like "Ooday ooyay onay utwhay ia eenmay?" when she was in our presence. We were asking "Do you know what I mean?" Apparently not. The expression on her face was really something!

Two weeks into our stay, Jack, John and I were strolling along an unfamiliar street when we heard English being spoken. We went into the building which turned out to be the police station. An Englishman and a Scotsman, former prisoners of war captured by the Germans and liberated by the Russians, had made their way to Lwow. They had been allowed to stay in the jail because they had no place to sleep. We took them back to the hotel, confronted the manager and told him to give them a room.

In the evening, our hotel restaurant became a night club with a band and good German beer. Our money had run out, so we signed checks with our name, rank, serial number, and US Army Air Corps. After three weeks or so, fed up because "tomorrow" never came, I thought I'd have some fun. I signed the check "Mickey Mouse." The next check I signed "Franklin D. Roosevelt." Then "Winston Churchill." No one noticed the difference.

Not long after that, an American salvage crew appeared in our hotel. Based at Poltava (the only US base in Russia), their job was to find American planes that had crash-landed and salvage whatever they could. They had been en route back to Poltava, when they landed at Lwow because of bad weather. They had no idea that we were there. Was that sheer chance—or an act of Providence? Whatever, they became our ticket out of that place.

As we headed out from the hotel, the local people we had made friends with waved and wished us well.

Those Russian soldiers were NOT our friends. We found out later that the letters we wrote to our families never left Lwow!

Our base had never been notified of our whereabouts! We had been declared "missing in action."

Haircutter and Gravedigger
by
Ed Adams
Newberry County, SC

I like to tell people that I've cut hair in more places than most anybody: in Newberry, South Carolina, in Army camp at Vancouver, Washington, in New York, when we went over to Europe on the Queen Elizabeth, then in England and later in France, Belgium, Holland and Germany.

I started cutting hair during the Depression when I was in a CCC camp. Back then, barbers in Greenwood were getting 25 cents. I charged 20 cents while I was learning. When I was drafted, I was 28, working in a cotton mill in Newberry and had been married two and a half years.

Before going overseas, I was at home on furlough after basic training. I decided I'd better take my tools with me when I returned to Vancouver Barracks.

I had been assigned to the Army Quartermasters, who provided service, supplies and sanitation. Sanitation, for us in the 605 Grave Registration Company, meant keeping the battlefield clear of bodies. I had a carbine (and later a .45), but I didn't ever have to shoot anyone.

Soon after we arrived in England in November, 1943, we were stationed in Tiverton, where, that summer, we were sent to a certain area to pick up bodies brought in by ships during the Normandy invasion. Fortunately, along the strip where my group was assigned, we never got any bodies.

After D-Day, we moved into Southern France. Our work intensified after that. As we went in a little late, there were not too many bodies, but we beautified a cemetery.

On the 18th of September, a Saturday night, the Captain called our company out about 9:30 p.m. I was already in my "two-man hotel" (pup tent), but he told us to get ready to go on a mission. By 10 p.m., the 3rd and 4th Platoons had been dismissed, and the 1st and 2nd (I was in the 2nd) were taking an all-night ride. We were attached to the 82nd Airborne and set up our "two-man hotels" in an apple orchard near Brussels, Belgium. From a distance, we could hear our big guns "softening up" the enemy.

At midnight on the 19th, the paratroopers went out. About 10 minutes to 10 the next morning, all guns stopped firing, like somebody had mashed a button. Our boys must be on their way, I thought. Then I saw them. Some of the C-47s had two gliders behind them. We saw six of those planes coming back. All but one blew up before passing us. It made a crash landing.

Two days later, we went to build a cemetery in Holland, 12 to 15 miles from Amsterdam, for the 82nd Airborne. Behind that was a German cemetery. We buried them, too. At the head of each grave, we put a white cross and attached an embossed plate with the name on it.

One day a Dutchman came with a two-tiered push wagon with pot flowers on it. He asked to put the flowers on some graves. He looked like he was smiling the whole time he was doing it.

There was enemy action all around us. Late one afternoon, English and German fighter planes got into a fight. A German pilot, whose parachute did not open, was still warm when we buried him. I don't believe he had a bone not broken.

About 80 German POWs were digging graves, when we heard that two German tanks had broken through the line. I don't know why I didn't move when I heard the first round, but I didn't. On the third round, when I heard the last balls whiz past, I went to tell the driver of my section, so he could deal with it.

Ed Adams in front of a 4-engine plane at the Eiffel Tower.
Paris, France. Summer, 1945.

Another driver took him to a nearby house, where he shot some windows out. The shooting stopped.

Another time, a young fellow in a paratrooper's work clothes was standing there looking at the graves of all his friends, the better part of a company. He turned to me. "What did you do to get in a company like this?"

"I was drafted," I said.

In all, we buried a little over 500 of the 82nd. The 101st Airborne buried theirs closer to Belgium.

As the war continued, our platoon was attached to the 17th Airborne in Germany. When we were crossing the Rhine River on a pontoon bridge, it was still dark at 4 a.m., and the big trucks had only "cat eyes" (small lights on the back and front). The man under the wheel of our weapons carrier couldn't see the edge of the pontoon. I leaned over to direct him with my mouth: "A little to the right, not too far." We made it.

We were supposed to build a cemetery there, but things were going so well, they didn't need one.

As we traveled on, we'd stop to dig up a few isolated graves beside the road or in a field, and take the dead back to a cemetery. Sometimes, we found bodies so decayed that they were sickening. We didn't eat much those days.

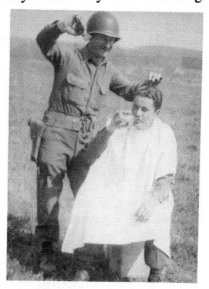

Once, we stopped at a place to pick up a few bodies that people were bringing in for us. Among them was a 16-year-old blonde girl. Germans were using them for decoys. I moved up the line, and the Lieutenant gave me a cross for her that said "One female German." I dug a grave in a corner of a garden, close to a person's home.

When the war was nearly over, we were stationed near Hanover by the Autobahn. A few bombs were still dropping nearby. Some of us walked over to where a pretty good-sized house had been and looked around. There was no house. While we were there, one of the GIs said,

Ed Adams trimming another GI's hair. Near Hanover, Germany. Spring, 1945.

105

"How about a haircut?" He pointed to a big rock and then sat on it. I pulled out my hand-clippers and cut two or three heads of hair while we were there. I was getting 40 cents a head by then and was picking up a little change.

As I was growing up, my dad used to say, "If you ever go to war, it's good to learn the 91st Psalm."

By the time I was a teen, I already knew it. In combat zones, I used it for a daily devotional.

One morning in Germany, about 3 a.m., German machine guns were shooting, and Americans were returning fire close by. For comfort, I began repeating the 91st Psalm. Before I got to the last line, I could hear no more shooting.

I want young people to know that, if you ever get into war, you need to remember the 91st Psalm. If you don't know it, read it now.

Blackout Danger!
by
Marcus Pride
Chester County, SC

A white reflective ribbon along the side of the narrow dirt road and the tail lights of a truck ahead showed us the way to the Rhine River in the blackout.

Our General Services Regiment did ordnance, demolition, building, engineering, electronics—whatever was needed to keep our troops advancing. We used to say, "We tear up and build."

This time, we were hauling square metal drums to put into the river for a pontoon bridge. We had left Luxembourg early that March, 1945 and, at 20 to 30 miles per hour, we had driven over poor roads all day and into the night. A few in our convoy turned back, as we'd been shot at on and off along the way, once from an unseen sniper. Somebody caught a blaze of a gun coming from a hollow tree. We took cover and used our .30 caliber machine guns to retaliate.

My assistant driver was taking a nap when I blacked out. I must have been asleep with my eyes open when I hit a huge oak tree. I snapped back awake and snatched that truck back on the road and kept going.

As we arrived the next morning, bullets and air raid bombs were coming in all around us. We drivers were taken to a big building and led three stories down, where I slept on an old car seat.

By the time we got up, our trucks had been emptied, and the pontoon bridge was partially built. Soon, we were returning to Luxembourg by the same treacherous route. We got back to camp at two or three o'clock in the morning. We got little sleep, because the whole company had to answer the call to reveille.

That was tough, but the good news was that everybody was there. No casualties.

A Medic's Surprises
by
Eugene B. Graeber, Jr.
Mecklenburg County, NC

At Fort Jackson, South Carolina, we of the 42nd Mechanized Recon Squadron of the 2nd Cavalry Group trained and we walked—up to 18 hours a day for four months. The last week of May, 1943, we had to walk 25 miles per day for five days, from Fort Jackson to Folly Beach, South Carolina. (I read several years ago that Marines walk 50 miles in three days; we walked 75 miles with full field packs in three days! Fifty miles? Kid stuff!) We were beginning to wonder if we were really in a mechanized outfit, for we had no vehicles until September.

I fared better than most in walking, since I had delivered *The Charlotte Observer* for four years while I was at Central High School.

About a third of the guys in our unit were from the New York area; a lot were of Italian descent. They thought they were in the boondocks! They were accustomed to riding subways, not walking. They couldn't believe our part of the country wasn't built up like theirs. And they'd never eaten food like ours before. Despite our differences, Silvio Sylvester Savatteri ("Sabu") from the Bronx and I became good friends.

He and I were among the 12 assigned to the Medical Detachment. Only one was a doctor, Capt. Robert D. Roane from Carlyle, Illinois; the rest of us had to train to be a medic. I never knew how I got picked. I thought I would be fighting a war, not pushing pills. I had heard that some medics were conscientious objectors. I was not. As I had qualified for officers training, I tried to get transferred to the Air Corps. But when I took the eye test, I found out I was partially colorblind. There was no way for me to become a pilot.

107

Medics Silvio Sylvester Savatteri and Gene Graeber in front of Sabu's half-track. Germany, 1945

One month before D-Day at Normandy, we arrived in Liverpool. Our bird colonel, Charles Hancock Reed, a West Point graduate, had trained under George Patton at Fort Riley, Kansas, and was Hell bent on getting our unit into Patton's 3rd Army. And he did.

Our outfit of light tanks and tank destroyers became part of the 4th Armored Division. Our reconnaissance job put us in first before a main thrust. The Medical Detachment was expected to treat whoever needed help (our own wounded, German prisoners or civilians), then we put them in an ambulance bound for a field hospital. We had four half-tracks and two ambulances. My half-track pulled a trailer with supplies. Capt. Roane had his own Jeep with a driver, but he said he preferred to ride with me because the half-track was more protective.

While we were still in England, a visiting general asked me what outfit I was in.

I told him "The 2nd Calvary, sir."

He looked at me squarely. "I thought that was where our Lord Jesus Christ was crucified."

I said, "You are quite right, sir. I'm in the 2nd Cavalry."

108

He smiled and went on.

We were not involved in the D-Day invasion, but six weeks later, we crossed the English Channel and went into action, first in France, then Luxembourg. Generally the wounds we dressed were caused by bullets, booby traps or land mines. Some were injured by a "bouncing Betty:" a wire stretched across a road or field. If you tripped on it, a grenade-like device on each end would pop up out of the ground, explode and throw out shards of metal in all directions.

One day, we were moving in a convoy when a German plane strafed the whole outfit. While most of us dived into ditches, the gunners operating the .50 caliber machine guns were trying to hit it. That pilot just flipped sideways and zoomed out unscathed.

In France, I had a totally unexpected experience. We were stopped by a woman, who wanted our doctor to check a girl in serious condition. I went with Roane and watched him deliver a baby girl. Very few American males at my age had ever seen such at that time.

One night in Luxembourg, I had another surprise.

Some of our troopers had shot down a German plane carrying two men. One was killed and the other had a leg broken. He was brought to us.

The prisoner had on a flight suit with many pockets and was moaning and groaning. While we were trying to help him, he was still moaning and fumbling with a pocket zipper. In an instant, he pulled out a miniature pistol, a Derringer. Six of us wrestled it away. We resumed bandaging his wounds. He picked at another pocket and pulled out what resembled a small box. With a jerk of his thumb, it became a dagger and he tried to stab us.

Ever after, we ordered everyone to check prisoners for weapons before bringing them to us. But we checked them again before treating them.

We were in Luxembourg from two days before Christmas, 1944, until March of '45, when we began chasing Krauts again across Germany.

On a spring night in the pouring rain, we could hear a German yell. Machine gun fire had sheared his legs almost off at the knee. The hefty blond guy was brought to us. As he was in extreme pain, Capt. Roane shot him with morphine and put plasma in both arms. Then he took some scissors, trimmed the remaining pieces of skin and flesh and handed the legs to me.

My job was to bury them, boots and all. It was grisly, and I really felt for that fellow.

He lived through the night, but we don't know what happened after sending him on to the field hospital.

The trooper who shot him and then delivered the poor guy to us asked, "Doc, why didn't you go on and kill him?"

Roane was angry. "You brought him in. If you didn't want him alive, why didn't you finish him off?"

The trooper turned white as a sheet. I'll bet he never shot at another German.

Another wounded German was brought in one night. I was going through his pockets to make sure he didn't have any weapons, when I pulled out a pack of Camel cigarettes. A tab on it said: "Smokes from the folks back home, Charlotte, N.C."

I mailed the tab to my parents in Charlotte with a note telling where I found it.

By V-E day, we were in Czechoslovakia. Two days later, we met up with a Russian unit. About a week after that, we crossed back into Germany to a small village named Lam, near Regensburg.

That's where I had another first-time medical experience.

To hear V-E Day news, some medics found a radio in a house in Stubenbach, Czechoslovakia, and hooked it up to an ambulance. L to R: Bob Olden, Gene Graeber, __Niementalo, Nick Sita, and __Wyer. May 8, 1945.

While we were playing ping-pong, one of the 12 in my outfit said he wanted to be circumcised. I assisted the doctor with the operation.

We remained in Lam until after V-J Day. On September 18th, I started on my way home with a one-day stopover in Paris.

That evening, I was waiting in a ticket line for the Follies when a captain came up. "Would you like to see the Follies?" he asked.

Of course I said, "Yes, sir!"

He invited me to be his guest, because his friend had passed out from too much wine. Our plush sofa seats were six rows back from the stage. I got to see about 50 of the most beautiful bare-chested young ladies I had ever seen! A welcomed sight after all that blood and guts.

Looking back on it, I was *glad* I served as a medic. I never carried a weapon. I never had to shoot anybody. I was never wounded. We helped people whenever we could. Only one man in our care died. (An American who had been caught in a booby trap was dying when we got him. It was the first time I had seen a person take his last breath.)

Besides, I probably wouldn't have survived flight training.

Liberating the Concentration Camp, Dachau
by
James F. Shrum*
Lincoln County, NC

There are people who say Dachau didn't exist, that Dachau didn't happen. I know it did, because I was there.

I was in the 48th Combat Engineers. On the 28th of April, 1945, we were just going along chasing Germans, clearing them out of houses. We were trying to get the war over. The 45th Division's front was moving very fast toward southeast Germany from the Heidelberg area. Dachau was located about five miles northwest of Munich. I was 22 years old, and I had never heard of it.

We were on this superhighway with our outfit. Other troops were behind us and ahead of us. It was just after noon when we suddenly came upon this place. We saw all these armored trucks, artillery units, infantry not moving, and soldiers were wandering around outside. We stopped and there it was. Inside the 10' to 12' walls were towering smoke stacks, with endless streams of smoke coming out and rows and rows of filthy, cramped barracks.

On arrival, we parked at the main gate. At first, all we saw were these people who looked starved inside fences milling around. Some of them were in good shape, because they hadn't been there long. Those who were able grabbed us around the neck. They whooped and hollered and jumped because they knew they were free after all those years.

In the barracks, they were motionless, just skin and bones, starving, too far gone to even move.

The smell of it! The smell of humans rotting in death is unexplainable—until you face it yourself.

There were details of men working, carrying the bodies out, laying them on little carts and hauling them out.

An inmate had scribbled on the wall: "This is the camp where you enter by the door and leave by the chimney."

Near the main gate was the crematorium. Nearby, there were two large buildings full of bodies waiting for the furnaces. And there were huge "shower rooms" used to gas inmates.

A man from Holland, a prison worker, who had been there about four years, told us that 3,000 per month were put through the furnaces. They were killed in many ways:

Theeee most unruly: gallows, hanging

Machine gunning, 12 to 20 at a time

Gassing, quickest

Starvation, the most common

Over 100 Russians, Poles and French escaped.

We saw prisoners empty a pail, defecate in it, empty it again, go to the nearby canal and drink from it. They had no other choice.

One man had a piece of bread. Others took after him like animal madmen.

May 1st we called "May Day at Dachau."

When we left the place, there were some 50 boxcars packed with 1,800 to 2,000 bodies frozen.

I went through World War II for three years. I saw lots of my friends die, myself almost in Cassino. But the last month of the war was the most memorable, most horrible. Ten days at Dachau.

Dachau. That was totally different than war. To me, that was the real hurt of the war. All those people in that camp...

* Editor's note: James Shrum died in 1999. His description of Dachau was taken from interviews by Stuart Grasberg of WTVI, Jacqueline Casey of the *Lincoln Times-News* and Dave Baity of the *Gaston Observer*, and from a detailed handwritten account left for his family.

The Pacific Theater and Beyond

From bloody island to bloody island, the Japanese attacked and invaded; the Allies (mostly Americans) counter-attacked and invaded. Meanwhile, the US Navy guarded island perimeters with the largest fleet ever assembled in wartime.

Some Americans went on to Japan. Others fought in North Africa, Burma and beyond.

But before all that action, a select few were sent to bomb Japan in retaliation for the humiliation at Pearl Harbor.

Doolittle's Raiders
by
Nolan A. Herndon
Lexington County, SC

"Hear ye! Hear Ye! This command is going to Japan," a voice on the loudspeaker of the USS Hornet's communications system announced.

When we volunteered at Columbia Air Base in South Carolina, Lt. Col. Jimmy Doolittle told us we were going on a very, very dangerous mission, but none of us really knew where.

A champion race pilot and well-known aviation expert, this pleasant fellow was the first to blind-fly an airplane, relying on instruments. When he had been told to train us and then take another assignment, he reportedly said, "Hell no! If I train them, I'm going to go with them."

We were all members of the 17th Bomb Group, from the 34th, 37th, 89th and 95th Reconnaissance Squadrons of the Army Air Corps. Our aeroplane had men from the 89th, 95th and 37th. Mine was the 89th Squadron.

Never before had planes as large as a B-25B been launched from an aircraft carrier in a military operation. Obviously, Roosevelt had been planning far ahead. Naval commanders followed up with the idea of bombing from an aircraft carrier in a surprise attack like Japan's on Pearl Harbor. The plan was to drop bombs on five cities in Japan and land at certain bases in China that were not occupied by the enemy. Large balloon fuel tanks had been installed in our planes to give us that range.

About halfway to Japan, Vice Admiral William F. Halsey, Jr. had come in on the USS Lexington with another fleet to join us. Before reaching our launching position, we encountered a Japanese fishing boat, which we took out. No one knew whether they had alerted Japan, so the big question was whether to abort the mission. Admiral Halsey was for throwing our planes overboard. The Hornet was crippled without fighters aboard to protect them, and our planes were too large to return and land on deck.

Col. Doolittle kept us informed, and we were against that idea. If we left early, 200 miles farther out, we knew we wouldn't have enough fuel to get to unoccupied China. "If you'll go with me," said Doolittle, "I'll go." He told us to ditch close to a ship, and "If they're Japanese on the ship, beat the Hell out of them."

We laughed, but we knew our chances of survival were not good. We wanted to go anyway.

Right before we had left California, a 16th plane was put on. It had a hand-picked crew and needed one more. I was asked to leave the crew I had trained with to join them.

As ours was the eighth plane to leave the ship on April 18, 1942, we were known as Crew #8. We were doing the opposite of the original plan. We took off in the morning instead of the afternoon to bomb in the daytime, not at night. Our plane's target was to be Yokohama, but, if necessary, we could find another.

As we were approaching Japan, our squadron commander, Ski York, said to me, the navigator/bombardier, "I want a course to Vladivostok."

"I can't do it!" I yelled back. I couldn't do two things at once. "Let's wait until we hit the target."

Meanwhile, I was questioning to myself: Russia? I thought we were going to China!

"I'll fly north and you won't have to," he said. Soon, he had picked another target, a large industrial building.

As planned, we flew in like a whirlwind at 100 feet, just above the water. That was so that their planes could only dive at us then wouldn't be able to pull up and would end up in the "drink."

The Japs *were* surprised. They were holding a practice raid and thought our planes were part of it. I dropped four 500-pound bombs and sought an island to get a coordinate for the course to Vladivostok. York just happened to have a map with him.

114

Over the years, I have learned that this was a prearranged plan, not from Doolittle, nor Halsey but from Washington. We were sent into Russia to see what they would do. Soviet Russia was not at war with Japan; they were fighting Germany. That's why the crew was hand-picked. Capt. York, a respected West Point graduate and pilot was Polish and could speak Russian, Lt. Bob Emmens, our co-pilot was a qualified pilot and had been operations officer of the 89th Squadron. The others were Crew Chief Theodore Laban, in charge of upper armament, and Sgt. David Pohl, the turret gunner. I had qualified as a navigator, bombardier and nose gunner.

It took us three-and-a half to four hours to get to the Russian coast, but we landed safely at a practice airfield ten miles from Vladivostok.

I also found out later that the others who became known as Doolittle's Raiders had various fates. Most had ditched in the water and managed to get ashore, bailed out or crash landed. Only three of those were killed, a remarkable statistic. Ours was the only plane not destroyed.

Eight got caught by the Japanese in occupied China. Three of the POWs were executed, one died of starvation and four survived, despite solitary confinement and terrible torture. The survivors ended up in Peking, where they were liberated. One of those men, Jake DeShazer, read a Bible, prayed and promised God that, if he were freed, he would forgive his enemies and go back as a missionary. Eventually, he did. One of his tracts converted the man who led the raid on Pearl Harbor. They met and began leading meetings together for Christ.

I did my share of praying, too. And throughout the ordeal, I was repeating in my mind, "Yea, though I walk through the valley of shadow of death, I will fear no evil..."

Herndon's B-25B near Vladivostok, USSR. April 18, 1942.

Interned in Russia
by
Nolan A. Herndon
Lexington County, SC

A Russian fighter was on our tail, as our B-25 approached Vladivostok. Our crew was one of the 16 who bombed Japan that afternoon (April 18, 1942) in retaliation for Pearl Harbor, but we were the only one now over Soviet Russia.

In his 30s, our pilot, Captain "Ski" York was authoritative but sensible, yet he was determined to land at Vladivostok rather than China, the others' destination.

Soon after our wheels stopped rolling, we headed for the headquarters building of what appeared to be a practice airfield around 5 p.m. As he was Polish (with an Anglicized name), Ski could explain to the Russian civilians that we came from Alaska and needed enough gas to get us to Chunking, China.

They looked at us and each other curiously, then put us into another room. About 6 p.m., the men called us back into the office. They had heard the news and were laughing about it. All their young people, men and women, were on the European front. Barrage balloons were overhead, but they couldn't stand to have a war with Japan. Nevertheless, they seemed glad that we were striking back at the country that was occupying China.

More people came in and joined us for a celebratory dinner, not with caviar but definitely some salmon eggs and a variety of foods we didn't recognize.

A couple of days later, the military sent a plane to take us to Khabarovsk, the headquarters of the Far Eastern Command near the eastern shore of Siberia. There, we were kept in a house with guards around us before being put on a train bound for Moscow.

The five of us, Capt. York, Lt. Emmens, the co-pilot, Theodore Laban, crew chief, Sgt. David Pohl, the turret gunner, and I, the navigator/bombardier/nose gunner, were ushered into a caboose with guards for the trip. Because we had to pull off on a sidetrack to give military trains priority, it took 15 days to get to Penza, 350 miles southeast of Moscow.

We stayed there until German planes began flying over us, anti-aircraft guns were shooting and shrapnel was falling on us. In the late summer, they sent us toward the Ural Mountains by rail and boat. We arrived at Okhansk, a village on the Kama River. Most everyone there was elderly, except the children in a large orphanage.

After we had been there several months, we nearly froze to death. (It got down to -42 degrees.) Until the weather got bad, we had guards. Obviously, we couldn't go anywhere, so they departed, leaving us an interpreter and two elderly women to cook for us in a large but primitive house.

The nearby river was frozen over, but, every day, we had to break the ice and drop a bucket six feet to get water. To get wood, we had to cross the river with a sled. Periodically, one of the older women had to go north of us in a truck, traveling more than 30 miles to get rations to keep us alive. Mostly, we ate rice, cabbage and black bread, which actually was brown and had straw and everything else in it. We drank something they called tea. Maybe it had tea in it. The women and the interpreter ate whatever we had. I lost 40-50 pounds while in internment.

Sanitary conditions were terrible. I had dysentery all the time. There was no toilet facility, just a stool over a hole in the floor. Now and then, a local would come with a sled and a barrel to get fertilizer.

Townspeople had it as tough as we did. Everything was rationed. Under Stalin, every person had a pass card, which said where he could eat, work and live. If he turned up elsewhere, he would be executed. Towns had guard posts where those cards were checked.

When an embassy representative came to check on us, we begged to be moved south. We complained about the cold, but we were thinking that maybe we could escape.

In early January, 1943, we were so desperate that we agreed to try something brash: a letter to Stalin asking for a secret release or, at least, to be sent to a warmer climate, where we might be given a job using our knowledge of planes. We gave it to our amazed interpreter to mail.

We were the ones amazed when it worked! In late March, when the weather improved, two officers of the Red Army came to the house to ask if we had written to Stalin. Ski admitted that we did. Our request for release was denied, but we left that very day on a long journey south.

Our crew was taken by car, then plane and train to Ashkhabad on the Soviet side of the Iranian border. We were housed in a two-room shack. An old man, who stayed in a shed behind it, provided us with food. We asked to work to pass the time, so we were directed to a big mechanical shop, where we helped repair airplane parts or do whatever was needed. To escape, we anticipated

117

that we should try to reach an embassy in Iran.

On the train, we had met a politically-connected resident who was very sympathetic with our plight. He knew a smuggler who regularly brought food in from Iran to people in the local government. Our friend asked the smuggler if he would take us back in his truck. "Yes, for whatever American money they have."

Among the five of us, we pooled about $300. York made a deal, and late one night, we met the smuggler at his sort-of-a-truck. He covered us with a tarpaulin, and we were off. Before we got to a guard post, he would put us out, and natives would take us around the post, where he would pick us up.

Whenever we stopped to rest behind some rocks, that rough and rugged guy was like a rabbit—he could move that fast. We would still be trying to rest, and he would dash back to his truck. York told me to "Hold on to him," so after that, I'd grip him by the feet until we were ready to go.

All of us were in bad shape with illnesses, lung problems and frostbite. It was especially difficult going through those mountains.

After daylight, when we were in seeing distance of Iran, we climbed out of the truck. Laban, Pohl and I hid in a bomb crater, while York and Emmens tried to make it across the border. From observation, we knew that, when an occasional truck came past the guard post, the guards turned their attention to the vehicle, while pedestrians streamed by. Our pilot and co-pilot joined a group of natives and passed through unnoticed.

Sometime later, a lorry stopped near the bomb crater and gave a little honk. Warily, we looked at the driver who motioned to us to get in the back. He took us across the border with no problems.

In Meshed, the people at the English consulate hid us in a barn east of their building, for Russians often visited there.

The English arranged for us to travel in another lorry headed for Quetta, India. There, we contacted the Army Air Corps, who got a transport plane to pick us up on their way back from delivering supplies to the Flying Tigers in China.

By that time, my dysentery was in such an advanced stage that I was passing a lot of blood. They wanted to leave me there in a hospital, but I would not hear of it. Instead, I stayed with our crew as we hitched a ride to North Africa, Ascension Island, then to South America and on to Miami. From our escape to our return to the States, about two weeks passed. We arrived in late May, 1943.

After 13 months in internment, we were surprised by our reception. FBI men met us at the plane and whisked us to Washington. They would not let us call our families or contact anyone. We were interrogated (they called it debriefing) for two weeks before being allowed to go home and then be relocated wherever we wanted to serve outside of combat.

Ski York and I chose the Columbia Air Base.

Even now, 60 years later, I am finding out more about our intentional diversion to Soviet Russia, secretly ordered by our government.

English Embassy representative meeting escapees, Doolittle's Raiders Crew #8: Nolan Herndon, Ted Laban, Bob Emmens, Ski York and David Pohl in Meshed, Iran. May, 1943.

Baptism of Fire
by
Charles Malvern Paty, Jr.
Mecklenburg County, NC

On 24 August, 1942, a few weeks following the Guadalcanal invasion by the Marines, our task force was operating a hundred or so miles off the eastern end of the Solomons. A radioman on the

USS North Carolina, I was alerted that a long-range patrol aircraft had detected a Japanese task force, consisting of several aircraft carriers, cruisers and destroyers, some 150 miles northwest of us.

Our carriers, the Enterprise and Saratoga, launched a full deck load strike of aircraft to attack the Japanese. Soon, the US and Japanese aircraft formations were passing each other en route to their targets.

Radio contact reports were coming in. At 1536 (3:36 p.m.): large group of enemy aircraft detected at 82,000 yards. At 1544 (3:44): large group now at 44,000 yards.

Although I was assigned to the radio division, at that time, radiomen were also responsible for the maintenance of radar. Radar was still very secret and very temperamental. My battle station was in a small compartment under one of our 5" anti-aircraft battery directors. My job was to watch the voltage meters and turn dials to maintain a constant voltage flow to the transmitter (not a very glamorous job).

The radar scope was above me, inside the director. I wore a headphone set and could communicate with a guy in the director, but we weren't supposed to carry on any unnecessary conversation.

At 1630 (4:30 p.m.), general quarters sounded, and we all ran to our battle stations. I sat there alone in the dark 4'x4' compartment with the temperature approaching 100 degrees. By that time, it was obvious that this enemy force of over 100 aircraft was going to attack us. It would be, as they say, our "baptism of fire."

I had seen the devastation of Pearl Harbor. On 10 July, 1942, we entered Pearl Harbor, our first exposure to the "real" war. As we proceeded down battleship row, we saw the battleship Utah upside down. The Arizona, a totally destroyed carcass, sunk at her berth with oil still oozing out and the flag still flying. The Oklahoma, turned upside down. In the next few days, we saw the West Virginia and the California in dry dock, with much of their sides blown out.

Would this now be our fate? My mind began to race, and I thought of home. It would be a terrible blow to my parents if I were killed this day. Furthermore, I had not experienced much of life. I had never seriously dated a girl. I had never held a job other than carrying a newspaper.

Now, I began to think of how I was going to die. Was it going to be quick—roasted alive in my compartment? Or was the ship going to be sunk, and I would go down with it? All of these thoughts raced through my mind in less than a second.

Charles Paty
Honolulu, Hawaii
1943

At 1710 (5:10 p.m.), I was jolted back to reality by our 5" AA battery just outside my compartment opening fire. This was followed by smaller AA guns opening up. The din was awesome! At the first sound of our guns, I sort of froze. But in a matter of seconds, my training took over. I began to adjust the voltage so that the director could still pick up the Japanese planes. I thought that any minute I would hear the explosion of a bomb or torpedo as we received a hit. My radar transmitter was cutting up, and the voltage and amperage was jumping up and down, as it reacted to the concussion of gunfire. I was desperately trying to adjust for this, but I don't think I had much success.

All the time I was thinking: "What a way to die, sitting in the dark, watching a bunch of dials and gauges."

We ceased firing. In about 12 minutes, we had shot down seven Japanese and assisted against seven more. Bombs and torpedoes had rained down on us, but we had not been hit.

The Battle of the Eastern Solomons was over. We had lost only one man to strafing and had no wounded.

Our ship had met the extreme test and passed. During those few minutes on 24 August, 1942, I probably said more prayers than I had said previously in my whole life. I also became a veteran.

On 15 September, 1942, our task force was still in the same area to protect the Marines on Guadalcanal. At 1400 (2 p.m.), I

121

finished lunch and went topside to get some air and observe fleet operations.

At about 1450, the Wasp (about 8 to 10 miles away) was emitting smoke, just a small wisp drifting astern but increasing rapidly. She made a port turn and headed for us. As she came about, we could see that she had a bad list to starboard. Smoke was pouring from beneath the flight deck. With a signal bridge long glass, I could see that the fire was all below decks, consuming most of the hanger deck. At 1453, there was a big red flash, and the ship was covered with smoke, which mushroomed to several thousand feet. About then, I saw a destroyer on our port side flashing "BB55" (meaning us) by light. I yelled to a signalman, pointing this out. A second later, someone shouted "Torpedo wake!"

Within a few more seconds, the torpedo struck the North Carolina.

I was knocked down along with everyone else on the signal bridge. A shower of water came down. As I rose to my feet, my first thought was that the ship was going to sink. My life preserver was stored two decks below. No way to get there, as general quarters sounded.

My battle station then was in Main Radio, two decks down below the water line and five below where I was standing. My training took over. I could feel the ship listing, as I raced toward Radio One. I was thinking that the ship might capsize and I was going in the wrong direction.

Unlike the Wasp, we didn't sink. In a short time, our list had been corrected, and we were making over 20 knots. That time, the North Carolina sustained five killed and no wounded. We returned to Pearl Harbor for repairs.

After that, we participated in the campaign for the Gilbert Islands and attacks on Nauru, a spec of an island with a phosphate operation, and the Kwajalein Islands before returning to the States for a major overhaul. Heading back to the Pacific in November, 1944, we ran into a typhoon, sustaining some damage, but moved on to our planned air attacks on the Philippines.

On the 6th of April, 1945, we were operating off Okinawa with a number of aircraft carriers, which were launching strikes against the island. The action was hot and heavy; enemy planes were flying all around and through the task force. At that time, my battle station was in Batt Two, high up in the foremast (main tower).

We had been firing several minutes when, at 1305, I heard a loud BANG! A large black cloud of smoke enveloped our tower.

Then it sounded like someone throwing a handful of marbles against the tower. Inside, I saw one guy fall over. I looked out on the platform and everyone was peering below.

Down on deck, men were lying everywhere: on the signal bridge, around the 40 mm gun mount, the director, and several other locations. Blood was running across the deck. I then saw the hole in the director base. It was obvious we had been hit by a 5" gun from one of our own ships.

The wounded man inside was our pharmacist's mate. He had been struck in the shoulder by flying shell fragments, the "marbles." It was a miracle that more of us were not wounded in those close quarters.

The net result was three men killed and 40 wounded.

On the 15th of August, 1945, we received the message to cease offensive operations against the Japanese.

In all, the USS North Carolina participated in over 50 battles. Many of these were minor in the sense that we might have fought off an attack by one Japanese aircraft. But the fact was: every enemy pilot was out to kill *me*, and I had to help kill him first.

An Incredible Christmas and Better New Year
by
Ralph H. Lawson, Sr.
Union County, SC

It was December 23, 1944. A Navy fighter pilot for an aircraft carrier, the USS Enterprise, I was shot down over the Philippines. I couldn't bail out; I fell out, because I couldn't move my left leg.

No, my life didn't flash before me, because I didn't have time for foolishness. Besides, I was too busy trying to guide my parachute. I knew pretty well where the Japs were and was determined to avoid them.

In fact, the Japanese had hidden units and ammunition dumps in and near villages, but the Filipinos would, by putting a lighted candle in certain windows, guide us on night flights by a row of lights to our targets.

I landed in a dry rice paddy, and within five minutes, two Philippine guerrillas got to me before the Japs. Wearing only shorts and each carrying a huge knife, the short stocky men had to carry me, because a piece of shrapnel was in my leg, and I couldn't walk.

123

They took me to a little village called Kiwan, and soon they were putting me into an underground shelter, which was normally used during a typhoon or a storm.

The shelter was about seven or eight feet deep, covered by a woven mat of bamboo sticks with shrubbery on top to hide it.

I was comfortable but scared.

All that first day and the next morning, I could hear Japs around me hunting and talking. I slept when I wasn't too scared.

The next day, a 5-year-old Filipino boy in a dark shirt and pants came in the shelter. He held out a bowl of probably two tablespoons of rice and a note from his mother. She said in English that they didn't have much, but they wanted to share their Christmas dinner with me. That was the best Christmas dinner I ever had!

Between midnight and 1 a.m. on December 26, the same two guerrillas came to get me. From our conversations, I learned that both of them and others had never been very far from me. They told me that Japs had killed the husband of the woman who shared her dinner.

The Filipinos had a great underground, although the Japs had many snipers, who would sneak around and shoot anything that moved. When the guerrillas heard the shots, they would go out to find the source. When they returned, they'd have his head on a stick.

My rescuers put me on a little boat, which carried me into the bay, where one of our submarines came up and took me to the USS Mercy, a hospital ship.

The shrapnel had gone through my knee, and I was afraid my leg would have to be amputated. My leg was bent under me and was badly infected.

At the beginning of the New Year, after a few days of poking a big long fork in and pulling out dried blood, the medical corpsmen finally got it to drain. There would be no amputation, but meanwhile, I was really in pain.

In the ward, in a bed across from me was a sailor who had lost a leg.

A chaplain came in one day and said to the amputee, "I see you lost your leg in the cause."

"No, sir," said the sailor. "I didn't lose my leg. I gave it for the cause."

That eased my pain.

Flying the Hump
by
J. Ruffin Bailey
Wake County, NC

At first, they said we couldn't fly through thunderstorms. One day they told us to go anyway. I found out we could do it! Weather and wind were our most dangerous enemies, but with some skill, a lot of luck, and relying on instruments, we *could* survive.

I had been sent over with a large group of pilots assigned to the Air Transport Command in April 1943, to the China-Burma-India (CBI) Theater, based in the upper Assam Valley of India. We were to fly the Hump (over the Himalayan Mountains) to supply the troops in China, a result of a visit by Madame Chiang Kai-shek to our President.

When we arrived, there was very little to do for three or four months until more of the four-engine airplanes (C-87s, converted B-24s) were sent. We had to get minimum flying time in to be paid, and there were not enough planes to do that. The rest of the time we sat on the ground. I spent time exercising, jogging, playing poker, reading mail from my family in Raleigh, and just doing nothing. Sometimes, I helped censor the mail of enlisted personnel and officers, cutting out references to where we were and other sensitive information. I read some *very* intimate and interesting letters.

Soon, though, we got into a routine like a truck driver, flying loads of cargo (gas, guns, ammunition, bombs, depth charges and PX supplies). I even took three loads of Chinese money, printed in New York City. Inflation was rampant in China, and, compared to US dollars, theirs were worth about 100+ to 1. Among the most hazardous cargo were the 55-gallon gas drums. Small leaks the size of pinholes caused gas to spew out at a high altitude. A couple of times, I returned to the base to have them removed.

The danger was not from anti-aircraft or enemy aircraft, for we flew at a high altitude. We had only a radio compass, not the kind of navigational beam used in the United States to keep us on course. We would tune to a station, and the needle would point to that station and we would head toward it. Navigation was not too difficult if we didn't have foul weather. Often, we never saw the ground until we landed. The Himalayas contain some of the highest mountain ranges in the world with a very high timberline and dense jungles. Three rivers wound north and south, so we could not follow the valleys but had to fly between the peaks. With no visibility and high winds, a pilot could get lost and run out of gas with no place to land. The crew could bail out but would find it very difficult to walk out. One crew, who crashed in Tibet, took 37 days to walk back. They brought in a five-gallon crock of whiskey given to them by a group of civilians who had helped them. A lot of people on the base were a little bit hungover that day.

I was flying along one clear night, when a head wind became so strong at 17,000 feet that I couldn't believe my instruments. Despite the 100 to 150 miles-per-hour winds, I finally got in, but we lost seven or eight crews that night.

A test pilot for airplanes on our base, I was in a position to see that I got missions. We often flew the three or four hour trip, one way, to Kunming, China. A crew was leaving every 30 minutes or so by day. At the Kunming field, planes would stack up every 500 feet, and move down to land. We did supply some Merrill's Marauders, although that was not our responsibility. Mainly, we supplied the 14th Air Force's Flying Tigers.

For awhile, we supplied our B-29s when they were flying from Chengtu on raids to Tokyo. Those were interesting runs, for Chinese laborers were building a big long runway, doing everything by hand. They first placed stones into the surface, hammering them down, then used tung oil as glue before pulling rollers with long ropes to pack it. Masses of workers in harnesses or using the ropes guided the rollers. Villagers or clans would work in groups of 100 or so, each with their own flag.

As we would come in to land, we didn't look for the 12,000 foot runway but the big mass of people. Someone would spot us, blow a whistle and the workers would scatter and clear the runway.

Usually we stayed only long enough to unload and eat a snack, generally bread and "flide" (fried) eggs. But one day, a buddy and I took a trip into the large village of Chengtu, where we saw some troops of the Red Army. They were not under Chiang Kai-shek, nor did they fight the Japs. They were getting ready to take over.

Later, we transported Chinese soldiers, 45 to 50 at a time, to our base to be trained nearby by General Stillwell before being sent back to clean the Japanese out of Burma. At the altitude we flew, it was cold—the cockpit got close to zero—and the oxygen supply was low. Many of them would get airsick or pass out. Those soldiers had no parachutes or oxygen masks. We were told to jump if we had to, but I don't know that I could have done that.

Only one sighting of an airplane concerned me, as single-engine fighters didn't come into that dangerous mountainous area. I never lost an engine and never got close enough to ground troops to be fired upon. The Japanese in Burma were fighting guerilla warfare, without anti-aircraft guns.

During those 16 months and 650 hours of flying (230 in the last month and a half), I was very fortunate.

"Hit and Run" Outfit: Merrill's Marauders
by
Fred C. Agner
Edgefield County, SC

Our main objective was to cut off the Japs' supply line that February, 1944. They were coming down the Kamaing Road. The Chinese were fighting but getting pushed back into India. We would have to cut our way from Ledo around the foothills of the Himalayan Mountains and get behind the Japanese line. On America's first mission on the Asian continent, we would spearhead the Chinese Army in that region.

Not just any soldiers could do it. We had all been trained in jungle fighting and survival. I had trained in Panama for nearly three years before 3000 of us (three battalions) had volunteered to help General Frank D. Merrill penetrate Burma's jungles and mountain terrain to reopen the Burma Road. A sergeant, I was one of four machine gunners in the 5307th Composite Unit's 1st Battalion, which had 900 men and 400 pack mules. We were originally called "Galahad," but soon became known as "Merrill's Marauders."

Merrill usually marched with the 1st Battalion until he had a heart attack and had to be airlifted. He acted like an ordinary Joe but was well respected, especially when he came back after his heart attack.

When we reached an access trail to the Kamaing Road, we unloaded the .30 caliber machine guns from the mules, set them up hidden from view, stationed riflemen around to protect the guns and waited. The other two battalions would sneak up on the enemy at other locations. The next day, some old trucks and Japanese troops came up. When they were all in front of us, we opened fire. We knocked out three trucks loaded with ammunition, food and supplies and many Japs, but we didn't have enough men to hold the position. We could only "hit and run" before they brought in replacements.

Farther south, we got word that more Japanese supplies were coming, so we set up our machine guns off the road and began digging foxholes. Mine was nearly dug when our radioman came by. "You take this hole and finish it. I'll dig another," I said. About dark, we began to hear artillery from two miles away. Before morning, the radioman had been hit by shrapnel. I felt really badly about that, but I helped him find a medic.

The Japs moved in the next day, and we opened fire. If we could just hold them off for four or five days, the Army could bring in Chinese troops, so we could move out. When that time came, we estimated that we had killed 250.

As we were cutting our way through the jungle, we sometimes would encounter a Japanese outpost or native headhunters. (The headhunters gave us the right-of-way, and not one of us strayed from our group.) Occasionally, we'd have to build a temporary bridge to cross a river, walk along an ankle-deep stream or carry part of the pack mules' load so they could climb a mountain with us. But those difficulties would have been easier if we didn't have to battle devastating tropical diseases, foot blisters, snakes and leeches along the way. Every evening we'd have to check for leeches and burn them off with a cigarette. If I missed one, he would be the size of a penny, full of my blood, the next day.

Our food and supplies came in by air drop, with colored bags designating contents (red for ammunition). But first, we had to find a suitable clearing and then radio for the drop. At least we could usually get a rest while awaiting the drop. We lived on mostly K-rations (a small can of meat, some energy crackers, soluble coffee, a fruit bar plus four lumps of sugar, four cigarettes and one stick of gum). At times, we roasted and ate a wild animal or one of our mules that had gotten shot. We'd explode a hand grenade in a river to get fish. When we didn't have fresh water, we cut a piece of bamboo and sucked on that.

When the fighting got really fierce, some guys would shoot themselves in the foot. Eventually, word got passed around that "If you shoot yourself, you won't get out."

Once, when we were ready for a rest, we got a call that the 2nd Battalion was on a large hill surrounded by the enemy 40 to 50 miles away. We marched that day and night and another day, taking only a break or two to rest. There was only one water hole, and the Japs had it. We found where they were and set up our machine guns. As our men went up, I had to shoot over their heads. As the Japs came out of their foxholes, we'd shoot them. With four machine guns, four mortars and the riflemen of our battalion, we eliminated enough of the enemy to get to what was left of the 2nd Battalion. Those men up there were starved and exhausted, wounded or dead. Nearby, about 100 rotting mule carcasses and 200 unrecovered Japanese bodies littered the hillside. The smell was so bad that we could hardly breathe. We named that place "Maggot Hill."

The Flying Tigers came in, and we used mortars to throw up a smoke screen to show where the Japs were. The Japanese began evacuating, a few on elephants, and all three battalions had to move on to take the airfield Myitkyina. But first, we found a valley and waited four days to get the wounded out and receive food, clothing and ammunition.

A hundred or so miles from there, the 1st and 3rd Battalions split, and ours was headed down a mountain when I heard a baby crying in a ravine. The Japs were taking "pot shots" at us, but I set up my machine gun, and while someone fired it over our heads, a scout and I crawled down to find the dead Burmese mother and pick up the baby. The child was taken to a nearby village.

Among our supplies was a new .37 caliber machine gun that fired bullets and pellets, which were more effective against Japanese "Banzai!" attacks. We dug in and let the 3rd Battalion go around. Snipers continued. I couldn't sleep at night, only dozed off day and night.

Two days later, a guy I knew only as Jim and I were sitting on a log, smoking a cigarette. Suddenly, a sniper fired. One bullet hit Jim in the shoulder. Two more hit the log between my legs and the ground between my feet. I took Jim to the medic's dugout.

The doctor turned him over to his helpers and then looked at me. "How much did you weigh when you came in?"

"Oh, 165 pounds," I said. By that time, I was down to 116.

He put his hands on my chest and torso and checked my mouth and teeth then put a tag on me that read "Enlarged liver, enlarged heart, typhus or malaria."

If it were typhus, I knew nobody lives with that. I'd had malaria twice in Panama, which gave me hope.

I spent an anxious two days waiting for the 3rd Battalion to secure a rice paddy for C-4s to land and pick up the 25 wounded and diseased, one man at a time. I was among the last.

At a larger field where we were to be transferred to C-47s for the flight to the field hospital, the C-4 pilot had to circle five times. Each time, the Japs shot at him. I could see the bullet holes, but we made it.

In May, 1944, the month I became an adult, I got the good news that I did not have typhus. Neither my heart nor liver were enlarged. The doctor had just felt them inside my emaciated body. They gave me medication for malaria, hookworms and fungus, fattened me up and sent me to an R & R in India.

I expected to go home after that, but the 475th Infantry Regiment needed experienced replacements. I went back to Burma for another eight months and finally helped complete the Marauders' mission to the Burma Road.

Bougainville Blast
by
James Claude Blair, Jr.
Stanly County, NC

A siren burst the silence of night. Japanese bombers had been spotted, so we dived into the nearest foxhole.

J. C. Blair
Guadalcanal, 1943.

For months, while we were in Guadalcanal, that happened over and over.

Following my training at Camp Croft, I had been sent as a replacement to the 52nd Field Hospital in in early 1943. Our Air Forces were using Henderson Field and another smaller field for our bombers and fighters in the Solomon Islands.

In February, the remaining Japs, who had been driven to the hills, abandoned the island.

We Army medical corpsmen worked 24 hours a day, catching sleep when we could at the tent hospital, mainly tending patients with shell fragment wounds, malaria and battle fatigue. Only the doctors amputated limbs; we treated and bandaged the other injuries.

130

But more of our casualties were from malaria than enemy attack. Despite the spraying of DDT, that contagious disease was a serious problem. As for those who were shell-shocked, we could only ship them back to the States. A while after Guadalcanal was secured, some of us corpsmen were sent with the troops to another Solomon Island, Bougainville.

The Japs were there, but we set up a perimeter around an airfield and our tent hospital. One afternoon, I was taking a break with another fellow or two, just "chewing the fat." I was sitting on the ground leaning against a wooden box, with my arm draped over the top. With no warning, a mortar shell exploded propelling a fragment through the box. I dived for a foxhole.

Wow! Had it gone only three inches either way, my arm or chest would have been hit, and I would have been a patient at our hospital!

You Can't Duck Kamikazes
by
James C. Davidson, Jr.
York County, SC

On March 26, 1945, the USS Loy arrived off Okinawa to deploy one of eight underwater demolition teams (UDT—we call them SEALS now) to set underwater charges to remove obstructions along the western beaches of Okinawa. The Japs had embedded concrete emplacements and other obstacles, including old boats, to keep small craft from landing.

On March 29, our convoy came under attack by kamikazes. One dived into a landing ship, killing the commanding officer and seven of the crew. We put our doctor aboard their ship and assisted getting it to the Kerama Retto anchorage. Some of the less injured crew were moved to our ship and a number of our men boarded theirs to get it back under control.

In the mid-afternoon of March 31, the day before our D-Day, from my watch station on the 40 mm gun mount, I witnessed the remarkable coordinated effort of UDTs setting off tons of charges all at one time. Each charge was about two feet long and two inches square linked by primer cord. They had been placed by several hundred men along eight miles of the beach. It looked like the entire beach went up in a spray. In an instant, a single geyser, a sheet of water shot up 25 feet high with all kinds of concrete, sections of coral reef and other debris flying.

On Easter Sunday morning, April 1, a beautiful clear day, the invasion began. We dropped off our UDT to assist during the landings. Our ship, a part of the largest armada in history, remained a few miles off the beach to render needed support. We remained underway at all times. During the invasion, we were on battle stations. Mine was a damage control station below deck. My job was to see that all the hatches were closed and that area of the ship was watertight.

During those first two weeks of April, our UDT did work from time to time on other beaches, then on April 16, we took part in the invasion of another island, Ie Shima, west of Okinawa. The Loy continued to operate under kamikaze attacks day and night.

Three kamikazes approached us simultaneously. On our earphones, we could hear the direction and bearing of the planes coming in. Then we heard each gun as it fired. The 5" gun fired first, vibrating the whole ship with almost deafening noise. I felt the concussion of the explosion, and my knees buckled. The 40 mm twin-mount guns sounded like machine gunfire, while the ship vibrated. When you heard the 20 mm guns, you knew the planes were close, *very close*.

The Loy shot down two of the Jap planes. The third was destroyed by other ships in the area.

That day, we watched as ground forces advanced several miles inland. The next morning, the Marines were back on the beaches fighting for a foothold, having been driven back during the night. The American flag was raised on Ie Shima on April 21.

On April 25, we withdrew to escort a convoy to Guam, arriving May 2. The next day, we disembarked our UDT. By May 15, we had returned with a convoy and begun screening the anchorage area west of Okinawa. There were three screens of ships in circles around the island. In the second screen, the Loy would run 7,000 yards, turn and reverse that course. If a ship in the screen sank or was damaged, it was immediately replaced.

On the night of May 25, we picked up 15 casualties from the USS Barry, which had been hit by a kamikaze. Other ships evacuated the crew, and it was towed to the Kerama Retto anchorage. Our doctor treated the wounded before some of our boat crew transported them to another ship.

While patrolling on our screening station on the night of May 27, the Loy was attacked by two twin-engine enemy planes. The first one exploded in the air. The second one continued in with a damaged starboard wing. It fell behind the Loy a few hundred yards with a terrific explosion. At my battle station, I could feel the vibrations, more vehement than when the 5" gun was firing.

Our combat information center notified us on the intercom: "Splash behind us! Port side!"

A few minutes later, near midnight, a third aircraft, a Zero fighter (that's what the Japs called their small fighter) attacked on the starboard beam. The aircraft was nearly destroyed and set afire. It ricocheted into the water on our starboard side less than 50 yards out and exploded. Fragments went into our hull, causing considerable damage, killing three crewmen and injuring 15.

When this aircraft was approaching, we in damage control first heard the 5", then the 40 mm and then the 20 mm gun above the compartment we were in. A shipmate who was about my size, Paul Gouge, had been picking a mandolin the instant before this occurred. I had just asked if he was in tune playing "Maple on the Hill."

When the 20 mm began shooting, Paul and I ran to the other side of the ship. The area we just left was riddled with shrapnel. The laundry room we were sitting in front of was totally destroyed. The oil tanks below deck were penetrated. Fire started on the upper deck.

All five of us from our battle station rushed to assist in fighting a fire on the fantail of the ship by moving fire extinguishers to that area. The flames were caused by gasoline from the kamikaze.

Four of our casualties occurred on the 20 mm gun directly over the laundry room. The explosion bent the flak shield around this gun. Two men there were killed and two injured. The bunk area where our UDT had been quartered near the fantail was badly damaged.

One fatality might have been avoidable. Bill Logan of Beaufort, South Carolina, a big red-headed boatswain's mate, always wore his helmet cocked to one side and never fastened the strap. As first-loader on a 20 mm forward on the starboard side, he bent down to retrieve a magazine. His helmet fell off at the moment the plane exploded. A small piece of shrapnel struck Bill in the head and killed him.

Relieved at our screening station by the USS Abercrombie, we extinguished the fires, assessed our damage and determined that we could continue on our own power to Kerama Retto for temporary repairs.

That night, I realized our imminent danger, as several of our

133

guns were inoperable. When I saw another enemy plane approach, I felt real fear and wondered if we were going to make it to the safety of the anchorage. But the guns that *were* working shot down the plane before it could hit us.

When I left the USS Loy, our scoreboard on the flak shield of the open bridge indicated the destruction of three twin-engine Jap planes and four single-engine ones. We had destroyed six floating mines and participated in six different island invasions.

Occupying Okinawa, Then China
by
L.A. Tomlinson, Jr.
Durham County, NC

The morning we Marines landed on Okinawa, April 1, 1945, Ernie Pyle was on board my transport ship. It was the first time this popular war correspondent had been in the Pacific Theater. The night before, a fellow Marine had told him "You'll really see a different kind of fighting out here—island-hopping is not like the war in Europe." On April 18th, Pyle was killed, becoming one of the early casualties of the Battle of Okinawa.

This operation was one of the first times the Marines Corps and the Army made a joint landing supported by the Navy's ships and planes. Part of our overall plan was to stage a fake landing several days ahead to draw the Japs to the south end of the island. Navy ships had fired rounds at the coast, and their airplanes had dropped some bombs. Because of this diversion, we were relatively unopposed, when we came from the west and entered north of Kadena Airfield.

Our 1st Division's charge was to hit the middle and cut the island in two, separating the Japanese troops on the south end from the ones left on the north. Okinawa was 60 miles long but anywhere from 2 to 15 miles across. Navy planes were overhead, while we first moved on the ground. It was supposed to take us a week, but because of the fake landing, it took only a couple of days.

That first night, while on a high bluff, I saw kamikazes for the first time. Those Japs were flying right into the stacks of ships, whether they were carriers, cruisers, battleships or transports. Meanwhile, our anti-aircraft guns were firing on them, knocking them out with great success. Every time one got hit, our Marines on the bluff yelled and clapped.

134

One of my University of North Carolina classmates, Emmet Sebrell from Charlotte, was on a cruiser during the battle. His ship was hit, and he was knocked into the water, where he floated until rescued.

Kamikaze fighting was a new concept. Japanese soldiers had extreme loyalty to their country and commanders. To wipe out many enemies while losing your own life was an honor. To be captured was a disgrace; to surrender, unthinkable.

To get the Japs out of the multitude of caves on Okinawa, we had to use flamethrowers. If the liquid fire didn't burn them up, it would evaporate the oxygen. I watched this on one occasion when the infantry attacked. As expected, no one ran out.

We saw very few locals in the countryside. Oriental males and females in their drab cloth slacks and hats were difficult to tell apart. Most were farmers or lived in tiny villages, but sometimes they would crop up in the line of fire.

As the commanding officer of Able Battery (1st Battalion, 11th Marines, 1st Marine Division), I was headed south in a convoy of jeeps and trucks pulling Howitzers one day, when we drew enemy fire. As the first shell hit, I instinctively jumped down into the ditch by the road. A shell exploded and fragments hit the pack on my back. Although I had some close calls at Guadalcanal and Bougainville, that's the nearest I came to being injured in Okinawa.

Fifteen miles from Naha, the capital, was Shuri Castle, one of the main Japanese headquarters, high on a hill with a myriad of caves beneath. As of June 1945, it seemed invincible.

As Able Battery was in that vicinity, I went up to check on a forward observer, Ben Reid, a lanky 2nd lieutenant from Richmond, Virginia. His foxhole was on a military crest of a hill several miles from the castle.

"Be careful coming over to OP," a radioman warned me. Radiomen were often American Indians, whose language served as a code to be interpreted by another Indian on the other end.

It's important to stay out of view when you come over a crest near an observation point (OP), so as not to give the observer away. When I arrived, Ben was calling for rounds of fire at the castle. After checking with him, I scurried back across the crest and headed to my jeep.

Just then, I saw a huge entourage of vehicles pulling up. "Who is that?" I asked, assuming someone important was being escorted.

Sure enough, it was General Simon Bolivar Buckner, the

commander of the 10th Army Corps, who was in charge of all the troops on Okinawa. With him were various other officers, press people and a photographer.

"Y'all be careful now. There are Japs out there," I warned no one in particular. "Don't put my forward observer in danger." I, a mere major, was not going to tell a general what to do, so I climbed in my jeep and moved on.

That night, I got word from Ben that the general was hit by a 77 mm shell. The Japs had seen the commotion and fired. The only person killed was the general, I was told.

On another occasion, I was at our observation post with Ben, helping him direct the fire of a battleship, which was out in the ocean about eight or nine miles, firing at Shuri Castle. Our artillery of smaller caliber could not do much damage. But the ship's 16" shells looked like jeeps with vapor trails flying through the air. They blew that castle to smithereens and damaged some of the catacombs of caves, as well.

Shuri Castle was the final major engagement and turning point of Okinawa, which was the bloodiest battle of the Pacific. Our occupation resulted in the largest number of casualties on both sides. In all, more than 109,000 Japanese and 12,500 American forces were killed.

We pretty well finished off the Japs at Shuri, so we went on to the capital, Naha, which was in shambles. We established order there and then went to the north end of the island for rest and recreation.

We were preparing to invade the main island of Japan when the United States dropped the atomic bomb. After the resulting Japanese surrender, we immediately stopped training and started playing baseball. All of us rejoiced that we'd been spared a massacre and awaited orders to head home.

In October, 45 days after the end of the war, the 1st Marine Division was shipped to China, which was supposed to have been neutral.

But the Japanese had taken command of the two largest cities, Peking (now Beijing) and Tientsin (now Tianjin), so our job was to enter Tientsin and take over the Japanese troops, confiscate their weapons and ship them back to Tokyo.

There was not much resistance to our green uniforms, only a little fire from the Communists, a small band that would fight anybody. Some potshots caused a few casualties, even though the war was over.

Larry Tomlinson and Granville Clark
American Samoa, June, 1942

We located the Japanese headquarters in a French arsenal near town, moved the Japs into a tent city and then we occupied the arsenal.

As I was among the few married officers in Battalion Headquarters, I spent a lot of duty at the camp in the evening, while the bachelors enjoyed the city.

In the nice officers' quarters, I had a Number One Boy and a Number Two Boy to do my laundry, clean up and fetch things.

I was surprised to see that Tientsin was not unlike a great American city with a business section, restaurants and cars. This Chinese metropolis still had a number of non-Chinese residents and many "white" Russians rather than Mongolian Russians. In short, there were more Caucasian people there than I had ever imagined.

Just in time for Christmas, 1945, I got to go home, rotating out as an individual. I was up for promotion the next week and loved the Marine Corps; it was a great organization. But my bride didn't want me to stay in.

How Can I Thank Them?
by
Ralph S. Ross
Union/Mecklenburg Counties, NC

In a matter of ten seconds, seven of us were on the ground. Flamethrowers, our squad of ten was making a flanking move to the right while our company was going to the left up a high grade of plateau on Okinawa. The step-like hills went up to conical peaks overlooking the town of Yonabaru.

Our job, as a part of the 10th Army, 96th Infantry Division, 383rd Regiment, was to locate pillboxes, caves and holes among those plateau hills where the Japanese were hiding for surprise attacks. We would throw napalm gas into those places and back off.

This time, on the 15th of May, 1945, we were getting a cross fire from northwest to southeast. The Japanese were rolling us off that hill. I got hit below the left knee. The bullet shattered my tibia, and I had flesh wounds from shrapnel on my leg and in my side. My fatigues had holes where more shrapnel had missed the skin. I was 6'3" and raw-boned strong, but I was helpless. I was almost going into shock.

The Japs hated flamethrowers, but they had quit shooting at me, so I crawled about 20 feet and shed the heavy apparatus we carried (two tanks of gasoline, a tank of air, and a firing mechanism that weighed 75 to 85 pounds).

Another sergeant crawled to me. "Take my rifle and shoot me," he pleaded. "I can't stand this anymore. I've been wounded twice at Leyte. Just shoot me."

"Soldier," I said, "please don't talk like that. Retreat to the lines. Tell somebody where I am."

He disappeared.

Soon, I went head-first into a bomb hole. The soil on Okinawa is bluish-gray clay inches below the surface. It holds water. I about strangled from the moisture before I could crawl under an upper ledge of the hole. I had wrapped my jungle sweater around the wound, and then I raked off as much earth as I could and lay down there.

At about 10 o'clock in the morning, I was looking east and could see the tip edges of where the moving forces were. Then they fell back, and I was beyond the view of any American personnel. I lay there until night. All evening, they bombed and strafed those hills right above me. The ground beneath me was rocking. Shrapnel was sizzling everywhere. Then there was a terrible boom.

I was beneath the back edge of a knoll like an umbrella and did not get hit again. But I overheard Japanese soldiers talking. They didn't know I was there or they would have finished me.

Soldiers carry a little rubber-like bag in a fatigue pocket. I put some personal things and a message to my girlfriend (Betty Forbis of Mint Hill) into my bag and buried it. On my back, I began sliding when I heard feet moving. Friend—or foe?

Two guys grabbed me under my arms. The crack, crack of bullets were overhead, but even while the Japs were shooting at us, they carried me down. Then they were gone.

"What happened to those two guys?" I asked someone nearby.

"I don't know."

"I never told them thank you!" I said, dismayed.

While waiting to be transported out, a young corporal, Horace Mitchell from Louisiana, asked, "Soldier, where's your flamethrower?"

"Over beyond that ravine," I said.

"Oh my God, what am I going to do?" shouted a captain. He turned. "Sergeant, can you get a detail to retrieve it. I can get another guy to carry a flamethrower, but we've got to find it."

That hurt my heart.

"Have you had any first aid?" Mitchell asked me.

"Absolutely not. I'm cold and I'm hurting."

"Captain," he said, "We've got to get this man to an aid station."

The captain ordered him to find two to carry me and two to go along as guards.

Along the way, we could hear the ping-ping of bullets. At about 11:30 p.m., the stretcher-bearers dropped me upside down into a swampy creek. They got me out of there and kept walking until we came to an aid station, which was a cleaned out tomb. By the light of a lantern, they filled me full of morphine.

By the next morning, all the Red Cross vehicles and equipment outside had been destroyed. We patients had to wait until they could bring in a truck to haul us out.

En route to the field hospital, the guy next to me was moaning, "Mama, Mama, help me!" He had been shot two times in the stomach area. The fellow turned to me. "Mama tried to tell me. I shouldn't be here. I'm only 16 years old."

It took all day to get to the field hospital: row on row of injured men in big field tents. The patients were protected by sandbags. Because I was wounded in the leg, I was put in a ward surrounded by men with limbs torn off, arms blown off, faces gone, total body casts. I was slightly wounded compared with them. In fact, the casualty rate was so high that they didn't touch me for 36 hours. Way into the night, someone put a temporary cast on my leg and told me I would be flying out soon.

The next day, a ward medic came to me and said, "Fellow, I'm sorry. So many Marines have been burned so badly with phosphorous and the hospital ship is full." He cut off the tag that indicated I was scheduled to fly out.

Eventually, I came out by ship to a field hospital in Saipan, where they finally operated twice on my leg. All the while, I was looking around me, knowing how much better off I was than so many of the others, mostly GIs in the infantry.

In fact, 80% of the war casualties were inflicted on line troops. We represented 20% of the troops in battle but 80% of the casualties. Of our squad of ten, four were killed, three wounded.

Since those days, I have come to realize that, whatever you do in life, there's no other experience better than to say "Thank you for what you did for me." I still regret that I never said "Thank you" to those guys who risked their lives to climb that plateau to save me.

Enola Gay's Bombardier
by
Thomas W. Ferebee
Davie County, NC
From UNC-Charlotte Special Collections
Oral History Program

Col. Thomas W. Ferebee, who grew up on a farm about six miles from Mocksville, North Carolina, was the bombardier on the Enola Gay, the B-29 that dropped the first atomic bomb on Hiroshima on August 6, 1945. This is an edited and condensed version of Ferebee's account of that event when he was interviewed by LeGette Blythe on October 16, 1966.

When I first entered into the program, which was August of 1944, I had been in Europe for two years. I had been in the first B-17 group that went to Europe in 1942, and I flew 63 missions there.

After a couple of months in the States, they told me that they would like me to do this. I went to Wendover, Utah, a rather isolated air base out in the salt flats about 120 miles due west from Salt Lake City, to start training for this specific mission.

They didn't tell anyone everything, but I had to know enough to continue the tests I had to do. It took about one year to the day almost from the time I started testing the different units until it was perfected to where we could deliver it.

As we would develop a certain phase, we'd have to drop a unit to prove that portion of it. Then they would go back and make another unit to prove another problem. It would usually take about two or three weeks to get another one developed. And I would go back and drop it. I did a lot of traveling to different places while they were developing another unit. I'd drop them in the air where they

140

get their instrumentation, so they could pick up the information that they required.

On the 14th of July, I went to Tinian Island in the Marianas. Actually, we had 15 crews that went to Tinian, where we delivered it from, but only two crews actually were programmed to do this—my crew and the one that dropped the Nagasaki bomb.

After I dropped the two units that I had to test over there (at Tinian), and everything proved it was working, I went to Guam and was briefed by General (Curtis) Le May and General (Nathan) Twining on just how we were going to run the mission and the different targets that were available. We lined the targets up in priority. Then I went back to Tinian, and they briefed the whole crew on as much as they could.

The main thing they told the crew was that this cloud would be there, and that we were definitely not to fly through. We were to turn about 155 degrees and lose about 2000 feet to pick up some speed, which would put us at the farthest distance from the impact when it went off. We would be at 35,000 feet going away from it so the flash wouldn't bother us.

The pilot, Paul Tibbets, had been a good friend of mine, continues to be a good friend. The plane was named for his mother. The rest of the crew were just selected from another that had brought the airplane to Tinian. I was a major; the pilot was a colonel. The navigator and co-pilot were captains and the rest were enlisted personnel. Admiral (William Sterling) Parsons, a Navy captain then, and Lt. Jefferson were there to arm the bomb.

It was a 13-hour flight. The bomb was actually armed in the air. Myself, Parsons and Jefferson were back in the bomb bay. All I did was observe, but the rest of the crew were not allowed to see in the bomb bay. They didn't actually know what was there. The Lieutenant did most of the assembling. It was approximately seven feet long. Weighed approximately 7000 pounds. It was a smaller weapon than the second one.

The one at Nagasaki was around 10,000 pounds, because the method of explosion was different. The one that I dropped was what they call a gun type. The other one was an implosion type weapon.

We dropped it on Hiroshima at 9:15 a.m. Japanese time, August 6th.

I used a plain, ordinary bomb sight like I used in Europe for two years prior to this. It was more or less automatic. You just set a switch, and when your lines come together, it automatically released. I had a manual salvo that was mechanically hooked to the weapon that, if it didn't go off electronically, I could have pulled.

Earlier, we had dropped several units perfecting the device to make it go off at a certain altitude. It was set for about 1400 feet above the ground.

Everybody was supposed to have dark glasses on, but I had a problem being able to see to do my job. The pilot had the same problem following his instruments in the turn, so the two of us had our glasses off. There was a tremendous flash, but it didn't do any damage to our eyes.

I felt a shock, and I turned around to the pilot and said, "They're shooting at us!" And then a few seconds later, it dawned on me that was the blast effect instead of flak. The plane shook, but nothing bad. You could definitely feel it. To me, it was just about the same thing that I had felt in Europe. Just a close burst of flak.

It was a real clear day. Everything was set up perfect, and there was no enemy action whatsoever. As we released it, I wanted to make sure it had left the airplane, so I actually moved forward, where I could visually see it in the air. And at that time, I turned the tone on, which notified the other airplanes. There were two airplanes orbiting, one with the photographic ship and one had the instruments to detect the blast effect.

Some people said it was dropped on a parachute. In fact, the parachutes were on the instruments that were dropped from another airplane to pick up the blast effects. After the war, there were a lot of articles that said it was dropped by a parachute, but the parachutes the Japs picked up came from those instruments.

It hit about 900 feet from the center of the bridge, our target, almost exactly in the center of the city.

We turned about approximately two minutes, where we could see it. The cloud was already up to our level. I had seen a lot of bombing, but this was much different than anything I had ever seen. It was just a gray boiling cloud, and you could actually see debris in the bottom of the cloud. It was just boiling. You could see it was beginning to continue to edge on out and cover the whole city. The first look I had, I'd say about half the city was in the cloud, and it was moving out real fast over the city, the smoke... The edge of the city was still visible when we first saw it, but within a few seconds, there was nothing. You couldn't see the city at all.

We immediately started preparing a message that we had to send through back to the President to report whether it was successful or not. They delayed the message a little while before

Thomas W. Ferebee and the Enola Gay. Circa 1945

they sent it to President Truman.

Some of the crew didn't know exactly what was going to happen. They were real excited. Only three of us had ever been on a combat mission before, so the others had never seen a bombing.

The second one was dropped on the 9th, and that was about the end of the war.

LeGette Blythe asked how Ferebee felt about it psychologically.

It never bothers me at all. I don't think of it any differently than any other missions I flew. And I never actually think of it unless somebody brings it up.

Blythe noted that President Truman believed that he had saved a lot more lives by ending the war. He imagined that Ferebee had the same feeling.

I definitely do, because I visited Japan immediately after the surrender, and I saw enough that convinced me that they had intended to go all out on the last stand, which would have cost many American lives as well as Japanese.

Blythe asked whether he had been to any reunions since this history-changing event.

The pilot, Col. Paul Tibbets, the navigator, Captain Ted Van Kirk, and I had flown together in Europe before. I wasn't allowed to mingle with the others too much, so if I went to a reunion, I wouldn't know the other people there.

I intended to go to Tinian. They have a monument there where we actually loaded this weapon, but I didn't get up there. The runways are all grown up, but there is still enough that you could land a small airplane.

When asked to contrast the atomic bomb he dropped with those of "present day standards" (i.e. 1966), Col. Ferebee admitted:

It was more or less a firecracker compared to what we have today.

Meanwhile, on the Home Front

Everyone did something for the war effort, even children. Some left the region, but most stayed.

Vast numbers of area workers were employed in industries vital to the Allies' success. In addition to those designated as "defense plants," hundreds of local industries of all sizes were manufacturing materials to fill military contracts: airplane parts, parachutes, other fabrics, clothing and machine tools. Throughout the Piedmont, females were operating machinery and doing other jobs formerly done by men. Of course, local women were already well qualified for assembly lines, for females had labored in Piedmont textile mills for nearly a generation.

All citizens were expected to buy war bonds, use ration stamps and volunteer to help however possible. Some ended up doing some really surprising tasks.

Their stories follow. But first, it is important to emphasize the significance of the involvement and contributions made by the Piedmont of the two Carolinas. This summary shows only a glimpse of the scope.

EMPLOYED WORKERS

Probably the home of the most typical "Rosie the Riveters" in the Piedmont was Alamance County's Fairchild Aircraft. In January, 1942, the *Times-News* announced that a former rayon plant would become the site for building training planes. Fairchild purchased the privately-owned airport, Huffman Field, nearby. By May, 1943, the AT-21 Gunner, an all-wooden twin-engine training plane had made its first flight, watched by thousands of people, including Gov. J. Melville Broughton.

Meanwhile, Kirkpatrick Heights, a complete town, was being built near the plant to house the plant workers. But as of May, 1944, the Army ordered Fairchild to curtail production.

In December, it was announced that Firestone would occupy the plant to make 90 mm artillery pieces, which they did only from March to August, 1945.

Female workers at Fairchild Aircraft. Burlington, NC. 1943. Courtesy of Don Bolden, author of *Alamance: A County at War.*

Operated by the munitions division of US Rubber, the Naval Ammunition Depot (commonly called the "shell-loading plant") had a contract with the Bureau of Ordnance to assemble 40 mm shells. With 272 buildings linked by 32 miles of gravel roads on 2234 acres along Highway 49 nine miles south of Charlotte, the plant employed approximately 7,500 (three-fourths women, one third of those black) from a radius of 60 miles.

With three eight-hour shifts, workers were expected to rotate every four weeks. To accommodate this work force, the plant provided a laundry which handled 8,312 coveralls and towels daily, a main cafeteria plus six smaller ones, a hospital and a fire department with four fire trucks and one ambulance. Two diesel engines moved freight over 23 miles of track.

Although 60% of the workers relied on bus transportation (64 busses per shift), the others came in cars from 72 surrounding towns. One woman, who lived 50 miles away, traveled the five miles to the bus line by horse and buggy. The most extraordinary means of transportation there were the "angel buggies" (which trucked gunpowder) pushed by girls with bells on their shoes.

* * *

Many factories changed hands or switched over to make other products to meet war demands.

In what had been Carr's Durham Hosiery Mill No. 7 in Carrboro, the National Munitions Corporation opened to assemble anti-aircraft ammunition in 1942. It eventually employed as many as 16,000, and had only one major accident. That, however, caused a chain reaction, explosions, one fatality and literally shook the small Orange County town.

And what do you suppose Penn-Carol Hosiery Mill in Concord made? Machine gun mounts and fuel pumps! Dr. Frederick Smetana says that their machine shop produced the fuel pumps for an English engine, the Rolls Royce Merlin, which was used in Navy PT boats and P-51 fighter planes.

The former Darlington Fabrics Company plant in the Thrift community off Mt. Holly Road near Charlotte was bought in early 1942 by the Defense Plant Corporation for a dry battery factory to be operated by National Carbon Company. It was estimated that 800 men and women would be needed. The batteries would be used for radios and communication devices.

National Carbon opened another battery plant in Forsyth County and an electrode plant at the edge of the Piedmont in Burke County's Morganton.

Stanly County's Aluminum Company of America (ALCOA) plant in Badin made 50-pound aluminum ingots which were shipped out to make products such as plane fuselages. J.C. Blair estimates that 750 people were employed there.

Kline Iron and Metal Company of Columbia, Greenville Steel of Greenville and B.L. Montague of Sumter joined with Southern Engineering of Charlotte and Carolina Steel of Greensboro to form a consortium to make parts for LSMs (Landing Ship Mechanized) which were assembled in Charleston.

Raleigh's Peden Steel made Navy barges.

R.H. Bouligny, Inc., a rural electrification company in Charlotte, produced armament for the Army, Navy, Engineer and Signal Corps and parts for Curtiss Wright and Martin Aircraft. Materials they had made for a government plant in Oak Ridge, Tennessee, were used to make the first atomic bomb.

Greenville's Poe Hardware and Supply and Poe Piping and Heating companies were involved in mechanical work at the

147

government installation at Oak Ridge and many military camps. Daniel Construction Company moved from Anderson to Greenville, as they were one of the contractors building the Greenville Air Base.

* * *

Textiles, nevertheless, were still the principal product of the Carolinas' Piedmont. But the main customer was the military.

Gaston County's Firestone Mills made tire fabric for military vehicles. Textiles, Inc. (the old Loray Mill) made thread for military uniforms. According to Howard Whisnant, 70% of the world's combed yarn came from Gaston County.

In Cabarrus County, Cannon Mills of Kannapolis was a major supplier of textile products for the military forces. While they were making sheets, towels and washcloths for the government, their "Cannon Girl" was appearing in ads as a bride, wife or mother, urging customers to make their own towels and sheets last longer. A machine-gun belt manufacturer estimated that his company had made 15 million belts for the war effort from Cannon and Wiscasset yarns. Cannon also produced heavy duck cloth. Kerr Bleaching and Finishing Company in nearby Concord finished eight million yards of that heavy duck cloth for tents and other purposes.

Cone Mill in Guilford County began making cloth for tents and camouflage as well as osnaburg for sandbags.

Surry County's Chatham Manufacturing Company in Elkin stopped production of their other products to make Army blankets, recalled Minnie Arnold Brown, who used to commute from Yadkin County to work in the weaving room on the second shift at the Old Mill near the Yadkin River.

Amazon Cotton Mills in Thomasville (Davidson County) made underwear for the military and millions of pounds of merino yarn (a combination of wool and cotton) for socks.

In Spartanburg County, Beaumont Mills, Fairforest Finishing Company and Mills Mill of Woodruff made fabrics for the military.

Newberry County's Oakland Mill produced gauze for bandages. Newberry Mill made sheeting and rope.

The Columbia Duck Mill made canvas for cots, stretchers, tents, vehicle covers, knapsacks and uniforms.

Not all the clothing produced in the Piedmont was of fabric. A Marine, Frank A. Dusch, Jr. now from Concord, wore what the guys called "boondockers" combat boots made by McRae Industries in Mount Gilead (Montgomery County). These were high top shoes with laces unlike Army boots with leather straps and buckles.

148

The Shell-Loading Plant
by
Frances Pruette Falls
Mecklenburg County, NC

Because of my bad heart, I couldn't get into the WAVES (Women Accepted for Volunteer Service), but I wanted to do my part in helping to win the war, so I got a job at the US Rubber Company's shell-loading plant in Charlotte, where they made 40 mm anti-aircraft shells.

By August, 1943, I was working on the night shift in Area 6 doing primer inspection. The primer head had to be put in and out of a gauge that told if it were the right size. At that time, they were still using the screw primers. The parts had threads so they could be screwed into place, but those were soon replaced by press primers.

The primer is the part of the shell that the gun hammer hits first. The primer head had a hole in the inside of it, and every one had to be visually inspected to see that the hole was open. If it were not open when the shell was put into a 40 mm gun, it wouldn't fire. A dud like that could cause a serious delay. The rack, which contained three or four shells, would have to be removed from the gun. That took several minutes to do before the weapon would be in firing condition again.

Each set of parts came with a lot number. From each lot, we had to check 250 random samples. The inner parts of a primer head were a plug, a powder cup, an anvil-shaped piece and a 3" brass tube with 12 holes in it. Every little or big part in the 250-sample set was gauged. These samples were always checked on the 7 a.m. to 3 p.m. shift.

Everyone except those in the administration building had to rotate shifts. For some reason, after about six months, regardless of what shift I was on, I was the one they chose to check the samples. Maybe it was because I found the most bad primer heads.

One day, I was asked to do a special sample. England wanted to buy US 40 mm anti-aircraft shells, and they wanted a demonstration. Every detail of the 500 shells had to be inspected. Each primer part had to be visually checked and gauged. I made sure that everything was perfect when I got through with them. We never heard anymore about the English purchase, but while watching the newsreels at the movies and seeing the British shooting shells at German planes, I envisioned our work saving the lives of some of our Allies.

Our bosses told us that, if we worked a year without missing a day, they would give us a tour of the plants in that huge complex. As a rule, we were only allowed to go into our own building, the cafeteria and the change house (where we showered and dressed).

Area 6 Primer Inspection Department workers: Ola Stratt, Lizzie Feagins, Aggie Johnson, Eva Gant, Ada Hamilton, Daisy Carroll, Martha Stephenson, Bertha Stephenson, Marie Rast, Lottie Wilkinson, Cecil Z. Smith, Ella P. Gordon, Mildred Seegar, Louise Howey, Lydia Phillips, Pansy Boyd, Annie Neely, Jessie Orr Gordon, Frances Pruette, Maude Thomas, Annie Rose Redd, and Dallie McIntyre. Charlotte, NC. 1944.

I took the tour to see some of the eight areas with large buildings, which were accessible along a gravel road off of York Road. Each section had a lot of buildings with covered walkways between them. A railroad track ran through the property. Freight cars were loaded with crates of shells and sent to Pineville. From there, they were shipped to their destinations.

We got the word back that the young men who operated 40 mm guns always liked to see "Pineville, North Carolina" stamped on the crates. They knew that they would find very few duds.

Most of people who worked at our plant were females of all

ages or men who were 4-F, somewhat disabled or too old for military duty. We women enjoyed the "hen parties" and never did have any fusses or fights. We had to buy our coveralls (blue with a pocket). The ladies liked to see what beautiful handkerchiefs they could display in those pockets. They probably wouldn't allow anyone who worked on the load line or around machinery to wear those handkerchiefs. For safety reasons, they had to wrap their long hair around a "rat," put it up in a bun or fix pigtails into a coronet. Later, the women in my area chose to wear their own clothes.

About 12 to 20 of us worked at two long tables in one room. Usually, after it got dark, someone would start telling dirty jokes. One of our supervisors, usually Eva Gant, would close the door to the warehouse. When the laughter died down, we began singing hymns. I wondered who started that. Then I realized it was Aggie Johnson from McConnell, South Carolina. She was the one who never participated or laughed at the jokes.

Two of my co-workers, Mrs. Stephenson and her daughter, Martha, worked eight hours a day like the rest of us and also ran their family farm along with Mr. Stephenson, who worked in another part of the plant. Mrs. Stephenson did all the canning and other farm-related chores as well as her inspection job.

Our salaries started at 55 cents an hour and went up to 65 cents. My typical paycheck for a 40-hour workweek at 65 cents an hour plus eight hours of overtime at time-and-a half was $22.80. Calculated with the other amounts withheld was $6.25, which was set aside to buy war bonds, just one more way I could do my part.

War Work Night and Day
by
Mary Ellen Suitt
Spartanburg County, SC

World War II had a great influence on my career. At Spartanburg High School, I asked to take mechanical drawing but was not permitted to because I would have been the only girl in the class. I went on to Stratford College and then to Ringling School of Art and Design.

After receiving a teacher's certificate in art, I was unable to find employment. This being June of 1942, I became aware of the fact that draftsmen were needed in the war effort. I went to the Civil Service Office, which is located in the post office, and was told,

151

"Mr. Orsini across the street is in great need of help. Go see him."

Mr. F.W. Orsini was the Cartographic Division Chief of the Soil Conservation Service. He gave me a field map to draw. After looking at my drawing, he said, "The job is yours. Since Converse College will be offering a drafting course at night, you will be expected to take that."

I began working on land use maps. Field men, who dealt with the farmers, would bring in a land plan for a farm, and we made the maps, showing which fields were for crops, pastures, woods, etc. Then one day, Mr. Orsini told me not to take that course at Converse. "This is private," he said. "Don't tell anyone."

At dinner that night, I proudly told my family what he said.

My mother asked, "Is he going to *fire* you?"

I thought I was doing well, but all night I worried. The next morning, I went to Mr. Orsini and told him Mother's reaction.

My boss laughed. "Mary Ellen, you're not going to get fired, but that's all I can tell you."

In early 1943, he called about 20 people into his office. "This group has been cleared by the FBI to do war work," he told us. "You have one week to get your affairs in order. If you need time off, you can have it."

For the next three years, we worked 11 hours a day, seven days a week. We would work a normal 8-to-5 day, then take an hour for supper and come back for three more hours in the evening.

Later, when the Japanese maps arrived, our hours changed so that we worked on shifts from noon until midnight or midnight until noon. A guard with a gun was posted outside the door at all times. The work was so secret that our own co-workers in the Soil Conservation Office didn't know what we were doing until after the war.

At first, our office was assigned to make maps of Italy. When the work began, Mr. Orsini traveled to Washington to make a study of the mapping requirements of the Army Map Service for this assignment. The source material was provided by Army Intelligence from a complete set of Italian maps that had been produced between 1865 and 1938.

We had to reduce the scale of the old maps and remove details not needed for military planning purposes, such as land uses. We used overhead projectors and drafting tables for this purpose. The original maps were black and white but were later converted to color.

As the war progressed, we would view aerial photos of

152

bomb damage and revise the maps accordingly. When a map was complete, one of the men from the office would ride the train to Washington and hand-deliver it to the Army.

The maps we made were used by intelligence officers in planning campaigns, by engineers to plan the best route of advance, by the Signal Corps in setting up communications, and later by the occupation army.

Sometimes we got edgy, and any unusual activities in the office were immediately suspect. In one instance, a co-worker and I saw a man bending over a big box."Nosy, nosy, nosy!" she said, bashing his head down into the box. When he came up, we saw that it was Mr. Orsini!

On another occasion, very late one night when I went to the ladies' room, I found a man resting on a cot located there. "Mary Ellen, go on," he said. "I'm not going to bother you."

I ran him out of there.

Some of the ladies in our office had taken drafting at Clemson or Converse and had come to Spartanburg to work. Apartments weren't available due to the influx of soldiers at Camp Croft, so they rented rooms and had to eat out. However, on Sundays, there was no place to go. One of them, Musa Jones, had an aunt who lived across the street from our office, and three or four of us would go there to fix breakfast and take a break about 6:30 a.m. Her aunt graciously used her ration stamps to buy meat for us.

Immediately, after completion of the Italian maps, we started mapping strategic Pacific islands and certain Japanese cities like Tokyo, Nagasaki and Hiroshima, mostly aeronautical charts. I was assigned to do the lettering for those Japanese maps.

After V-E Day, the Spartanburg paper ran the headline: "A Job Well Done and a Secret Well Kept" and an article about what we had been doing. We were relieved that we could finally talk about it.

When the atomic bombs were dropped, we had no radio in the office, but we received the news from outside. Everyone stopped work. We were stunned by the devastation of the bombs, but we then knew that our maps had been used.

Throughout those three years, I worked so hard that I had no social life and was hardly aware of what had been going on in the war—or even at home. I did not regret all the sacrifices.

Ten years after the war, I took a three-month Brownell Tour to Europe. On a river trip in Holland, I got a hint of the hardships others had felt.

The waiter, seeing food left on my plate, commented, "If

you'd been as hungry as we were, you wouldn't leave that. We lived on tulip bulbs."

After seeing more of Europe, I realized that the sacrifices we made at home, such as rationing, lack of sleep and no social life for three years were insignificant compared to what they had been through.

Anyone for Chess? Craps?
by
Mary Evelyn deNissoff
Moore County, NC

At Pinehurst's Holly Inn, I was taking dictation when Dr. Stone, my new boss, commented, "I learned to play chess when I was in jail."

For murder? Robbery? I wondered, horrified.

I didn't know that conscientious objectors, who had been drafted but refused to bear arms, had been put in jail. The government didn't know what to do with them. Some conscientious objectors who would not fight for religious reasons were given other jobs. The actor Lew Ayres was one. He went into the service as a medic. Others went into Civilian Public Service. Then there were those who volunteered for medical experiments.

Stone was one of three directors of a temporary research center, where a group of "conschies" from Fort Bragg were involved in experiments with a dangerous, contagious disease, atypical pneumonia. The other two directors were medical officers stationed at Fort Bragg.

Like a Kelly Girl, I was a freelance secretary working at the resort where I had gotten my first job at 17. In 1940, I had been secretary to Ed Horne, the manager of the 1890's vintage inn. Owned by Pinehurst, Incorporated, Holly Inn's eight-sided Victorian Room, the big dining room on the left of the entrance and the wainscotted bar behind the stairs had been the place to have parties and be seen. As columnist Dorothy Parker said of her office with colleague Bob Benchley, "Had the office been one square inch less, it would have constituted adultery."

After gas rationing was put into effect, most resort hotels shut down. Holly Inn was open to residents for meals, but the locals could take only officers as guests. It was closed to enlisted men.

Because summers were hot as Hell, Holly Inn and the other

Pinehurst, Incorporated facilities always closed down in the summer. The company owned another resort up North, where employees could go during the months they were laid off.

The government took over the inn in the summer of '43, and I was working three days a week to do reports and letters. The office was in another (much larger) location, and the Victorian Room, dining room and bar were closed off. The patients, who were quarantined, had to stay in their rooms.

But when I walked from my home three blocks away, I could see them sitting on their window sills, talking to each other. The ones in the dormer windows over the porte-cochère would wave at passersby. You could tell that they didn't feel well, and some had grown beards. Only one, that I know of, became very ill. To my knowledge, none died. To pass time, they put out their own newspaper, *The Guinea Pig News,* and tied up the switchboard playing chess between the rooms.

When I wasn't working at Holly Inn, once or twice a week I would roll bandages for the Red Cross. Located in an office building where the ABC store is now, the Red Cross was run by a general's wife, Louise Wyche. Before the United States got into the war, I knitted a few sweaters for Bundles for Britain.

After Pearl Harbor, many servicemen came to town from Fort Bragg or Camp Mackall. Southern Pines, which is six miles from Pinehurst, is almost on the reservation of Fort Bragg, although about a 45 mile drive. Camp Mackall was in Richmond County near Hoffman. Bragg was the home of the 82nd Airbourne Division. Camp Mackall trained paratroopers, the 101st Division. Those guys just wanted to get away for awhile. A favorite eating spot was the Gray Fox (now Theo's), where they'd fill the patio and the bar downstairs. One of those enlisted men, Harmon Nelson, who used to play the piano, had been the first husband of Bette Davis.

There were a lot of young, good-looking guys around, unlike today. Older people would invite them into their homes for dinner and to spend the night. I lived with my mother and grandparents in a five-bedroom home, and sometimes I would date one of the guys who stayed with us. All most of those boys really wanted was home-cooked food and a bath.

The mini-USO Center was in the Pinehurst Theater Building, which had been a shop. They didn't have dances, but girls from town would go shoot the breeze. I used to shoot craps on the floor with them.

A Job I Couldn't Leave
by
Betty Alexander Cardo
Mecklenburg County, NC

I was 20 years old and just out of Duke when I was hired by National Carbon to run the control laboratory.

National Carbon was making batteries for "walkie talkies" and radios for the military. Basically, they coated large sheets of metal with carbon, stamped them, and stacked them together in cells. Those were encased in dark green wax-covered cartons.

Most of the employees were women, who worked the assembly lines. A few men ran the office. I was the only one in the lab. My job was to get samples and test them to be sure the metal was coated properly. If there was only a pin-hole not coated, acid could get through, and the battery wouldn't work. I had taken a course in chemistry in college, so I got the job.

For about 18 months, we worked six days a week. We didn't even get Thanksgiving off. I really wanted to work at a bank, but, as a defense employee, I wasn't allowed to leave.

Then shortly before Normandy's D-Day, a general with his entourage came to inspect the plant. If we did well, they would run a flag up a pole in front. Apparently, he was anxious to ship out as many batteries as possible immediately, but I wouldn't pass on a run of the metal sheets. I knew the batteries would be dead before they got there, but he got very outdone with me.

There I was in my school skirt and sweater with my bobby sox telling them all that I wouldn't okay one of the runs. I won.

Not long after that, one of the men who ran the plant signed a slip allowing me to leave. They found a middle-aged high school chemistry and physics teacher, an authority figure, to take my place, and I soon became one of the first women tellers in Charlotte at Union National Bank.

Not Exactly Rosie the Riveter
by
Margaret Homesley Marrash
Gaston County, NC

After riding all night with very little sleep on a train from Cherryville, North Carolina, suddenly I heard the conductor saying,

156

"Next stop, Washington, DC." My three friends, Delores and Katherine Black and Dottie Beam, and I were to change there for Baltimore, where we would seek the riches that work in a defense factory would bring. Schoolteachers at Cherryville High had worked at Glenn L. Martin, an aircraft building company, during the summer and made *big money*—much more than I was making working at the Royal Cafe.

Getting a "redcap" was out of the question. It cost 20 cents, which was a lot then. Our country was coming out of the Depression, but as of September 1942, our families had not reaped the benefits. So we carried our luggage for what seemed like a mile into the station and back out to the train to Baltimore. What an ordeal! We were tired, sleepy and dirty.

In Baltimore, we took a taxi (for the first time in our lives) to an address where we thought we had an apartment waiting for us. SHOCK! No one knew anything about it, but we thought our former teachers had made the contacts. There were no vacancies. What to do? We were deserted and homeless in a strange city!

We started to walk and ring doorbells. The first one was at a synagogue. We had never seen one before. There were only two Jewish families in Cherryville, the Goldiners and Galloways, who owned department stores. A well-dressed, rather stocky bald middle-aged man came to the door. Somehow, he reassured us by exuding an innate sense of kindness. After his initial amusement, Rabbi Epstein said to us with a twinkle in his eye, "You had better come with me."

Like sheep, we followed and piled into his dark sedan, while he stuffed our luggage into the trunk. He drove us back to Union Station and introduced us to a rather weary young woman at Travelers Aid. With her help, we found a room rent we could afford, and Rabbi Epstein took us to a brick home in an old neighborhood, where we could stay until we found an apartment. Then he drove into the night. We never saw him again.

On Monday, Dottie and I took an hour-long bus ride to the Glenn L. Martin Company at Middle River, Maryland, where they made B-26 bombers and Navy planes. My job was in the finishing department in Building B, where the cowling (covers for the engine) were cleaned and painted.

We worked at long tables, wearing huge heavy gloves. With rags, we cleaned the cowlings with some kind of acetone. Then they were taken to the paint shop. Dottie worked in the engineering department on the first shift; I was on third from 10:30 p.m. to at least 6:30 a.m., but often overtime. We made 56 cents an hour.

I enjoyed most of my co-workers: Margie from High Point, five older ladies (two sisters from Virginia, the others from Maryland), two men who were painters from Pennsylvania Dutch country and another gentleman from Frederick, Maryland, in particular.

One woman in her forties with decayed front teeth loved to repeat filthy jokes. One day, she started telling them, and I walked away. "Oh, Little Miss Innocent," she taunted, "pretending that she doesn't like to hear dirty jokes." That really hurt!

I had taken a commercial correspondence course, so I also did some clerical work for our manager and took the reports upstairs, where hundreds of men and women were crawling over unfinished planes, riveting and hammering.

Every night, I heard the "wolf whistles" and "hubba hubbas," which were frankly disconcerting and embarrassing—but also pleasing. We did not need coveralls, but I usually wore slacks and a sweater or blouse.

By 1943, Baltimore was a prime target for enemy submarines. I joined a large group of Coast Guard volunteers known as the Volunteer Port Security Force (VPSF). The males, mostly older men, were stationed in the harbor. But I served two six-hour shifts in the personnel department as a yeoman first class before going to my job at Glenn L. Martin.

It was like being in the regular Coast Guard, as we wore the uniform, had to salute the officers and learned Navy talk, such as "eating in the galley," and we marched in front of many, many reviewing stands.

While in Baltimore, we moved more than once a year. Yes, we paid our rent. Every time we got settled, a serviceman came home, and we had to move. All our landlords and landladies treated us like their children except one.

Even so, during all that time, I was very, very homesick for Mama and my family. (Papa had been dead for years.) We never called home unless there was an emergency. My sister Anne wrote every week, and Mama wrote often, too. Mary Ruth and I wrote and sent care packages to our brothers (Bynum, who served in the Navy in the Pacific and A.P., who was in the Army Air Corps in the States), our brother-in-law Claude, in the Army infantry and several other young men we had met in Baltimore.

All of us Cherryville girls attended church regularly every Sunday.

Dottie Beam, Margaret and Mary Ruth Holmsley and Angelita Beam from Cherryville sip fruit punch at a ritzy restaurant in Baltimore. Winter, 1944.

We didn't get home very often, but when we did go, the trains were crowded with soldiers and their duffel bags in the aisles. Once we stood for the 12-hour ride.

The highlights of our stay in Baltimore was when our youngest sister, Nellie, came to visit and when our youngest brother, Don, happened to be there on V-E Day and marched uptown with us and thousands of others.

We *did* have some fun with our new friends in town and Cherryville boys, who were stationed at Fort Meade and Camp Holabird. My sister Mary Ruth and Dottie's sister Angelita, whom we called "Poodle" and a friend, Joyce Leatherman, came to work at Martin and joined us at our apartment. Our favorite places for fun were the indoor ice skating rink and the Hippodrome, where they had the latest movies, famous orchestras and vocalists.

VPSF put on two minstrel shows at the Armory as fund raisers for war bonds. My sister, Mary Ruth, and I sang "Harbor Lights," "In the Evening by the Moonlight" and "Kitchen Mechanic" in black face, a la Al Jolson. This was perfectly acceptable in those days as part of the culture.

At a bowling alley on North Avenue, VPSF had a very large

league. A terrible bowler, I was more than compensated when I met a black-haired handsome young man. After a couple of years of courting, we were married in old St. Paul's Church on Park Avenue. David Marrash brought me back to North Carolina in the late 50s to raise our daughter, Susan.

View from Town Hall
by
Louise Allen Smith
Chesterfield County, SC

In 1940, a classmate and I indexed library cards at Pageland High School for $4 a month on the National Youth Administration (NYA) federal program established during the Great Depression. Of that $4, I spent $1 for a typing fee, which helped me get a job when I graduated that year. I was the secretary at Pageland's Town Hall, still under NYA, until that program expired. According to the Town Council minutes on May 5, 1942: "Council voted to pay Miss Allen $4 per week." I became the first woman hired on the town payroll.

During my six years there, I witnessed many war-related activities. In 1940, Fort Jackson met Fort Bragg in maneuvers in our area. The soldiers would line up to use the cold showers in the basement of Town Hall after a day's skirmish. Only 16, I flirted with all of them.

One evening some of the Pennsylvania guys stopped by my front porch to visit. They really liked our pecan trees and sat hulling and eating them the whole time. When they came another evening, they refused the pecans. Something about diarrhea.

Another night, a handsome blonde soldier from Chicago took me to the movies and walked me the two blocks home. He became so obnoxious that I ordered him off the property. The next time I heard about that Chicago steel worker, he was in the jail at Town Hall for intoxication. That night, he stomped the one and only water spigot into the floor and flooded the jail.

One day, a tank stopped dead in the middle of the intersection of West Maynard and South Cedar. The men pulled it aside off the road to fix it. Some local people wondered if was really broken, because those boys knew the women in town would feed them—which they did.

The maneuvers' final battle climaxed two blocks from the Square. It was a little bit dull after that, but some girls had met their husbands in those maneuvers. The prostitutes who had followed the men to South Carolina and stayed in Pageland's only hotel, left, too.

After the United States got into the war, we began having air raid drills, summoned by a siren installed up under the water tank behind Town Hall.

The Town Hall became a busy place.

The Chesterfield draft board had one representative, R. W. Outen, at the Town Hall. Sometimes, a person who couldn't read or write would ask me to help fill out the registration papers. One day a mother brought in her son. "I don't know when he was born," she said, "but I think he's 18."

I had to ask Mr. Outen what to do. He said to establish a birthday, so I subtracted 18 years from that day's date and said to the physically-fit teenager anxious to serve his country, "This is your birthday. Celebrate it and share it with others."

One day a week, a federal public health nurse and a TB nurse would come to Pageland to see patients. They didn't maintain an office but used the jail when it wasn't occupied. They would get me to type up the VD cases. Periodically, a few women went upstairs to fold bandages for the Red Cross. Sometimes the Town Council would allow USO square dances in the courtroom upstairs. I had to sneak off to go, because my parents disapproved.

As Camp Sutton in Monroe was only 18 miles away, they had a rifle range and obstacle course in Chesterfield County on Highway 9 west of Pageland. Part of the obstacle course was a snake pit, where the soldiers would learn how to protect themselves in foxholes all over the world. I went down to see that and even hung a snake around my neck. I trusted someone enough to believe him when he said it wasn't poisonous.

One night coming home from the theater, I heard the police phone ring. It was set up to ring loud enough to be heard within three blocks of the business district, because we had only one policeman per shift. I had the key to the clerk's office and went to answer the phone. The police chief's brother, Lee Russell Cato, was calling from New York to ask his brother to tell their parents that he was home from overseas. I caught a ride to deliver the happy message.

Soon after V-E Day, Sanford Smith came home from Germany, where he'd been in the Army infantry. He was five years older than me, but I knew his family. Sanford came in to Town Hall to find out how much it would cost to open a deli. I took one look at him and knew I was going to date him, but I didn't know how or when. We were married six weeks later before V-J Day.

On April 23, 1946, I resigned and, according to Town Council minutes, "Miss Sarah Middleton was hired at $15 per week."

I'm still getting teased about that. They say she was worth more than I was. I say: Inflation!

THE SELF-EMPLOYED

Farmers were also laboring for the war effort!

Bobby F. Edmonds in his book, *McCormick County Land of Cotton,* expressed the dilemma of farmers in his area, particularly after the disastrous drought of 1941.

The Farmer's Quandary

Cartoon printed in *McCormick Messenger*, March 18, 1943.

"Young men left the cotton fields...as they answered the call to serve in the war effort and the Armed Forces. Ernest Harvey, county supervisor for the Farm Security Administration, called on farmers to bring land-power and manpower together for crop production, utilizing every acre of land possible. War loans for purchase of equipment, livestock and other operating goods were made available in order that every farmer could increase his production."

Edmonds referred to another phenomenon which was happening all over the country: "People planted 'victory gardens' to grow vegetables for the table and the war effort. Clemson Extension sponsored community contests to spark interest and competition."

He also included an advertisement from the *McCormick Messenger* run by R.M. Winn of Plum Branch noting that "The nation looks to the South for pulpwood." The ad indicated the importance of wood for packing materials to transport supplies and equipment overseas. The plea from the Winn sawmill was: "We need every cord we can get and we need it now," with the admonition: "Never let it be said that the South failed in its duty to back up our boys on the fighting fronts."

Food and Fiber for Soldiers
by
Victor W. Crosby
Iredell County, NC

When Pearl Harbor was attacked, my wife Ruth and I decided that we'd better go to Iowa, where my family was, for Christmas that year, for we might not be able to return until after the war.

By then, I was buying a farm in Iredell County next to my father-in-law's farm. Robert Lee Alexander had only two girls, so he and I worked together to produce cotton, wheat, hogs, cows, sheep (and later, corn) on about 600 acres.

When Ruth and I got back to North Carolina, I went to Harmony High School at night to take a government course on agricultural production for the war effort. Basically, the emphasis was on food and fiber to feed and clothe soldiers. Through the Farm Credit Administration (FCA), we could borrow what we needed, and we'd have a guaranteed price based on the cost of production plus a parity price. We also learned how to manage the rationing system.

That year, I tore down an old farmhouse on the property and used part of the lumber to build us a new house. Because of shortages, I bought the kind of windows available. We couldn't buy concrete blocks, so we built forms and poured concrete to make the foundation. We used weather boarding and some rafters and joists off the old house as well. The rest of the lumber we cut from the farm.

I already had a 1940 two-door Chevrolet coach, and I was able to get a ton-and-a-half truck. I knew the former owner and his widow, but the rationing board handled the sale and set a price of $275 for the 1934 truck with a V-8 Ford engine. I put in an order for a Case tractor, but they said I couldn't have it. Somebody else had a priority. Instead, they found a John Deere I could buy for planting and cultivating. It was supposed to have six gears. Metal was scarce, so it had only four. That meant I had to crank it by hand.

Later, I built a tractor. I bought an old Fordson tractor that had been partly converted, and overhauled a Model A car engine to go into it. I cut the steel cleats off the wheels and put rubber tires on it. Then I found some Chevrolet truck brake drums and hydraulic cylinders to put on the rear wheels. On the front, I put Plymouth wheels. The tricycle-type tractor was what I needed to pull a combine and a disk.

As the work progressed, I bought planters, cultivators and chisel plows. Eventually, I got the first corn picker to come into the county. The next year, you couldn't buy one here, because all corn pickers were sent to Kansas, after heavy rains produced a bumper crop.

We had one family of sharecroppers, and, when needed, I hired day help. They were paid by the pound picked or by the hour for work done. I got three or four of my regular workers deferred for a time, but when they left, my nephews were getting old enough to work.

Our production varied depending on the year. That first year, I had bought corn at 75 cents a bushel from a Mr. Harmon to feed the stock, But after I was producing it, Mr. Harmon went into the chicken business and needed more than he could grow, so I sold my corn to him at $2.25 a bushel.

If the market couldn't buy our products at the guaranteed price, we would store it and deliver it later to a government collection point. The wool we delivered to a mill at Mouth of Wilson, Virginia. The cotton went to approved cotton gins at Jennings Store in Iredell, Mayberry at Houstonville, John Gill's at the edge of Statesville or the Harmony Milling Company.

At Christmas, 1944, my sister, Alice, who worked for the War Rationing Board in Washington, and two girlfriends wanted to go to Iowa for Christmas. My brother-in-law, Will Campbell, and I put a 15-gallon drum of gas in the trunk, took the spare wheel off Will's car and took what gas stamps we had left to make the trip. My 3-year-old son Erik went with us, but my wife, who was pregnant, stayed home. Will's brother-in-law had promised him an overcoat, so we detoured to Statesville to find him. It was snowing, but he pulled off the overcoat, and we left him with an overall jacket.

When we got to Reidsville, the road was caked with ice. We didn't see the road again until we got back to the East Coast. It took about eight hours to get to Washington. The capitol city had no street signs (a civil defense measure), so it took us from 2 a.m. to 5 a.m. to find their apartment and get back on the road. We spent one night in Chicago with a cousin, but a train passed the house every hour, so we didn't get much sleep. The whole trip took three days each way, but it was good to see my folks again. It was the last time our whole family was together.

In early 1945, I got a draft card. I was informed that, if I wasn't 26 by the first day of June, I'd be inducted into the Army to fight Japan. I turned 26 the first day of May.

Oscar Blackwelder's Revelation
by
Alex Patterson
Cabarrus County, NC

After Oscar Blackwelder, one of Concord's town characters, retired, he used to hang around downtown to pass the time of day visiting friends. My father and I ran an insurance agency, and, during the 1950s, Oscar was one of our insureds. He stopped by a day or two every week when he was in town. In his early 70s, Oscar had the ruddy complexion of someone who spent a lot of time outdoors. No farmer, he always wore an ordinary businessman's coat and tie and a felt hat in the winter, a straw hat in the summer. Occasionally, he would tell us one of his tall tales. That's what they seemed to be at first, but later I found out that they were true!

A few things I knew: he was an expert with dynamite, and he knew a lot about the history of gold in and around Cabarrus

County. For example, there were only two mines where the gold was found in veins, Reed Gold Mine and Gold Hill Mine. All of the other mines had gold found in pockets—very rich, but when it ran out, that was it.

Quite often, I'd see Oscar driving uptown in his old Essex convertible. He had been a salesman for the Essex dealer before the company went out of business. Beginning in the 1930s, he was a prospector for the Vanderbilt Laboratories out of New York.

His work was in the general vicinity of Moore County around Robbins and was to find a mineral called talc, better known as soapstone. It has about 500 uses, including making lubricants, talc powder, paint and as a base for insecticides.

Oscar told my father and me that whenever he found a stone he couldn't identify, he would mail it to the Vanderbilt lab in a cigar box. They would send him a postcard with its name and a brief description of its uses. Such had been the situation one day somewhere around Robbins. He found a vein of black rock running across a creek branch out in the country, so he shipped a chunk to the lab. That time, he didn't receive the usual reply.

A rather expressionless fellow, he said, "They didn't send me a postcard."

"They didn't? Well, why not?" I asked.

His answer was "They came to see me." He explained further, "A couple of the fellows from the lab were waiting for me at the hotel one evening, when I came in from the field. They showed me the black rock and asked, 'Mr. Blackwelder, do you remember where you found this rock?'"

Oscar used the same flat tone when he was telling us his story as he undoubtedly used with them. "Yeah."

When the men wanted to go see the location, Oscar gave them another flat reply: "Nope."

"Why not?"

"It's too far to get there before dark. We'll go first thing in the morning."

After Oscar showed them the site, they told him to "mine it, weigh it, and ship it by rail to this address."

Oscar had asked, "How much of it do you want me to ship?"

The reply was "All of it, down to the thickness of a butcher knife blade, if the vein tapers that thin."

Just before they left, one of them asked, "Mr. Blackwelder, do you have a pistol?"

"Yeah, I have a .38 Smith & Wesson back at the house."

166

They told him he might ought to start carrying it.

"I'll need a permit," Oscar reminded them.

"Don't worry. We'll take care of it" was the response.

About ten days later, Oscar received a big manila envelope from the Department of Interior, United States Government, Washington, DC.

He told Dad and me his reaction. "The first thing I noticed was a big gold seal at the bottom of the letter. It gave me permission to carry a pistol and what would happen to anybody if they interfered with my business. Very impressive!"

As his work progressed, word got around that Oscar was carrying a pistol, so it wasn't long until the sheriff stopped by the dig. After a while, he said, "Mr. Blackwelder, I see you are carrying a pistol."

Oscar interrupted with "Sheriff, I believe you are a pretty good fellow and wouldn't want to see you get in any trouble, so before you go any further, I would advise you to go read that letter up there in the car pocket of my Essex."

The sheriff was gone for a while.

The old-time prospector chuckled a little just thinking about it. "When he got about halfway back down the hill, I could see he was two shades whiter."

All the sheriff had said was, "Blackwelder, please do me a favor and just forget I was even out here!"

That got Dad's and my attention.

Oscar Blackwelder with his Essex. Concord, NC. Circa 1955

Oscar said that one of the men from the Vanderbilt lab paid him a visit a few weeks later to ask if he'd had any problems.

"No problems, but I'd like to know one thing," Oscar said. "Just what in the heck is this stuff I'm mining?"

"It's called pitchblende" was an answer that didn't mean anything to Oscar.

His next question was, "Yeah, but what is it used for?"

All the guy would say was "Some people think it can be used to make a powerful explosive."

According to Oscar, it was several years after World War II that he learned the whole truth. He had been mining the richest uranium ore found in the US to date. The ore he had shipped to Oak Ridge, Tennessee, was used in making the first atomic bomb.

THE BUSINESS ASPECT

Many businesses were affected adversely during the war.

For example, the Southern Furniture Exposition Building in High Point was taken over by the Demobilized Personnel Records Branch of the Adjutant General's Office of the US Army as of December, 1942, so there was no furniture market during that time. Furniture manufacturers were dismayed, however, that they did not get their building back until May, 1946, and, unlike their competitors, they could not schedule an exposition until January of 1947.

In his book, *Alamance: A County at War*, Don Bolden, the retired executive editor of the *Times-News*, gives a month-by-month report of how businesses were affected in their county. Here are some of the highlights from 1942:

* By January, farmers were urged to increase production of sorghum, because sugar would soon be rationed. At that time, there were 35 sorghum mills in their county.

* One month later, the City Machine and Welding Shop had been taken over by state and federal vocational organizations to prepare citizens for work in defense plants.

* Auto companies were changing over to defense production, so by April, Spence Motors began selling phonograph records and Hughes Motors had horses, saddles and farm equipment for sale. Rubber was no longer available, so Kelly Springfield Tires had to close.

* Because of gas rationing, Melville Dairy, in May, had to start delivering milk by horse and cart.

* In August, the *Times-News* announced that there would not

be as many photographs because of a zinc shortage.

* As of November, Burlington Dyeing and Finishing Company had to shut down because of higher costs and the lack of labor.

* Burlington had no Christmas parade that year, but downtown merchants decorated their windows in the spirit of the season.

INVOLUNTARY SERVICE

Although rationing was nationwide, Piedmont people were sometimes affected in unique ways. As early as January, 1942, tires were rationed. Soon thereafter, the automobile industry converted to war production and remaining cars were rationed. In April 1942, gas and sugar were added to the program. Citizens were required to attach a sticker to their vehicles, which allowed limited amounts of gasoline per month. Most drivers were required to have "A" stickers, which allowed for short in-town errands. People who needed vehicles to make a living might get a "B" and those doing war-related or public health jobs could have the coveted "C" sticker, which allowed more (though still limited) amounts of gasoline. The alternatives were walking or public transportation. Unlike the large cities in the North, Piedmont towns and cities lacked enough public transportation. Housewives who needed extra sugar for canning could apply for it, but many found that inadequate, as Southerners generally did more food-canning.

By June of 1942, food supplies were placed under the control of the War Production Board. The Office of Price Administration issued ration stamps for such items as butter, meats, cheese, canned foods, and, of course, sugar, all based on a point system, which became a huge source of consternation for housewives and grocers. The program was discontinued gradually, beginning in October, 1945.

Black market sales were vehemently condemned verbally but were, nevertheless, popular. "Hoarding" was a dirty word—very unpatriotic. Meanwhile, Carolinians found other ways to cope.

Clyde Bigger, a farmer from York County, South Carolina, traded shoe rationing stamps with his brother in New Jersey for sugar stamps. His brother's child, Randy, needed shoes for school and Sunday school; his wife needed sugar for canning.

"When someone had a family emergency, we would round up extra gas ration stamps to help out," said Clara Danielsen Wertz of Newberry County, South Carolina.

"It used to be that every time I had a date, I could say to my mother, 'We had a flat tire and couldn't get home on time,'" recalled Louise Allen Smith of Chesterfield County, South Carolina. Later, she bought tire patches at the dime store. "And then if my soldier date had a flat, I'd pull a tire patch out of my purse."

When Henrietta Castlebury Auman's husband was drafted, her sister and brother-in-law came to live with her in her Hillsborough, North Carolina home. "We were planning what to do with our extra sugar rations," she said. "But we had to use it in my baby's supplement and didn't have any for ourselves."

VOLUNTEER SERVICE

War Bonds

By buying war bonds, citizens were giving the needed funds to the government. True, they could expect a return years later, but citizens gladly sacrificed not just to win but, as many a mother would say, "to bring our boys home!"

As of April of 1942, Americans were asked to use 10% of their salaries for war bonds. Many large companies made it optional but withheld that amount from employees' paychecks. Bond drives were held throughout the Piedmont, often featuring celebrities.

In Alamance County, cowboy movie star Wild Bill Elliott came in July, 1942. In mid-September of that year, John Payne and Jane Wyman raised $49,325 on an East Front Street stage. On January 25, 1944, Ann Savage and Lon Chaney sold personal items such as earrings and cuff links to sell $143,000 worth of bonds.

Rutherford County's war bond drive was so successful that a B-17 was named for it.

On December 9, 1944, 5000 people from the Piedmont saw a War Bond show at Charlotte's Armory-Auditorium featuring Lt. Tyrone Power. "Shoot the Works" was put on by the AAF ORD of Greensboro with a company of 70.

A Bond Drive sponsored by South Carolina's Columbia High School raised enough money to purchase 29 jeeps.

Civil Defense

Civilian Defense organizations in both states trained citizens to be auxiliary firemen, auxiliary policemen or air wardens. In cities large enough for an airport, they gave civilian pilot training. Some adults spotted unidentified aircraft from watch towers. North Carolina was known for having the most volunteers in the region.

In Guilford County, the Civilian Defense Volunteer Organization enlisted hundreds and provided a rescue truck.

When air raid sirens went off in a community (whether as a warning of an unidentified aircraft or just as a test), a blackout was strictly enforced. One night, air raid wardens in uptown Charlotte couldn't find anyone to turn off the neon lights of Haverty's, a furniture store, so they broke the sign.

Community Collections

Patriotism was personalized by the spirit of giving. And junk made great gifts! Scrap metal (even the foil from cigarette and gum wrappers), used kitchen grease (which contained glycerine needed for explosives) and scrap paper were all needed for the war effort. One of the slogans was "Collect Scraps and Beat the Japs."

One year after the United States joined the war, a Salvage Award was given to North Carolina counties that had collected more than 100 pounds per capita. The Piedmont winners were Caldwell, Catawba, Davie, Forsyth, Guilford, Mecklenburg, Lee and Stanly.

Alamance County's War Production Board salvaged 445 tons of streetcar rails from a route from Graham to Burlington. The city of Burlington took up their Big Gun, a World War I Navy weapon that had been on public display at Webb Avenue and Anthony Street. By October 1942, local residents had donated more than a million pounds of scrap metal.

Cabarrus County's Reed Gold Mine donated *their* scrap metal. Gold? No, the nation's first gold mine gave up their old boilers.

North Carolina's Salvage Committee asked the Junior Chamber of Commerce to organize the Junior Commando Army of North Carolina. Although the Jaycees started the first chapters, they had the cooperation of the state's Parent Teacher Congress, who assisted in school systems where there was no Jaycee chapter. Children were encouraged to collect metals, fats, rubber, rags, newspapers, magazines, corrugated boxes and scrap paper, all properly bundled or boxed. Each child would be rewarded with a rank and an arm band for 25 to 350 pounds (private to master sergeant). Those who collected a cumulative 500 to 2000 pounds earned the rank of 2nd lieutenant to colonel. They received a sweater, cap and arm band. Each one who exceeded 2500 pounds earned stripes for his or her sweater. Five service stripes entitled the Junior Commando to a service plaque. The schools were expected to buy the awards but could keep the cash earned from the sale of the scrap.

171

JUNK
needed for War

"What's it good for?"
"Guns, tanks, and maybe part of a plane"

In the barnyards and gullies of farms and in the basements and attics of homes is a lot of Junk which is doing no good where it is, but which is needed at once to help smash the Japs and Nazis.

Scrap iron and steel, for example.

Even in peacetime, scrap provided about 50% of the raw material for steel. It may be rusty, old "scrap" to you, but it is actually *refined* steel—with most impurities removed, and can be quickly melted with new metal in the form of pig iron to produce highest quality steel for our war machines.

The production of steel has gone up, up, **UP**, until today America is turning out as much steel as all the rest of the world combined. But unless at least 6,000,000 additional tons of scrap steel is uncovered promptly, the full rate of production cannot be attained or increased; the necessary tanks, guns and ships cannot be produced.

The rubber situation is also critical. In spite of the recent rubber drive, there is a continuing need for large quantities of scrap rubber. Also for other waste materials and metals like brass, copper, zinc, lead and tin.

The Junk which you collect is bought by industry from scrap dealers at established, government-controlled prices.

Will you help?

First—collect all of your waste material and pile it up.

Then—sell it to a Junk dealer, give it to a charity, take it yourself to the nearest collection point, or get in touch with your Local Salvage Committee.

If you live on a farm, consult your County War Board or your farm implement dealer.

Throw YOUR scrap into the fight!

This message approved by Conservation Division
WAR PRODUCTION BOARD
This advertisement paid for by the American Industries Salvage Committee (representing and with funds provided by groups of leading industrial concerns).

LOCAL SALVAGE COMMITTEE
PHONE: McCORMICK 52
JAMES M. DORN, Chairman; R. L. DENDY, W. P. PARKS, MRS. R. L. FAULKNER

JUNK MAKES FIGHTING WEAPONS

One old disc will provide scrap steel needed for 210 semi-automatic light carbines.

One old plow will help make one hundred 75-mm. armor-piercing projectiles.

One useless old tire provides as much rubber as is used in 12 gas masks.

One old shovel will help make 4 hand grenades.

MATERIALS NEEDED

Scrap iron and steel.

Other metals of all kinds.

Old rubber.

Rags, Manila rope, burlap bags.

Waste Cooking Fats—When you get a pound or more, strain into a large tin can and sell to your meat dealer.

NEEDED ONLY IN CERTAIN LOCALITIES: Waste paper and tin cans—wanted only in certain areas, as announced locally; NOT NEEDED (at this time); Razor blades—glass.

JUNK bulletin in August 6, 1942 *McCormick Messenger*

The Country Club Grease Caper
by
Eric A. Jonas, Sr.
Mecklenburg County, NC

The Junior Commandos were a big deal among the boys at Charlotte's Myers Park Elementary School. I was proud to wear a military-style cap that showed I was a Junior Commando.

We could earn points by collecting various things, such as tinfoil, for the war effort. You could advance in rank (up to, at least, colonel), depending on how many points you earned. Friday was the day we turned in what we had collected and found out whether we had earned a higher rank.

My friend Carter Terrell even got a wooden plaque with a gold-embossed eagle signed by Governor Melville Broughton. His father, an owner of Terrell Machine Company, had donated an old boiler in Carter's name.

You could really rack up beaucoup Junior Commando points by collecting grease, too. My dad had an "in" with the kitchen help at Myers Park Country Club, so I acquired the grease franchise there.

The first week, I pulled a wagon laden with a huge pot of grease from the club to our home on Sterling Road. The next day, my dad delivered the grease in his car to the collection point downtown. It must have been a real mess. He declared that there would be no more grease collections. End of franchise.

Even Kids Helped the War Effort
by
Henry Shavitz
Guilford County, NC

A siren on a telephone pole rolled around, piercing the night sky over High Point's streets. As it rolled in our direction, it would be louder, then it would fade as it pointed away from us. It signaled a blackout drill (in case bombers came over), time for us Boy Scouts to spring to action.

I had been active in Scouting before I was old enough to be one. The Scout Executive, Bunn Hackney, a friend of our family, let me go to camp, and I hung out with Kermit Cloniger, the Scoutmaster of Troop 20 at the First Presbyterian Church.

Soon after I turned 12, Kermit became a Naval officer, and I joined Troop 55 at First Methodist. Not long after Pearl Harbor, we were Junior Air Raid Wardens to assist the Wardens during black-outs in our neighborhoods. Red-haired Frank Montgomery, our leader who was in his 30s, would be tipped off, and he would get word to us before the sirens blared. With special arm bands on our uniforms, we worked in pairs, patrolling two or three blocks, checking to see that people's draperies or black shades were drawn. If we spotted any light at all, we would knock on the door to remind them.

We felt real important, but when there was no moon out, no street lights, not even stars if it was cloudy, in all that darkness, I was a little bit scared.

Our work for the war effort did not stop there. As soon as gas rationing was announced, everyone had to go to a voting place, a school or a church to sign up for their stickers. We were stationed there to help register people. Drivers had to fill out a form to determine whether they were eligible for an A, B or C sticker to go on the lower left side of their windshield. Then they would be issued rationing stamps based on those codes. Doctors and people with jobs important to the government got the C rating. Ordinary citizens like my dad, who drove a four-door Chevrolet, got an A.

While I was helping out, a heavyset white farmer sat down at my table. He seemed to be in his 60s, which, back then, I thought was unbelievably ancient. He handed me his form. "I can't read or write," he said.

"I'll do it for you," I offered.

When we finished, I handed it back to him. "Now you can sign it."

"I can't write my name," he said solemnly.

I told him what we had been trained to say, "Well, make an X, and I'll sign beside it, 'his mark.'"

The bib-overalled farmer shook his head. "How do you make an X?"

At the time, I thought that was funny.

Our Scout troop also collected scrap needed for military purposes, especially scrap metal, grease and tinfoil (from cigarette packs and sticks of chewing gun), which we rolled into big balls. We went door-to-door asking for them. Housewives donated old pots, pans, metal tableware and used cooking grease.

As a student at High Point Junior High, I participated in a talent show to sell war bonds. After telling a few jokes, I grinned when one of my teachers said, "Henry, you ought to grow up to be a comedian!"

I've always been a fan of comedians, and I've made a hobby of studying them. I have never been a comic but occasionally do a funny routine for my friends.

Later, I was in several other shows, which helped raise money for war bonds. My favorite was "HMS Pinafore," when I wore a sailor uniform.

On V-E Day, I was at a summer camp in Maine. My father sent me a melodramatic telegram, which my counselor delivered. He praised me and the other scouts for our efforts to help win the war.

I entered the Army (Signal Corps) toward the end of the Korean War. I did think often of his telegram telling me the war had ended. I wondered why there was another war so soon.

A lot of boys had to grow up too quickly!

Switch
by
Phil Hammond
Guilford County, NC

A week before Christmas, 1942, Van, one of my buddies at Greensboro's Aycock Junior High appeared at my front door. Shorter than my other best friends, he always stood out, as he had very blond hair. "Phil, here is your present," he said, handing me a small rectangular box wrapped in bright paper with ribbon tied neatly on top.

In turn, I handed him mine, and he left.

Too excited to wait, I tore off the paper and stared at a dark handsome box. Inside was a beautiful black knife with a Boy Scout insignia emblazoned on the handle. The three attached blades would give me many hours of pleasure on overnight camping trips in nearby forests or at Camp Greystone, the area Boy Scout camp, some 30 miles away. "Wow!" I said to myself. "Van has really given me something of value."

A few days later, our doorbell rang again. Van in coat and gloves looked me in the eye. "Could I please have the present I gave you? I've made a mistake. That present is for someone else. Yours is in my coat pocket."

As I returned the box with the treasured knife, out came a gift which looked similar to the package I had given him.

175

To do my part for the war effort, I had bought war bond stamps. For each of my five best friends, I had put four 25-cent stamps into a booklet so they could start saving for a bond.

Down the steps he went. "Merry Christmas!" he called out.

Curious, I tore open the paper from his gift. There in front of me was a very familiar booklet with a fifth stamp attached.

Local Hospitality

Even before American forces were in the war, soldiers were appearing in the Piedmont with not much to do during free time.

In the fall of 1941, more than 400,000 soldiers fought a mock war from Charlotte, North Carolina to Laurinburg, South Carolina. On weekends, they headed for the nearest town seeking entertainment and lodging. Movie theaters and YMCAs were overwhelmed. Some cities abandoned their "blue laws" to allow movie-going and the sale of beer and wine on Sundays.

Acres of pup tents popped up in places like Charlotte's Independence Park and Memorial Stadium. National Guard units bivouacked in open fields. The USO later set up 10,000 mattresses in the Charlotte armory and school gymnasiums, and the city built a "soldiers' rest room" across Mint Street from the main post office.

Churches, civic groups and individuals rallied to be accommodating. That was the beginning of the Piedmont's commitment, especially of their churches, to welcome the military with open arms. Jewish homes were also opened to servicemen. At one Kol Nidre service at Charlotte's Temple Israel, 700 Jewish military men attended. The town's entire fleet of Yellow Cabs was recruited to deliver the men to members' homes.

The majority of soldiers who came to Anson County on maneuvers were Catholic. Their chaplains held services in Wadesboro's Ansonia Theater, and, by 1941, a Catholic recreation center with volunteers from the faith community was operating on West Wade Street.

The Red Cross sponsored canteen corps, motor corps and nurses aide corps and used volunteers to prepare surgical dressings and knit socks and sweaters.

Many volunteers packed Red Cross boxes and "CARE packages" for POWs and men who served in combat, but, in North Carolina's Orange County, some women made "dream bags" full of little surprises for soldiers abroad. In the basement of the Confederate Memorial Building, where the library was located, a high school home economics teacher, Henrietta Castlebury Auman and other local ladies sewed small bags with drawstrings (like marble bags but larger).

"We used old sheets," she said. "I even took one of my good sheets. I bought up all the little peppermints that were individually wrapped," she added. Then Auman told how a restaurant would bake the bags at a certain temperature in the oven (presumably to sterilize them). "The first bunch I forgot to take the candy out, and it stuck to the paper and was a mess."

Other items they packed included toothbrushes, toothpaste, soap, a needle, thread and the kind of buttons needed for uniforms. Auman says the items and ways of packing them changed. They had been told not to include scissors. "And when the men started coming home, they told us to thread the needle, put a button on it and tie a knot at the end." Henrietta Auman always added something personal: a poem attached to the back of a calling card.

Usually located in train stations and bus depots, trained volunteers from Travelers Aid helped travelers—especially servicemen and their families—with multiple problems, such as lost children and wallets. Meanwhile, both YMCAs and YWCAs provided rooms and recreation for military personnel.

The United Service Organization (USO) was a joint effort of the Salvation Army, YMCA, YWCA, National Catholic Community Services, National Travelers Aid Association and the National Jewish Welfare Board, offering hospitality in the communities where they were present with literally thousands of volunteers.

Due to the proximity of Fort Jackson and the Columbia Army Air Base, Columbia had five USOs, three for whites, two for blacks. The largest, a new building which opened in May, 1942, overlooking what is now Findlay Park, was regarded as "swanky" by *The State* newspaper.

Soldiers from Newberry County, South Carolina who found out they were to be shipped out of Fort Jackson would notify relatives which train they would be on en route to a collection center, according to Clara Danielsen Wertz. Word would spread, and when the troop train made a ten-minute stop at the Newberry Depot, women would be there to hand them little brown bags of sausage biscuits and other goodies.

In 1942, soldiers from Camp Sutton with a weekend pass were turning up in Concord. "On Sunday mornings, they'd be seen sleeping on the grass," recalled Alex Patterson. He told of residents opening their homes and putting cots in the local armory for them.

"In the early days of the war, they had nowhere to go on weekends," added Helen Arthur-Cornett. "A lot of them were Yankees." She described the Canteen Community Center set up in what used to be a YMCA beside Central Methodist Church near the Square. "It was a beautiful old place with a huge ballroom, an organ, and a mural of Cabarrus County from the time of Indians to the early 1930s."

People used their ration stamps (meat and sugar) to fix supper on Saturday nights, breakfast and lunch on Sundays. Sometimes, Army bands or an occasional jazz group came to play, but usually record players or a jukebox provided dance music. Local girls (well-chaperoned) were on hand to entertain the young men. None were allowed to leave the canteen with a date. "It was strict as a nunnery," said Helen, a senior at Concord High that first year.

As the war continued, soldiers came longer distances for Concord's well-known hospitality, food and friendly people. Word had certainly reached Fort Bragg and beyond. The feeling must have been mutual, for above the Canteen's door was a sign: "The world's greatest soldiers come through these doors." Perhaps in response, soldiers sang "I left my heart at the Concord Canteen..."

Sis Dillon of Monroe says that local churches opened their meeting halls every night as recreation centers for Camp Sutton soldiers, and many of the military men who attended church services were invited to homes for Sunday dinner. "Women would drive girls (called Military Maids) to and from dances, which were held in the old Bank of Union Building and at school gymnasiums. Even after a USO was built, the civilian recreation program continued."

Burlington opened a Service Man's Center on West Davidson Street In July, 1942, noting that more than 100 men from their area had already joined the military.

Through Guilford County's Community Planning Council, they organized entertainment for black and white servicemen and operated the only United Service Organization (USO) under local direction. They set a national precedent by including the Red Cross in their comprehensive program. The Central Y in Greensboro provided recreation for as many as 5,000 soldiers and housed up to 300 on weekend nights. As in most communities entertaining soldiers, "blue laws" (no retail sales on Sunday) were suspended in Greensboro—excluding pool halls.

Charlotte was also considered a recreational center and transportation point for servicemen from throughout the Carolinas. On weekends, soldiers were seen sleeping on the court house lawn.

178

As of June of 1943, Charlotte's Enlisted Men's Club, sponsored by the War and Community Chest, had counted 90,000 visitors since it opened a year earlier. Two months later, the Business and Professional Women's Club (BPWC) opened an Enlisted Women's Club on the same floor at 208 South Tryon. Servicemen could visit "for one night only" during the opening reception.

The Charlotte Defense Recreation Committee reported at the end of 1942 that 1191 homes provided hospitality, 6781 soldiers had been weekend guests and 8431 had eaten Sunday dinner in those homes. Meanwhile, 31 churches had put on 124 parties and 48 suppers honoring 20,000 soldiers, and the committee (featuring 1611 registered "Victory Belles") had hosted 242 social functions to entertain 119,361 soldiers, all white. However, they had a separate division for blacks. From May to December, that division had 110 homes where 1132 soldiers were weekend guests and 100 ate Sunday dinners. With the help of "Cheer-ettes," they sponsored 148 social functions and 24 service functions to entertain 19,500 men.

That September, more than 150 Victory Belles put on "Jingle Jangle Jingle Review," a free show for 1000 soldiers from Morris Field and Camp Sutton the first night. The next two nights, they sold tickets to the community with proceeds divided between their committee and American POWs. Victory Belle Marion Carter Childers, who had a singing/dancing act and comedy routine, recalled that the girl who sang "Don't Sit Under the Apple Tree with Anyone Else but Me" with a soldier ended up marrying him.

Charlotte's Little Theater also did USO-type tours. Betty Alexander Cardo appeared in one at Camp Sutton. Their audience was delighted with "Warrior's Husband," as the almost-all-female cast portrayed Amazons in very short Greek costumes.

OTHER PATRIOTS

A unique defense group officially called Citizens Service Organization (CSO) but also known as "Guerillas" or "Cox's Army" sprang up in Alamance County in answer to the call of a minister, Rev. James S. Cox. More than 3000 men between 16 and 85 (two regiments of whites, a battalion of blacks) and a women's auxiliary volunteered to protect the home front when needed. Rev. Cox accepted the rank of Colonel and deferred to Everett Jordan of Saxapahaw, who was named General.

Conscientious objectors served their country in other ways.

Proud to Serve My Country - Another Way
by
Clarence Ray Thomas
Randolph County, NC

Quakers don't have creeds. We have queries. In the query on peace, we are asked: Do you consistently practice the Christian principles of love and good will toward all men? Do you work actively for peace and the removal of the causes of war? Do you observe the testimony of Friends against military training and service?

I've been a Quaker since I was 15. Originally a Baptist, I was invited to sing with my quartet at a Quaker Sunday school in my hometown, Asheboro, and I just kept going there. That's where I met Pauline. We married in 1937.

Because of my marital status, I wasn't drafted until March, 1943. I went to talk with a member of the draft board and gave my testimony. Soon after that, I was declared 4-E and got my notice to report to the Civilian Public Service Camp 19 close to the Blue Ridge Parkway.

The rustic wooden barracks at Buck Creek Camp had been built by the CCC boys. Originally a Civilian Conservation Corps camp, it had been taken over by the Department of the Interior and was under the supervision of the National Park Service.

Civilian Public Service for conscientious objectors was new. It took lots of meetings, conferences and traded ideas to work this out. But the Mennonites, Church of the Brethren and the Quakers took the responsibility of feeding and caring for 12,000 or so COs. We were to do work of national importance for no pay, no free food, no travel expenses. We provided our own clothes, and those who could were asked to pay $35 a month for board. We signed papers that the US Government was not responsible for anything that happened to us.

While at Buck Creek, we cut dead trees, made rail fences, developed Crabtree Meadows campground, crushed rocks and worked on the roads of the Blue Ridge Parkway.

Conscientious objectors were often asked to participate in medical experiments. Some of our fellow workers got atypical pneumonia germs sprayed into their throats. I served in a control group. We were checked frequently to see if we caught it. Two or three of the men ended up in the hospital, but they all recovered.

After five months, I was transferred to Smoky Mountain

Park near Gatlinburg, Tennessee, where I spent all of 1944. There, we did a lot of maintenance work, keeping up the walking paths, horse trails and roads. When needed, we put out forest fires. And at the carpentry shop, we made signs for the Appalachian Trail.

Our crew ate pretty well there. Now and then, we would buy a cow at an auction in Knoxville to butcher for meat. Once, Art Little, a vegetarian, found out what we were doing. He came and put his arms around the cow's neck and hung on. We had to secretly set another butchering time.

A woman in nearby Knoxville somehow found out that I had a wife in Asheboro. Charlotte McPherson, who was a school teacher, called and asked me if Pauline would keep house for her and take care of her little girl, Janet. Later, I got kidded for answering "yes" without asking Pauline, but we were so glad to have time to be together again—and the McPhersons became our friends for life.

By mid-1944, more service opportunities became available at state mental hospitals, state agricultural experimental stations and, in Florida, a hookworm project (building and installing outdoor privies), and out west, smokejumping and forest fire control units.

Ray Thomas, Joe Allred, Al Wolfgang. In truck: "Stormy" Vetter. Gatlinburg, TN. 1944

In 1945, three of us from North Carolina opted to work with the Delaware Dairy Herd Improvement Association.

Each of us was assigned a county. Frank Teague of Snow Camp went to Sussex; Larry Williams, who was from near Yadkinville, to New Castle and I, to Kent County.

We were supposed to stay overnight in the home of each farmer we served. Our routine was to take samples from each dairy cow during the afternoon milking, spend the night, then get up to take more samples and test them.

After we calculated the milk production for each cow, we would move to another farm, 28 days a month.

Only one Amish farmer, Sam Beachy, requested testing. Their bishop had not approved the service. His defiance, though, became the Lord's way of answering my prayers.

I was sitting on the milk stool, when Sam asked, "Are you married?" Then he wanted to know where she lived. "We've got to get her up here," he said and began making plans for us to move into an empty house nearby for $8 per month rent.

Neal Miller's family, who lived across the street, took us into their hearts and became more friends for life.

Frank Teague went to North Carolina for a visit and brought back Pauline. Not long after we had settled in, a farmer took sick and needed help while he was in the hospital. We were offered the house rent-free, if Pauline would tend the chickens and water the lambs. When we had to move again, our Amish neighbors found us another house.

Incidently, the fee for my services paid by the farmers all went to the US Treasury to be used for relief and reconstruction in Europe and Japan after the War. From what I've heard, that money is still in the US Treasury!

However, the Mennonites and the Brethren sent young heifers with volunteer caretakers to Europe to help the farmers start over again. The Quakers' American Friends Service Committee went to help organize and oversee reconstruction.

Conscientious objectors were not particularly popular during World War II. A man on the draft board made unpleasant comments to me. Another one, giving out gas rationing stamps (so I could transfer to Delaware), was pretty rough on me, but I learned to just let it roll off and keep a'going.

A military officer, who was inspecting Buck Creek Camp said to us, "I hate your guts!" Then he added, "But you don't cause any trouble."

In Delaware, one farmer would not let me test again after he found out that I was a CO.

All in all, though, people were kind—like the McPhersons, Sam Beachy and Neal Miller. We named our first daughter Janet, after the McPhersons' child. And our first son is named for Neal.

Oh, and several Amish boys are named Ray now.

Stateside Service

Not everyone in the military went overseas. Those who did, trained in the United States first, many in the Piedmont.

Yes, the Armed Forces had a significant presence in this part of the Carolinas, and many civilians got jobs on regional bases or moved to other states to help out.

First, a summary of local military installations.

NORTH CAROLINA

Greensboro was the only city in the United States with an Army camp having more than 30,000 personnel within its city limits.

It opened as Basic Training Center #10, where new soldiers were sent before entering an Air Corps technical training school. Later, BTC #10 became one of only three Army Air Force Overseas Replacement Depots (ORD). An estimated 87,000 men were trained there from 1943 to 1944. Close to the end of the war, it was designated a Separation Center.

The Greensboro camp had the unique distinction of having the lowest number of venereal disease cases in the country.

* * *

Northeast of Monroe, Army engineers established Camp Sutton (named for Frank Sutton, who enlisted in Royal Canadian Air Force and was killed in North Africa December 7, 1941). Previously, Monroe had been used as headquarters for a major military exercise from the Catawba to the Pee Dee rivers a month before US involvement. When it opened in early 1942, the camp was for overflow troops from Fort Bragg who were training to go into Europe, but it was later expanded as an engineer training facility. Although 133 cooking units with showers and latrines were built, the soldiers slept in tents on 12'x12' wood frames.

From 1944 to 1946, Sutton housed about 1000 German POWs, who did farm labor and wood-cutting as civilian contract laborers in the community. For only three months, 3,500 Italian collaborators were held in a compound there, but they proved to be too difficult to handle and were transferred to other locations. When Sutton closed in the spring of 1946, Monroe annexed the area with infrastructure and the rest of the land was returned to farmland or used for industrial purposes. The base hospital became a state mental hospital then a facility for polio patients before being transformed into what is now the Union-Memorial Hospital.

* * *

Camp Butner (named for Major General Henry Wolfe Butner of Surry County) in southern Granville County was activated in March, 1942, as a training facility for 40,000 troops, a hospital and, later, a POW stockade. Workers labored day and night to make the camp operational in three months. Post Headquarters was completed in a week.

The 78th Infantry Division, known as the "Lightning," did combat training at Butner as did the 89th, 35th and 4th Divisions. When the Army released the property, the state purchased it for $1 and renamed the medical facility Umstead Hospital and turned some of the barracks into Butner Training School for the Mentally Retarded.

* * *

In January, 1942, Charlotte Air Base was named Morris Field for a World War I flier and aerial instructor, Maj. William C. Morris of Cabarrus County, much to the consternation of Charlotteans, who had recommended and endorsed Mecklenburg County's 2nd Lt. James Sykes, a World War I ace killed in action in France.

The US government had taken over the local airport for the Army Air Corps to form an advanced base for training bomber pilots and maintenance crews before going overseas. A sub-depot was added, where technicians began operating lathes and drill presses, welding, dispensing parachutes, testing delicate electrical equipment and reconditioning aircraft. More than 600 people, including wounded vets and women, also repaired 100 planes per month urged on by their motto: "Keep 'Em Flying!"

* * *

The Raleigh-Durham Airport was designated an Army Airfield and served as a training center and an air defense base. The Army Airfields at Raleigh-Durham and Charlotte were filter centers where sightings of aircraft from town watch towers were plotted.

* * *

On 72 acres formerly occupied by a Ford plant on Statesville Road, the Charlotte Quartermaster Depot opened May 16, 1941. At the peak of operation, 80 Army officers and 2500 civilian workers in six enormous warehouses supplied Army installations in the two Carolinas, Virginia and West Virginia with everything from "tooth-

184

picks to battle gear" and filled emergency needs overseas.

In 1943, a Salvage Branch opened on the property providing lumber for studs and pallets (some from dismantled CCC camps), steel and other metals, cloth (including osnaburg) and paper such as tabulator cards. The Depot eventually became an Inspection Headquarters to check on and improve efficiency at Quartermaster Depots throughout the Southeast. In 1944, the Charlotte Quartermaster Depot set a national record for purchasing more war bonds than any other large establishment, military or commercial.

After the war, the American Graves Registry Division operated there from August 1946 to 1949, delivering bodies of more than 5,000 soldiers to their next of kin in surrounding states.

* * *

Camp Mackall, located on the edge of the Piedmont in North Carolina's Hoke, Richmond, Moore and Scotland Counties near the town of Hoffman, was used for maneuvers by troops under the command of the 3rd Army, National Guard, ROTC and Marines and as the Hoffman Airborne Command Station. A rather primitive camp, Mackall trained the 511th Parachute Infantry, which joined the 11th Airborne Division in 1943 and, in '43 and '44, the 555th Parachute Infantry, known as "Triple Nickles" [sic] For a while, Mackall housed POWs. It is now used by Fort Bragg for training.

* * *

Moore County (the Pinehurst area) was also the home of Knollwood Army Airfield, a communications training base for the Army Air Corps in 1942-43.

* * *

On the North Carolina Piedmont's other edge was the Lake Lure Army Air Force Distribution Rest Camp in Rutherford County.

SOUTH CAROLINA

By 1938, the Army decided to transform the idle Camp Jackson outside of Columbia into Fort Jackson, named for Major General Andrew Jackson, who was the 7th President of the United States. After opening in August, 1940, it became an induction center and was soon known as a pioneer in training environment for the infantry. The Richland County facility trained the 30th "Old Hickory" Division as well as the 4th, 6th, 8th, 26th, 77th, 87th, 100th and 106th during the Second World War. The original buildings were temporary, but Fort Jackson eventually became a permanent Army Training Center.

* * *

185

Originally the private Lexington County Airfield, Columbia Army Air Base began construction of wooden barracks less than a month after the bombing of Pearl Harbor and soon became a transition and training base for B-25 bombers. It is best known as where the Doolittle's Raiders volunteered for a "very dangerous job," later known as the first US bombing of Tokyo in retaliation for Pearl Harbor.

This 21st Sub-Depot provided support and training for a base in Pennsylvania. When B-25 pilots were taking advanced training and making bombing runs over Lake Murray, Lunch Island got the name Bomb Island. One bomber crashed into Lake Murray; another in Lake Greenwood.

* * *

The Greenville Air Base opened in 1942, and thousands of airmen were trained there. Renamed Donaldson Air Force Base in 1951, it closed 12 years later.

* * *

The Army built Camp Croft near Spartanburg on 22,000 wooded acres to train 20,000 or more infantrymen at a time (every three months). Named for Major General Edward Croft, it took only four months to build with the help of 12,000 construction workers and the hinderance of a flu epidemic that affected 2,000 of them. The first group to train there was B and C Companies of the 33rd Battalion. Others included the 32nd-40th Battalions, and the African-American 50th.

Although the community, like other Piedmont cities, provided many services for the trainees, a chaplain on the base set up a variety of learning programs (including elementary German) and interest clubs (such as glee club, public speaking and drama). As for sports, the Croft Crusaders football team gained local fame.

* * *

Camden's Southern Aviation School had a private contract with the Army Air Corps to give 60 hours of primary training in ten weeks. From 1941 to 1945, Southern Aviation's 100 instructors trained 6000 American cadets and 300 British.

Owned by civilians (World War I pilots Frank Hurst and Ike Jones), it was supervised by Army personnel and was the home of the 64th Army Air Forces Flight Training Department at Maxwell Field. The main base for operations was Woodward Field with 200 acres, three hangers and more than 100 PT-17s. By 1943, three auxiliary fields (Bateman, Trotter and Stevens) had been added in Kershaw County.

Recruited by Mary McLeod Bethune
by
Dovey Johnson Roundtree
Mecklenburg County, NC/Chester County SC
Co-Author (with Katie McCabe) of *Healing the Brokenness*

Mary McLeod Bethune was a friend of Grandma's. My grandfather was Clyde L. Graham, the pastor of East Stonewall AME Zion Church in Charlotte and a Mason. My grandmother, Rachel R. Graham, was very active in the Eastern Star—treasurer for 46 years—and other women's organizations. My mother, sisters and I lived with my grandparents at 921 East Hill Street after my father died. Grandma introduced me to Mrs. Bethune when this women's woman was here to speak on Emancipation Day.

When I graduated from Second Ward High School in 1931, Mama got a job in Atlanta and took me with her, so I could work and go to college. After two years, I got a NYA (National Youth Association) loan. Spelman College was just what I needed at that time. It had the best teachers, and I got so many NYA jobs that I parceled some out to other students. Meanwhile, I again met Mrs. Bethune, who had founded the National Council for Negro Women, when she was a speaker at Spelman. She encouraged me and, for the rest of my life, she was my mentor.

I was a good student and I hoped to get a scholarship to medical school. But back then, all the spaces in med school seemed to be for men. Mrs. Phern Rockefeller, the treasurer of Spelman, had even written a letter of recommendation for me.

While waiting to get a scholarship, I taught seventh grade and counseled senior students at the Samuel L. Finley School in Chester, South Carolina for two years.

By 1941, I was discouraged. I went to Washington to look for a job and see our family friend at her office. This champion for women was heavy and not as tall as I, with mixed gray hair and nice features. She had a pleasantness about her that could wrap you up. Yes, she was *Dr.* Bethune, but I called her Mrs.

I stayed and worked for her at the National Council for Negro Women, doing whatever needed to be done. I went out and got Cokes, picked up the mail and did other chores. I would do anything for them.

Mrs. Bethune would guide women to forge down a valley to a sanctuary, where they would get their strength and understanding before they ventured forth. She believed that you needed thoughtful

187

women, who had points to make and made them, and the National Council worked through mission departments of churches and the YWCA to get women to be active in their communities. She'd tell them with so much enthusiasm, "You have to read, you have to go to the library, learn all you can before you speak." That helped me a lot later, when I became an attorney.

While I was there, she had a tea. That was the first time I met Mrs. Roosevelt.* Later, when she said "We know a secret but can't tell you yet," I knew that if Mrs. Bethune said she had a dream, you'd believe her, because she was influential from the White House to the outhouse.

Sometime later, Mrs. Bethune revealed her secret to me, "It's women in the Army." Both black and white women would be a part of the Women's Auxiliary Army Corps, and she was helping to handpick the first blacks to attend Officer's Candidate School. She expected me to go and told me I'd have to start at the Charlotte Army Recruitment Office.

When I told the family, Grandma's reaction was that it was "fine" with her, but it wouldn't be "okay" downtown. Mama thought it would pass off.

At the recruitment office, a woman took my name on the sign-in sheet. On the paper, I wrote "I want to join the WAACs." She asked if I could be reached by phone. We didn't have a phone, but I gave her the number of our neighbors across the street. I asked, "Will I hear from you?"

She went to the back, and a man came out. He said this was not the recruiting office for the WAACs. I told him the law had been passed for women to be in the Army, but then he said, "If you don't get out, I'll call the police."

Soon after that, at Mrs. Bethune's suggestion, I went north to Richmond where my cousin Ally Bryant Lowery lived. I applied at the recruitment office there, and they took my name and said they would check it out. They called and wanted me to come take a test. I was disappointed in the slow process, but one day a man came in a car to check me out. He brought more papers that had to be notarized. That day, they cleared me, and on Saturday, I was sworn in. Several white girls and a couple of black girls joined, too. My whole Richmond family went down to the station to see me off.

At Fort DesMoines, Iowa, it was cold, although it was summer, 1942, when we arrived. We began training the next day. My feet hurt, my head hurt and I was homesick. We marched everywhere we went. In class, we were all together, but signs on the tables in the mess hall were marked "colored" and "white." We talked and moaned and groaned. I contacted Mrs. Bethune to complain.

"You're on a mission, Baby," she told me.

"Yes, ma' am."

"But I'll look into it."

I knew that meant she was going to dial Miss Eleanor. People didn't know it then, but those two women were running the country. Those signs were soon gone.

After commencement, I was sent out on a recruiting job in the Southeast with another 2nd lieutenant, Ruth Lucas. It was poetic justice, I thought, when I returned to Charlotte. But, at the recruitment office, the male officer wouldn't let me come in. I called Mrs. Bethune.

"Do nothing. Don't go back. I'll open the door with a key up here," she said.

Ruth Lucas and Dovey Johnson, who were sent to the Southeast as recruiters for the WAACs. Late fall, 1942

Grandma was afraid the house was going to get blown up, but by the next week, they gave me a cubbyhole so people could come to see me at the office.

Meanwhile, I contacted some of the local ministers and spoke at Johnson C. Smith University, Second Ward and West Charlotte High Schools, the NAACP and Brevard Street Library. I also went to churches, the YWCA and Eastern Star. Reporters came. And Grandma was proud. She'd tell me which ones she thought were "good girls."

I traveled by bus to other towns. At Chester, I went to the Samuel L. Finley School and spoke to an assembly. Mr. Finley was still there. I had been a little direct when I was in school there, so I was not his favorite, but when I went back, he had open arms.

When I got back to Fort Des Moines (in the spring of '43), the base commandant was wanting to re-segregate. Many of the white girls were concerned, as we were. We had friendships and cooperativeness. We didn't want to lose all of that.

At a meeting of black officers, when he was to announce his intentions, I spoke up against it. It was wrong, I told him. We've been getting along. All of that fellowship would be gone. Separate but equal was always separate but never equal. I found that troubling.

I took off my insignia from my uniform. I knew they were going to put me out as "unfit."

Other black girls didn't back me up. Some thought I was a troublemaker.

Later, I had to put my insignia back on to keep doing my job.

Of course, I made contact with Mrs. Bethune. It was an abortion of what she believed in. She gave me assurance not to worry and not to do anything.

A few days later, the base commandant sent a notice out that the Army had revoked the order.

The result: all that talk of re-segregation made us "one."

* Editor's note: In interviews with Katie McCabe for her forthcoming book, Roundtree indicated that, while she worked at the NCNW office, Eleanor Roosevelt visited Dr. Bethune frequently and that the two leaders were on a first-name basis. Dr. Bethune also directed the Division of Negro Affairs of the National Youth Association and was a special advisor to President Franklin D. Roosevelt on minority affairs. "Auxiliary" was dropped in 1944; hence, WAAC became WAC.

From a Plow to a Plane
by
Ernest Henderson, Sr.
Laurens County, SC

In 1932, I was in a field plowing on our farm in Laurens County when I heard a rumbling noise. I looked around and didn't see a car. (Cars were few and far between back then.) I looked up, and there was a little yellow airplane, a Piper Cub. Whoa! I stopped the plow and watched it until it faded away into the distance.

When the war broke out in Europe, I was a junior at Hampton Institute in Virginia. The US began to train men and were drafting them out of school. I was 22 and I thought, well if I go into the service, I want to do something I like, not just be a ground soldier. I'll join the Army Air Corps! I had the qualifications (two years of college, an A-B average and good health), but they wouldn't let us in because of our race. They thought black men didn't have the aptitude, technology or judgment to fly an airplane.

But six black colleges: Delaware State, West Virginia State, Howard University, Hampton Institute, A&T in Greensboro and Tuskegee Institute, organized some civilian flying classes under the Civilian Pilot Training Act. I enrolled at Hampton and got 40 flying hours.

On the morning of my first solo cross-country flight from Newport News to Norfolk, I had to cross a small part of the Chesapeake Bay. I looked down and saw that water. I couldn't swim! So I climbed that airplane as high as I could. I had prayed before the flight, but I remembered Jesus teaching Peter how to walk on water, and I thought, if I fall in the water and get out of the airplane, Jesus might not teach me how to walk on water, but he'd teach me how to swim real quick. Nothing happened, and I got my pilot's license.

The President of Hampton Institute told me to go to Tuskegee Institute in Alabama, where they had advanced courses. I took the advanced course and one for commercial pilots to certify me to fly a large plane. In 1941, I became the first black man from South Carolina to get a pilot's license, instructor rating and instrument training.

One day, a large group of high school students who were there to check out the college, came to the airport to see black men fly. My instructor, an Italian, said, "Henderson, take this airplane up," pointing to a WACO-UPF-7.

191

I showed those students what I taught others to do: straight-and-level, a loop, fly-over, slow roll, snap roll, a half snap, and two maneuvers to be used in combat: a vertical reverse and a lazy 8.

On another occasion, I tried two maneuvers that I brought into existence: a hesitation roll and a vertical 8. An instructor said, "Henderson, where'd you get that?" I did those to test my own ability; I taught the students strictly by the book.

Ernest Henderson, Sr.
Tuskegee, Alabama
Winter, 1941.

One student, Scott, could do maneuvers but was not good on landings. On the 12th hour, I told him if he didn't solo that day, he would wash out. I flew around the airport with him four times before I let him try it. He had to fly around the airport once, and I told him to come back to the wind-tee in the middle of the field, where I'd be waiting for him.

The boy did fine until he came in for the landing. He was heading straight to the wind-tee, where I was standing. I thought of Proverbs 3:6: "...acknowledge Him and He will direct thy path." The airplane was on a path northwest, so I took a path northeast. The lower part of Scott's wing hit the top of the wing-tee. I had to wash him out. I should have said, "If you stop flying now, the life you save may be your own."

My best student was named Wilson.

Before his graduation flight, I told him, "Wilson, I'm going to give you a present. You can be in the front seat. You be the teacher."

Soon he was pointing his thumb back to me and saying, "Mr. Henderson, climb to 3,000 feet." We took turns doing maneuvers. He'd touch his head when he was taking over and point his thumb with another order. After I did a half roll and a split S, he didn't do any signs or say anything. We dropped from 500 to 400 to 300 feet. A student isn't supposed to talk back, but I saw pine trees below my heels. In Ecclesiastes 1, it says, "There's a time to keep silent and a time to speak." I asked if he were flying this airplane.

"No sir, I thought *you* were flying it! "

I took the airplane, gave it full throttle and pulled the nose up away from those trees. When we reached the ground, I told him I would have been responsible if anything had happened because I was the instructor, but that he was still my best student.

Meanwhile, in Europe, the 99th Pursuit Squadron was joined by other black squadrons that we had trained to form the 332nd Fighter Group, which began escorting bombers. When I heard they had painted their tails red, I worried that, if they had a crash, everybody would know that a black man failed.

At first, some superiors tried to make our guys look bad. They sent out 16 bombers to Castelvetrano, Italy, with only six pursuit planes to protect them. Generally, each bomber is supposed to have four.

I shouldn't have worried. Throughout the war, those "Red Tail Angels" never lost a bomber to enemy fighters.

We trained more than 1,000 pilots at Tuskegee—and lots of them wrote to thank me.

A WASP Breaking the Barrier, Cracking the Ceiling
by
Kate Lee Harris Adams
Durham County, NC

When my younger brothers were building model airplanes, I was, too. I've always been fascinated with flying, so, while I was at Duke, I took advantage of the Civilian Pilot Training Program.

For every nine boys, there had to be a girl. My friend and classmate Jane Winters and I were happy to fill those spots. We thought it was thanks to Eleanor Roosevelt, who advocated women's rights.

We took classes on West Campus but had to go to the airport on the other side of Raleigh for our flight instruction. Our instructor, who was concerned about our safety, told us that we were in more danger getting to the airport than we were flying. After I graduated from Duke in 1941, I didn't use my new skills because it was too expensive to rent a plane.

Although the Women Airforce Service Pilots (WASP) organized in 1942, the original pilots were very experienced, but they kept lowering requirements. By the end of 1943, all required was a civilian pilot's license and at least 35 hours flying time. I had 42. At the air base in Greensboro, I took the physical. I had to stretch to get to the height (5'2") and eat bananas to get to the weight. My blood pressure was up (I can't imagine why!), but they were as accommodating as could be and let me stay overnight and be retested. Once accepted, I had to go home to Durham and wait to be called. Both my brothers, who were one and three years younger were already air cadets. Soon there would be three of us Harrises.

Did my parents object? Not then. The biggest problem had been getting them to allow me to enroll in the CPT Program. I cried, so they let me take it.

On September 5, 1943, I was notified to report to Avenger Field in Sweetwater, Texas. Avenger had been a training field for men, first the British then Americans.

In the middle of Texas, it was an excellent flying area. We had ground school as well as flight training there. How I loved it! The whole program! The only thing I wanted more: to be sure of graduating. We never knew when we woke up whether we would have to leave tomorrow. The washout rate was more than 50%. Women who were very good pilots were sent home.

The Army was preparing to send a few of us to B-26 school. Known as the "widow-maker," the B-26 was a very tricky airplane to fly. Men did not want to fly it, so the Army thought that female pilots who could master it would shame them into trying. Some of my best friends flew those twin-engines. It took only a few days to get checked out. The reason? Women followed procedures and instructions. After seven months, I was sent to Napier Field at Dothan, Alabama, an advanced single-engine flight school.

I flew 17 different single-engine planes. WASPS flew everything from the Piper Cubs to B-29s. Our safety record was a little bit better than the males. But still, many men didn't think women could fly and resented us generally. They didn't appreciate that we were releasing them to go into combat. We quaked in our boots when a military pilot checked us out.

We were the first women military pilots. Other females functioned in military roles only as members of an auxiliary. In the late 1970s, when women were first admitted to the Air Force Academy, we lobbied Congress to acknowledge this. One of the biggest objectors was a Texas Congressman. One day, during the hearings, a WASP pulled out her discharge card. He pulled out his. They were identical. He stopped fighting us. Soon, they were thanking us for breaking the barrier, cracking the ceiling.

At Napier, we were engineering test pilots to check out the repaired planes before turning them back to the cadets to fly. We were expendable. If anything fell off the plane, a cadet didn't die.

We also did some ferrying, some flying of administrative personnel around, taking people to get parts and even delivering mail to Eglin Field, Florida—any flying job that needed to be done. We loved it all.

One afternoon, I was testing some distance from the field when I saw a big, dark cloud. I called the tower to see if they had called off flying. With a very condescending attitude, the air controller replied, "No, we haven't called off flying," insinuating: "you female pilot."

So I continued to put more slow time on the engine before I decided to go in anyway. Then that dark cloud turned into a dust storm. The wind was shifting around. A gust caught me as I was landing, and my AT-6 nosed up and dragged a wing tip, damaging the prop and the wing.

Unhurt, I was unable to move because the air controller *did* call off flying, and cadets were landing their planes all around and couldn't see mine. I was afraid one might land on top of me! When the dust cleared, the airdrome officer of the day came out in a jeep to report the extent of my accident.

Kate Lee Harris signing a Form One flight report on an AT-6. Napier Field Dothan, Alabama. September, 1944.

An instructor, the handsome 2nd Lieutenant Bob Adams was kind, understanding and not at all condescending. Exceptionally skilled, he had been named the honor cadet of his class, and I was impressed.

When I got back to my quarters, I glanced in the mirror. I looked like a clown! There were two round white spots where glasses had been. Dirt everywhere else. I was still mad, too. I was mad at the air controller's condescending attitude and at myself for not coming in sooner.

Bob, the man I would be married to for 54 years, laughingly called it "fire in your eyes." After our children were out of college, we had two different single-engine planes and enjoyed many wonderful hours of flying time.

195

Sworn to Secrecy as a Code-Breaker
by
Elizabeth Hyatt Caccavale
Spartanburg County, SC

On December 7, 1941, I was standing in our kitchen at home getting ready to go to church. At 18, the oldest of six children, I heard my mother say, "Quiet everybody!" We all stood near the radio and listened, as President Roosevelt said we had been attacked. Right then, I knew my life was changed. "What can I do?" I wondered. "I'm only a woman."

Females were not in the military then. But Congress eventually passed an order allowing women to go into service. As soon as I heard that, I went downtown to the Navy Recruiting Office to register. The officer was shocked to see me, as I was the first woman in Spartanburg to enlist as a WAVE (Women Accepted for Voluntary Emergency Service). "Wait until I get a photographer over here!" he said. A photo of me, taking the oath and being sworn in, appeared in the newspaper the next day.

My mother was mad. I had to get Dad's signature, because I was only 19. My boss was mad, too. I would soon be leaving my secretarial job at Cecil Smith's insurance office. Actually, I had to wait a long time.

Meanwhile, I was attending USO dances at Camp Croft and had met Private Phil Caccavale from Brooklyn, New York the first day he arrived. When he finished his 13-week basic training, we had to kiss good-bye and promise to write. He was shipped to Casablanca, and, a few days later, I left for basic training at the State Teachers College in Cedar Falls, Iowa.

Soon, I was learning everything about a ship, guns and equipment as well as Navy history, doing calisthenics, running obstacle courses and marching all over corn fields. The "old salts" brought in off their ships to train us spouted a lot of verbal abuse at us. They didn't want to be there or to train women, of all things. We girls tolerated them and their ridicule. But we began to enjoy the benefits of wearing a military uniform: traveling at half price and, when in public, never having to wait for anything. People stepped back and let us go to the head of the line.

After a brief trip home, I was told to report to Washington. Not one of the other girls from Cedar Falls joined me there. Twenty women from all over the country were inducted in the Naval Communications Intelligence Organization.

196

Then we were taken to a church, where we had to face the altar to take a second oath, promising never to discuss our work with anyone, as we would be working with highly secretive material. The prerequisite was a fifth generation American with a high IQ. For my "cover story," I was given the name of a high-ranking official (fictitious, of course), and I was to say I was his secretary and leave it at that.

We worked on a campus of a former teachers college on Nebraska Avenue but were allowed only to go into one building and the mess hall. We were to wear a picture ID under our shirts and a ribbon that was the color of a sign over the door of each room we could enter. Our barracks, with ten bunk beds, was across the street.

Betty Hyatt at Rockefeller Plaza on her first visit to New York. Spring 1943.

For two and a half years, I worked with coded Japanese messages.

At first, I would count how many times the same group of five numbers appeared on a page. After we determined patterns, they would be read in Japanese and translated into English.

We were told that, if the Japs invaded Washington, our building would be the first place they would go. We must destroy whatever we were working on, and as a last resort, swallow the messages.

One day, I was given a bunch of messages and told to take them to Admiral Lee. As I prepared to enter, a Japanese man in an American uniform was standing near the door and started coming toward me. "The building has been invaded!" I thought. I saw other people working at desks. "And they don't know it yet!"

Noticing that I was ready to swallow messages, the man smiled, "No! No! I'm an American!"

"You don't look like one," I said dubiously.

He started laughing, "I'm a Japanese-American. It's my job to translate."

We worked swing shifts (8 a.m. to 4 p.m. for a week, 4 p.m. to 12 a.m. the next week and midnight to 8 a.m. the next) and would get a 48-hour leave every three weeks. I usually took the train home, but one weekend, I took my first trip to New York. Phil and I were still writing, although his letters were so censored that half were cut out. His sister, Maria, invited me to visit their home.

At her father's expense, Maria and I saw "Oklahoma," and dined at a fancy night spot. At dinner, we met two men in uniform. One asked me to give him my number. He said he had a friend in Washington who would take me to dinner there. I agreed, and, when I returned, Dr. Santa Lahara (I called him Joe) phoned. When he appeared for our date, he was the handsomest man I had ever seen! Not only that, he was the third secretary of the Dominican Embassy, who had once been engaged to Trujillo's daughter!

For the next year and a half, Joe took me to parties at every embassy on Embassy Row, where I met many famous celebrities, even John Wayne! Joe wanted to marry me, but I preferred Phil.

One night, when I was ready to go home from my "grave-yard shift," an officer came in to announce that a captured code book had just arrived. Anyone who was not too tired or sick would be expected to stay until every message in our office was de-coded. Most of us stayed *for two days and two nights!*

Once when I went in the bathroom, I was afraid to sit on the toilet for fear I would fall asleep there. We could be shot for sleeping on duty! Finally, they let us take 15-minute naps as needed until the job was done.

Once we were able to translate every message, the Allies began playing war games, so the Japs wouldn't know we knew the code. That's how we happened to shoot down the airplane carrying Yamamoto and other top officers.

In October, 1944, Phil arrived at a hospital at Mitchel Field, New York. He had been in the invasion of Casablanca, crossed into Sicily, and, later made his way from Rome into France and up to the German border, where he got hit by mortar shells on each side. He had bandages on his left arm and a cast on his right arm when we were married in Brooklyn in February, 1945.

If a husband were wounded, the Navy allowed the wife to be released from duty. I got out May 30, 1945. By then, I was confident that the war was nearly over, in part, thanks to that code book.

198

Although I had been released from duty, I was not released from my oath. The Chaplain had reminded me before I left and I received a letter confirming what he said.

So how can I tell this story now? We were released 10 years after the war.

Education, Compliments of the Army
by
Cedric H. Jones
Wake County, NC

When I graduated from Shaw University in 1941, the teaching field was crowded, so I found employment waiting tables at a dining hall connected to some tourist cabins near Asheville.

I helped a classmate, the son of a Shaw trustee and also a graduate, get a job where I worked, and at the end of the summer, I bought a used car (a Graham) to drive us back to the Piedmont. Degree in hand, I went to North Carolina State College in Raleigh to do the only job I could get—as a common laborer.

For doing lawn maintenance and knocking down an old NC State silo, I was making $12.50 for five-and-a-half days' work, but I was expected to pay 50 cents for lunch and eat in the kitchen. I took my lunch in a pail.

I finally had a white-collar job as an insurance salesman when I was drafted in 1942. Our early training for Quartermasters was at Camp Gordon in Augusta, where we learned how to unload coal and put it into an Army truck. We were sent to warehouses, run by civilians (mostly World War I vets), where we unloaded ships with goods needed to stock barracks.

At Camp Butner, I was part of a crew as a Tech/4. Our starting pay was $21 a month, but it went up to $54. Of course, I sent an allotment back home.

From January to August of 1944 at Fort Benning, I was finally able to use my degree. By that time, the Army needed more manpower and was accepting functionally illiterate men with the understanding that, if they could achieve a fourth grade level during a period of 16 consecutive weeks, they could serve in the military.

For about three hours a day, I taught reading and English with the Special Training Unit in a barracks with 15 desks and not much more than a blackboard. My students also took simple math, taught by someone else. In the afternoons, we had to drill and train with our group. But during my class hours, I found it a pleasure to be in the Army, to look at those young people, see the possibilities they could have with education and know the contributions they could make.

Many of those boys hadn't had the opportunity to learn. Some were slow, and a few were like the one who admitted he had been sent to school, but he would "slip and go somewhere else." He was stuck with me, and I was determined to do anything I could to help all of them read and understand what they had been reading. Our primary reader was *Private   Pete,* stories about a private who would do things the "Army way."

It was marvelous to see those boys go that fast through four years of education. Most, by then, were willing to learn, well mannered and followed instructions. They had talents they'd never used, and I didn't have any failures. Not only did they pass the Army test, but this was the opportunity they needed to start an adventure, a life more meaningful because they could read and explain themselves. They could get better jobs in the future and feel more comfortable in social gatherings. Some had a quick benefit to their achievement— they could write letters to their loved ones back home.

Meanwhile, other men with deficient educations were taking classes at higher grade levels and were encouraged to take high school equivalency tests.

I felt fortunate to be a successful teacher, but I had to move on to finish my training, first at Indiantown Gap, Pennsylvania, where, at the supply depot, we learned to load ships on dry land, take it all out and load it again. At Charleston, we practiced loading and unloading a capsized ship. The Army always advocated safety, and that was important to our training.

We were then sent to the Army's port of embarkation in Los Angeles, California, to load ships with ammunition, food and combat gear. We had the help of winches, but it was challenging to us. For safety, you had to keep your mind on what you were doing. Yet, you knew that as a result of your experience, you were helping others, and that gave you courage and enabled you to follow through.

Now and then, the fellows got hungry and would open a can or two. I never did that, but I shared some of the food, like peaches, once in a while. On off hours, we would take some trips to the Pacific, a nine-mile walk one way.

Because of my military experience, I saw both oceans, but I never sailed on either one. I was in the Army 47 months and never saw combat. But I came home.

And because of the Army's GI Bill, I got my masters degree at Columbia University before moving to Charlotte in 1948 to teach at Second Ward High School.

Busted and Back
by
Les Roark
Cleveland County, NC

From sergeant to guardhouse, to private, to sergeant, to overseas assignment—all within a 30-day period—still seems like fiction. It happened like this:

In the fall of '44, I was a sergeant, an aerial gunnery instructor, at Harlingen, Texas Air Base. A lifelong buddy from a neighboring farm showed up as a student. Back home, Frank Allen carried the nickname "Ham."

During his six-weeks course, Ham missed an opportunity for a pass to cross the border and visit Matamoros, Mexico, where a lot of action and excitement was readily available to service personnel.

As a good buddy is supposed to do, I decided to help. So I borrowed a pass from my friend, Sergeant Hardy G. Robinson.

We had a dilemma: the Military Police at that time were checking uniforms to see that appropriate stripes, etc., were being worn off base. No problem. I would let Ham wear my shirt. With Robinson's pass and my properly trimmed shirt, my buddy was ready to go.

After the 26-mile bus trip, we crossed the border for several hours of entertainment that GIs enjoyed on such occasions. To return, we used the standard method of hitch-hiking, quickly getting a lift with three inebriated Mexicans in the back of a beat-up pickup. Luckily, we made it to downtown Harlingen.

Around a corner was a taxi stand where we could catch a quick five-minute ride to the base. It was then several minutes after 11 p.m., and curfew at the gate was 11:30. No problem.

Just as we whirled the corner, we encountered two MPs exiting a restaurant. They were cordial enough, but one decided to check our credentials and asked to see our passes. We produced them. Then they asked each of us to state our military serial numbers. I reeled mine off quickly, and the MP returned my pass, admonishing us to hurry along and make curfew.

From Ham, nothing but silence. The other MP, holding his pass, asked him again. No response.

My suggestion that my buddy could have had too much to drink was not persuasive. The next step was to unbutton the shirt collar and check the name and serial number, printed indelibly on all uniforms. The MP saw my name and serial number, then looked at the pass that Ham had. It said Sgt. Hardy G. Robinson. He then looked at me. "Now tell me who you are."

I did. They checked my shirt collar, and it matched my pass. "Where and who is Sgt. Robinson?" he asked.

To protect my friend, I told them that I did not know him but "borrowed" his pass, because it was the one next to mine in the box where passes were kept in alphabetical order.

Further interrogation revealed that Ham was a buck private, that Frank Allen had my shirt and Sgt. Robinson's pass and that Sgt. Roark had removed Sgt. Robinson's pass without his knowledge. So the MPs gave us free transportation back to the guardhouse, the military's name for "jail." Locked up, we spent the remainder of a restless night.

Next morning, all inmates were marched to the mess hall for breakfast. Armed guards were at the front and back of the formation of "criminals." Along the way, several of my friends observed me in the ranks of that procession. That was embarrassing, to say the least.

After that, Ham and I were separated. A corporal took me to Squadron Headquarters, where I was asked to write a complete report of the episode. I was then escorted into the office of the Colonel, our squadron commander, who looked at my report and asked a number of questions. I was excused, saluted the Colonel briskly, did a proper about face and left.

My Class A pass was in the file box, so, for the next ten days or so, I returned to my normal duties and routine, even going into town a time or two. Then one morning, I received a Special Order issued by our squadron officer. It was then I learned that the session in the Colonel's office was a summary court martial.

I was reduced to private, which automatically removed me from flight status. Sergeant's pay, then, was $78 monthly. Flight pay was 50% extra for $117. Privates got only $50. A $67 reduction would have reduced the amount I was able to send home to my widowed mother, creating a real hardship for her.

At that time, five gunnery instructors were being selected to ship out for an overseas assignment with the 8th Air Force in England. I immediately got in touch with the officer in charge and made an appointment. I learned that the five had been tentatively selected. Based upon my previous work records and my unfortunate circumstance, the officer approved my request for transfer. My sergeant's rank and flight status were restored.

Frank Allen and I are both safely at home in Cleveland County and members of a seniors coffee club, where we are occasionally asked: "Tell us about your trip to Mexico."

Lifesaving Blimps
by
D. Kermit Cloniger
Lincoln/Guilford Counties, NC

I wanted to be in the Navy. I didn't want to sleep in fox-holes, so when I received orders for active duty as a Naval officer and a buck private in the Army, all in the same mail, it was an easy choice.

I had been working on getting a commission for the Navy, so I went to Raleigh as soon as I could to accept it. The procurement officer tore up the Army orders, and I was commissioned as a lieutenant junior grade, a jump in rank because I had very high grades on the tests.

By then (September 10, 1943), I was 30 years old and had been working for International Harvester in Atlanta since 1935. I had brought my wife back to her home in High Point, where I went to college my last two years.

I was ordered to duty at the Naval Air Station in Hitchcock, Texas. The procurement officer didn't know where that was; neither did the ticket master at the Southern Railway train station. It was about 50 miles south of Houston near Galveston, in a part of Texas where much of our oil is refined..

It was a new blimp base, commissioned in 1943. Its purpose was to escort oil tankers on the first leg of their journey to the North Sea, England and the rest of Europe.

When I reported for duty, I could tell that Capt. Roland was very disappointed, because I didn't know anything. But the first big lesson I learned was that *nobody* knew what they were doing. It was a new base, as we were increasing our military forces from practically nothing to 12 million almost overnight. So I became an expert after I was there a couple of weeks.

Soon, I was made permanent duty officer, then he assigned me as a junior division officer. My primary duty was the military life of the command.

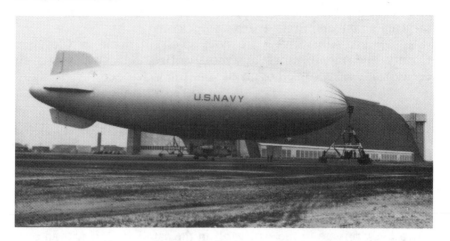

USN blimp at the NAS in Hitchcock, Texas. November, 1944.

Our base had hundreds of people and six blimps. Our only ships were crash boats. For a routine flight, we would get up at 0400 to load bombs, ammunition, depth charges and food. Each K-ship (blimp) was 250 feet long, had two 475 horsepower engines (one on each side of the gondola), twin .50-caliber machine guns in the nose and carried a crew of eight men and two officers.

Everything was weighed so that we could gauge the amount of helium needed to make it lighter than air. Generally, it took off at daybreak and received the coordinates to rendezvous with a fleet out in the Gulf. When it was time to moor, usually about eight to ten hours later, they would discharge some of the helium and then use the engines and controls to place the blimp in position for the mooring crew on the ground. They would pull the mooring line and secure it to a tripod on wheels. Then the K-ship would be moved into the hanger. Despite some rough weather, we never lost a blimp on our base.

Typically, ten to forty ships would form a convoy. Oil tankers, destroyers and sub chasers would be met by three or four blimps off shore. Our base responsibility was from the Mexican border to Louisiana. We escorted the convoy to somewhere south of New Orleans. Another squadron of blimps from Houma, Louisiana, would pick up the convoy, and another south of Key West, then Glynco, Georgia, Elizabeth City, North Carolina, and more until they reached their destination.

Before blimp protection, a tanker a day was being sunk off the East Coast. In the early days of the war, those big long tankers (mostly Merchant Marine) had what we called Armed Guards, a branch of the Navy, to protect them. That was a Naval officer and a few enlisted men with a 3" or 5" cannon. That was tough duty. One gun for each ship. Tankers were targets. A lot of men didn't want that duty again. A friend of mine had a nervous breakdown from that experience.

After radar came into use in 1943, a blimp could pick up a periscope ten miles away. Radar made a formidable weapon out of a blimp, which could travel at 65 knots and stand still in the air. The German submarines built for World War I had no anti-aircraft guns, only surface guns which could not shoot down a blimp. So after we got the blimp bases coordinated, we did not lose another tanker. Not a one! Think what that meant in winning the war!

One evening, a storm came up and a blimp was running out of fuel and had to come in. I ordered an emergency and called for all hands. The medical corps thought they didn't have to obey. Those off-duty corpsmen wouldn't leave the pool hall or the bowling area.

Kermit Cloniger with his staff car at the Naval Air Station, Behind him are SB2-C dive bombers, "Hell Divers" like the one President George W. Bush flew. Hitchcock, Texas. Fall, 1944.

A Marine told me, so I got in touch with their duty officer.

"Kermit," he said, "we don't have to do that."

"I'm a line officer," I reminded him.

"I'm going to report this to the flight surgeon," he said, although his men had obeyed by then.

The flight surgeon went to the skipper, and the skipper told me to meet with them. I did, and the flight surgeon demanded that I be reprimanded.

The skipper said, "I'm not going to reprimand him." He knew the rules, too. He turned to me, "Cloniger, I'm going to commend you."

Some time after that, a man was transferred in who was believed to be a "goldbrick," one who pretends to be ill to get out of work. He had served under a half-dozen commands, and I mentioned that when I was reading his jacket.

"I have migraine headaches," he said.

I smelled a rat, so I sent him to a doctor, who, I told him, had a cure for migraines. I called Dr. Hanson, another flight surgeon, to alert him. "Haven't you got some cure?"

"I've got a shot," he said.

Hanson gave the "goldbrick" shots of distilled water all the way around his forehead and had him come back for more the next day. That guy was healed!

By the first of 1945, we declared victory at sea and no longer needed blimps. Meanwhile, so many planes were coming off the assembly lines that we were storing some in our hangers.

In April, 1945, I was made Executive Officer of the Naval Air Station. By then, we had an excess of pilots coming to us from Pensacola. After V-J Day, 120 ensign pilots were there with no duty. I was trying to keep them out of trouble. I didn't know where to put them, so I gave orders for them to go home for a two-week leave then to send a wire requesting two more weeks emergency leave, so we could figure out how to get rid of them.

Although I had enough points to be released myself, I had some skills they wanted to keep, so I continued to serve at the pleasure of the President. I stayed until April of 1946.

I was no hero. There were 12 million heroes of World War II—and more! I don't think that we've ever given civilian workers credit for helping win the war. Many left their homes and went to work in defense plants and in other jobs—at least 25 million more heroes!

Accompanying Roosevelt - and Truman!
by
Dan H. Wolfe
Mecklenburg County, NC

Soon after President Roosevelt died on April 12, 1945, his body left Warm Springs, Georgia, by rail. The train stopped at every little place, where people viewed the casket and grieved. I was in the Marine Corps then. It was about two or three days before we were to graduate from OCS in Quantico, Virginia. When Roosevelt arrived in Washington, the Army, Marine Corps and other servicemen were to march down Pennsylvania Avenue.

I got in the line-up and went down there. Thousands of people were crowding along the route, crying. Our President really meant a lot to so many people. We Marines thought it was great being a part of history.

When we were preparing to go back to Quantico, the Marine headquarters, the officer in charge came to us and said, "We're not going back. We're going forward." He explained that Roosevelt's body has been taken to Hyde Park, New York, where he was to be buried. "We're going to go up and be the guard of honor."

We spent all night shining our shoes and everything else. They took us up to Hyde Park by train, where we did a 21-gun salute. Churchill, President Truman and other dignitaries were there. Although we had to hold our heads perfectly straight while standing at attention, I could see that the FBI or Secret Service were pulling down people who were climbing the fence around the graveyard.

Afterward, we got on a train with only two cars. We Marines were in the second car. Truman and others were in the first. In the Marine Corps, we are used to cattle cars. We all stand up wherever we go. In this case, we were seated in a passenger car and escorting the President. The train traveled at great speed and did not stop until we got to our destination.

When we arrived in Washington, the first car unloaded. We sat there thinking, "Aren't we big? We're doing all this with the President of the United States!"

We were supposed to wait to be taken back to Quantico, but no one came. They did feed us supper, but it was late that night before they got to us.

They had forgotten all about us. That deflated our balloon in a hurry!

THE MILITARY IN THE PIEDMONT

Ground Instrument Flights
by
Paul F. White, Sr.
Kershaw County, SC

In June, 1943, four months after I became a Link trainer instructor at the Southern Aviation School in Camden, South Carolina, Bob Morgan came to see his former instructor, Earl Friedell. Captain Morgan, who flew the Memphis Belle was a hero, the first pilot to come back after 25 missions. His outfit had lost 83%. I didn't get to meet him that day, but we were all very impressed. (After touring the US for three months, Morgan then checked out in the new B-29, flew 26 missions in the Pacific, and on November 24, 1944, led the formation for the first bombing of Tokyo since the Doolittle Raiders' attack.)

June of '43 was also memorable because the biggest glider and paratrooper maneuvers ever came in from Fort Bragg with more generals than I've ever seen in one building and so many colonels that they could've been second lieutenants. Gliders were landing in the field where DuPont is now, and there were thousands of parachute drops all over the county.

For months, local kids were picking up the dropped C-rations the size of Cracker Jack boxes. Right after that, I flew around the area to see all the crashed airplanes. Four or five had hit trees when they landed.

Southern Aviation, a privately owned primary flight school, had a contract with the Army Air Corps to give 60 hours of training in ten weeks supervised by Army personnel.

My commanding officer was 24 years old. A private first class, I was 22 and had 200 hours of flying. We had 100 instructors and 100 PT-17s, which had 220 horsepower Continental engines. The six Link trainers were in a hanger at Woodward Field, the main base. These cloth fiber trainers operated on bellows.

We instructors would run a recorder and give signals to help cadets practice flying the beam, which was the airway they had to follow. I worked with eight upperclassmen a day, an hour at a time. They would receive ten hours in the Link.

One day a cadet came in for his first Link training. I briefed him and was ready to put the hood down when he went over and got his parachute.

208

Paul White, Link trainer instructor, at Link desk. Southern Aviation School, Camden SC. February, 1943.

"What are you doing?" I asked.

"Isn't this a government trainer?" he questioned naively.

"There's not room for that," I said. "Besides, you won't need it."

Another time, I was at an auxiliary field in a building with some students when a cadet, who had been on a solo, came rushing in to tell us, "I just had a big emergency!"

"What happened?" I asked.

"My tachometer quit!"

"Was the engine still going?"

"Yes, but I had to make an emergency landing."

While the others were still laughing, I suggested to him that he not tell his instructor that he had to make an emergency landing because the tachometer quit. A "tach" only measures the rpm's.

We had a near emergency the morning that Lieutenant Charles Broome took a cadet up and told him to do a slow roll. Broome didn't have on his seat belt and rolled right out of the cockpit. He opened his parachute but got stuck in a tree.

When the cadet came in, someone asked how the check ride with Broome went.

"I forgot! He fell out of the airplane!" The cadet raced to the dispatcher and tried to explain approximately where Broome might be.

A truck went out to pick him up. A very frustrated Broome was still up in the tree.

After work one afternoon, I was going out the gate at 4 p.m. to thumb a ride home. (By then, I'd learned that by thumbing in a uniform, you could travel faster than by train.) An ambulance was coming out the gate, and I heard someone say, "Paul, get back in there. Two planes crashed in a traffic pattern!"

I hurried toward the crash site and pulled one pilot out. His leg had been sheared off. "Oh my gosh!" I gasped. That was the only time at the Southern Aviation School that I lived up to my last name.

We military people lived off the base. The cadets stayed in barracks. My buddy, Jack Osborn, and I stayed at the Magnolia Inn.

That's where I met my future wife, Mary M. Richey (with whom I spent 54 wonderful years). I was there only from February '43 to February '44, but out of my department of twelve, six married Camden ladies. Of the other six, three were already married.

My commanding officer, Leonard Hauprich, started dating Ann Whittaker, who worked in supply at the main base.

At first, some of the cadets were dating that attractive lady, too, but word soon got out that you might get caught in the washing machine (get washed out on a check ride) if the Captain found out.

Guess you could say we Yankees really loved Southern girls.

A Life-Saving Maneuver
by
John E. McIver
Darlington/Fairfield Counties, SC

An incident while we were on maneuvers in Fairfield County saved my life. I like to tell people that, because I believe it did.

Originally from Darlington County, I took advantage of the ROTC program at NC State. Although compulsory the first two years, it was optional the last two, but we got $20 a quarter (a lot of money then).

By the end of July, 1941, I was on maneuvers with the 8th Division out of Fort Jackson. We maneuvered for about six weeks through mostly-agricultural counties near Jackson, moving nearly every day, mostly on foot. Our movement was based on the opposing forces' tactics. We ate whenever we could from a company kitchen on the back of a truck and slept wherever we could, usually in pup tents with a preassigned tent mate.

A second lieutenant, I was an umpire, who had to help judge whether the blue team or red team were making the best maneuvers.

The infantry carried rifles with blanks, but the mortars were merely logs, which had to be transported. Tanks were vehicles with signs on them. There were no real mortars or cannons. A man who got "killed" by a blank had to leave the ranks.

The men moved wherever a battalion commander indicated. To my knowledge, no one asked the farmers' permission to use their land. But the residents knew what we were doing and why we were there and were very supportive and pleasant. A farmer's wife or small-town housewife might cook and feed whoever was around.

We seldom got to ride, but one day we were in a convoy on Fairfield County's Highway 21, when we stopped in the middle of the road, which was paved and normally used by a lot of local people. We were holding up traffic, so I got the trucks to pull off the road into a field.

Our regional commander noticed that incident and recommended me for Motor Maintenance School at Fort Benning, Georgia. That got me from being a platoon leader to being in charge of motor pool vehicles.

That, I believe, saved my life. The normal life span of a platoon leader in heavy battle was pretty short: a week or two. A company commander might last a day or so longer.

After Benning, I joined a newly reactivated division, the 90th, which entered Normandy on D-Day +1.

We had waterproofed our engines, so that when the landing craft let us off in four feet of water, our jeep had no trouble. By the time we got there, Omaha Beach had been secured, and we encountered only occasional artillery shells.

The 90th Infantry Division changed from the 1st Army to the 3rd about three months after D-Day. Because we were doing truck repairs, we were not on the front, even at the Battle of the Bulge, so our service company didn't see any heavy action all the way to Germany.

After V-E Day, I didn't have quite enough points to go home.

That's when the second event occurred which saved my life again. If Truman hadn't dropped the atomic bomb, we would have been in a bloodbath in Japan.

CIVILIANS ASSISTING THE MILITARY

Doing My Patriotic Duty
by
Gladys Hayes Sellergren
Lincoln/Mecklenburg Counties, NC

Our final exam at Lenior-Rhyne College Business School was a Civil Service test. At that time, in May of '42, there was a big demand for office workers in government facilities.

Only 17 years old, I opted to stay close to my home in Lincolnton. After having passed security clearance, I was hired as a clerk-steno at the Charlotte Quartermaster Depot and eventually ended up as secretary to Major Frank F. Cook, the new Officer in Charge (OIC) of the Zone Inspection Division. Located in the old Ford plant at the end of the bus line in the 1800 block of Statesville Avenue, the Depot supplied our troops with their basic needs, like clothing, knapsacks, food, textile products and equipment.

Most of our supplies went to debarkation depots such as New York and San Francisco.

One of my jobs was to dole out gas rationing stamps to the salesmen and those who inspected goods at factories. Those stamps were valuable, and I had to register and account for every one.

Our work week was six days. But it was not unusual to go in on Sundays, too. Patriotism was strong, and I don't remember complaining. I guess it was a norm for the times.

We were cautioned by posters all around. One depicted an enemy cupping his ear, with the caption: "Tojo is listening." Another warned us that "A slip of a lip sinks ships."

Our *Tarheel QMD News*, published monthly, ran an article by Perry A. Davis in the September, 1943, issue, reminding us how important it was to be there regularly, no matter what our job might be. "Every day that you are out without leave, you are handicapping our war effort and helping the Japs and Germans," he wrote. "Why you could even cause hundreds of troops to be without food or supplies that they are waiting for."

Davis called attention to a picture which hung just inside a Warehouse #1 door. It was of some men from a squadron, which was one of the first to fly over Sicily and did not have a plane or a man lost in their first combat. "We Negroes of this Depot should be proud of them. First, because they are Negroes. Second, because we probably shipped some of the supplies that they used in that

212

attack." He encouraged everyone to avoid being absentees, and to "give eight or ten hours a day plus 10% of our pay to bonds."

Actually, that 10% was taken out of our paychecks automatically. We probably had to sign something to authorize that, but it was expected.

Generally, the African-Americans worked in the messenger section (doing inter-department and other deliveries) or in one of the warehouses. Women were in most departments. In fact, *Tarheel QMD News* had female reporters in the stock control, general supply, subsistence and clothing & equipment units, as well as the incoming property, mail & records, service, stock record & accounting, warehousing and inspection branches, the signal office, transportation division and office of the chief clerk and the depot quartermaster. Male officers ran each department and trained other officers (who would do similar jobs elsewhere), but I believe 75% of the personnel were women.

Probably the reason I kept that particular issue of our newsletter was because I was pictured on page 7 as the just-crowned Depot Queen, receiving a war bond, and on page 11 were photos of our girls softball team.

And what else did I do for the war effort? Attended dances for officers!

The Charlotte Woman's Club, which had its own clubhouse, held dances for military officers similar to a "Stagedoor Canteen" and needed hostesses. A young woman had to be sponsored and then invited to join. I was one of the lucky ones.

Sometimes, out-of-town requests came through for 25 to 35 girls to attend dinner dances. I happily did my patriotic duty. Once, for a formal dance in Matthews, North Carolina, they sent transportation in the form of covered Army trucks. We just folded up our cleaners' bags and hoisted up. Dressing rooms were provided at the event.

My three roommates and I lived in the Frederick Apartments on North Church Street Our apartment had no kitchen facilities, so we ate out a lot, often at the S&W and the Ship Ahoy. Luckily, we didn't always have to pay for our meals, thanks to boyfriends.

One evening, a friend brought a guy by our apartment who later bought me many a dinner. Captain Bob Sellergren, who was OIC of the Test Pilot Division at Morris Field, had a charming smile and was a pilot—very impressive. On our first date, we went to the Morris Field gym to shoot some baskets. In December of 1944, we were married on the base.

Quartermaster Depot Girls Softball Team. Back row: Gladys Hayes, Lincolnton, first; Georgia Riley, Charlotte, middle blonde in striped top; Delete Drye, Albemarle, last. Official US Army photo. 1943.

Until V-E Day, we lived primarily day-to-day.

Suddenly, we knew that the war would soon be over. Morris Field began shutting down soon thereafter. By V-J Day, we were living in Valdosta, Georgia, where Bob was stationed. As we came out of a movie, we were, at first, frightened by the whooping and hollering. Then someone shoved drinks into our hands to celebrate. It was exciting, because we could more realistically plan a post-war life together.

People say that war marriages don't work. Bob and I are looking forward to celebrating our 60th Anniversary in 2004.

Typing for Victory
by
Lillian Spencer Steele
Guilford County, NC

After graduating from Averett and Radford Colleges and then working one year as a school librarian in Danville, Virginia, with a salary of $92 a month, I decided to make a change, for better or worse. I was game!

My aunt was on the faculty in a government school in

Greensboro, so my mother and I decided the move would be good for us. I invited my college roommate, Helen Mason, to move in with us and try her luck, too. In 1943, Helen and I took the Civil Service examination, passed it, and were sent to the Basic Training Center #10, which, by then was also an Overseas Replacement Center.

We worked as clerk-typists for the base's permanent party, the staff members who were never transferred. Our commanding officer, Col. Walter W. Pailing, was over the Division that transferred soldiers to other camps or overseas. Sometimes, we'd have to work all day Saturday and Sunday to get endorsements typed. When a group was shipping out, we'd have to put those in their service records.

Our office was in one of the barracks, crudely thrown up, which stood on concrete blocks. One of the men's bathrooms was set aside for us women. We hated having cubicles with no doors and urinals. A pot-bellied stove kept us warm most of the time, but in the winter, air came up through cracks in the plank floors. I can't talk or type when my feet are cold, so we'd get cardboard boxes from the grocery store, and, although I usually wore socks, I'd put my feet in a box to stay comfortable.

Stockings, made of nylon, which was needed for the war effort, were so scarce that we'd have to stand in line at Meyer's Department Store to get two pairs. If I got a run, I'd take the stocking to a shoe shop downtown to get it repaired. Some girls used leg makeup.

At one time, we were in an office that overlooked a training field. After marching, the boys would have to stand at attention. We'd watch them faint from the heat, but we could do nothing.

Lt. Emma Kirnen, who was tiny but mighty, took over our office for awhile. I never saw her smile. She was over twelve enlisted men and six of us female typists, and there were no jokes. I typed like crazy then.

The most nervous I ever got, though, was the day a visiting colonel from Seymour Johnson Air Base stood over me while I typed a letter for him. I was frightened until I realized he didn't know as much as I did.

Generally, we didn't wander far from our office. Once, Helen and I went to the base hospital to visit one of the fellows from our staff, who had had minor surgery. He was in a barracks ward with beds lined up on either side.

Some famous people rotated through our base. I saw Tony

Martin, who was here with Special Services, but I wasn't impressed. He sang with our pick-up orchestra. Apparently, he kept telling them they played too slow or too loud, and they resented it. Charlton Heston got married while he was here. (He's *still* married to her!) Sabu, the little guy from India who used to ride elephants, came through here, too, as did the movie stars Alan Baxter and Donald O'Connor.

Sometimes we would see the German POWs in their fatigues being exercised. They were assigned to only one barracks as far as I know.

In one of the larger barracks, they held dances. Helen and I would go by bus to the King Cotton Hotel, where Army trucks would be waiting. Soldiers would help us up into the back and away we would go to a dance. We danced with enlisted men who were from our office.

All the men respected us; none were "fresh," even in our office, where six or seven girls worked. But one of the permanent party, Master Sergeant John Richard Steele, found me interesting. Tall and thin, that "Yam Dankee" who graduated from Syracuse University was not the least bit handsome but very intelligent. He was 24 and I was 23 when we began dating.

Because of the gas shortage, we walked to town to the movies, and in June, 1944, we were married in the Church of the Covenant and took a quick honeymoon by bus to Danville and Richmond, Virginia. Even after we were married and had an apartment on McIver Street, I called him "Steele" like we did at the base. I never called him John or Richard.

Helen and I continued to work at the camp until the powers that be decided to close it and move the records to Fort Monmouth, New Jersey.

They asked me to go with them, but, by then, Steele had been discharged from the Army and was working as a quality control person for Sears. I soon got a job as Guilford County's first full-time school librarian.

POW Experiences

Prisoners of war take great offense when people deride them as cowards who preferred to "sit out" the war rather than die for their country. Vast numbers of POWs *did* die for America, not by a quick bullet but a slow painful death of starvation hastened by disease—or the cruel, prolonged agony of torture.

The first stories are from the ones who survived, often because they refused to give in or give up.

Then we look at their dilemma from the eyes of their spouses.

But what about POWs here in this country?

THOSE IN GERMAN CAMPS

"Dave, This Ain't No Place for You!"
by
David K. Helsabeck
Rockingham/Forsyth Counties, NC

The fall of '43 was a very dangerous time for B-17s. Our P-47 fighters would escort us to the German border, then Germans picked us up and "escorted" us to the target. It would be a battle royal from the time you got there until—if you were lucky—you escaped alive.

On January 29, 1944 at 11:30 a.m., we were 75 miles southwest of Frankfurt, where we'd already hit the target of our 23rd mission. On the 22nd, we were the only one of our squadron of seven who got back to Norwich, England, headquarters of our 96th Bomb Group, 339th squadron. Very few crew members made 25; the ticket to go home, but we were beginning to think we could.

KaBOOM! Our right inside engine got shot out, probably by a rocket. As the bombardier, I could look out the plexiglas window and see gasoline burning 15 feet above the engine. I thought, "Dave, this ain't no place for you!"

Brrinng! The pilot, Claude Farris, rang the battery-operated bail-out bell. I sprang into position.

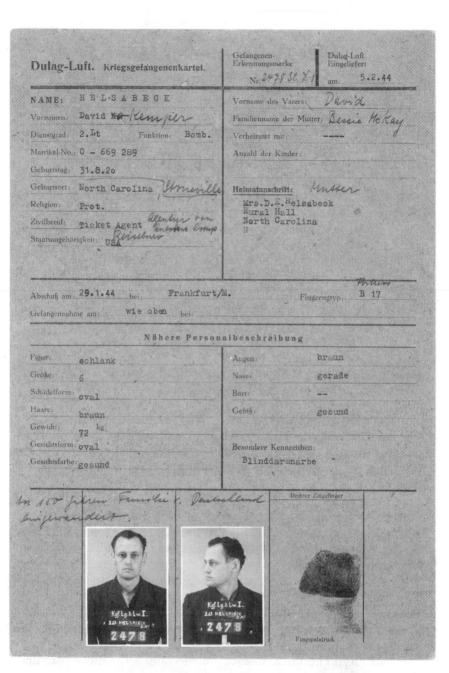

Dulag-Luft. Kriegsgefangenenkartei.

Gefangenen-Erkennungsmarke	Dulag-Luft Eingeliefert
Nr. 2478 St. Z.	am: 5.2.44

NAME: H E L · S · A · B · E · C · K

Vornamen: David K. *Kempler*

Dienstgrad: 2. Lt   Funktion: Bomb.

Matrikel-No.: O - 669 289

Geburtstag: 31.8.20

Geburtsort: North Carolina *Asheville*

Religion: Prot.

Zivilberuf: Ticket Agent *Agentur von Greyhound Reiselinie*

Staatsangehörigkeit: USA

Vorname des Vaters: *David*

Familienname der Mutter: *Bessie McKay*

Verheiratet mit: ----

Anzahl der Kinder:

Heimatanschrift: *Mutter*
Mrs. D. E. Helsabeck
Rural Hall
North Carolina
N

Abschuß am: 29.1.44   bei: Frankfurt/M.   Flugzengtyp: B 17

Gefangennahme am: wie oben   bei:

Nähere Personalbeschreibung

Figur: schlank		Augen: braun
Größe: 6		Nase: gerade
Schädelform: oval		Bart: --
Haare: braun		Gebiß: gesund
Gewicht: 72 kg		
Gesichtsform: oval		Besondere Kennzeichen:
Gesichtsfarbe: gesund		Blinddarmnarbe

In 100 Jahren Familie v. Deutschland eingewandert.

Rechter Zeigefinger

Fingerabdruck

David Helsabeck's prisoner-of-war record.

Marcus McWaters, the navigator in the nose, saw me coming in a dive. I was at that bail-out door. He was right behind me. I yanked the emergency release. Nothing happened. The two of us finally got it open. The door was supposed to fall off. It didn't. We jumped anyway, hoping the handle wouldn't catch our parachutes.

Bullets were flying in every direction. I was so glad to get away from all that lead, that I floated calmly for more than 1,000 feet, then pulled my chute open. Just then six German fighters headed for us. One came within two yards, cocked his wing and waved at me. I could see the whites of his eyes!

Whump! I fell into a young apple tree, knocking a limb off, as I flipped to the snow-covered ground, feet first, before landing flat as a pancake.

The tree was in a rural area. Five middle-aged farmers with their World War I Lugers came running over, followed by a bunch of young'uns. They took me to the nearby barnyard, then put their Lugers up. More fliers joined me, as about 30 others landed in the same area. One farmer carried a pitchfork, in case someone got out of line, while another called the military to come pick us up.

I rode into town in a six-year-old Ford sedan to the town dungeon. Cold. Bitter cold. None of us had enough clothes. All were damp. One was hurt, bleeding badly from shell fragments in his neck. It was our engineer, Arthur Sicliano. I held his head in my lap all night. Our captors tore up his parachute and let us use part of it for a bandage.

The next day we were put on a train to take us to Frankfurt. Although it was only 75 miles away, with all the stopping and starting it took us a couple of days to get there. Frankfurt was a glorious mess. The RAF had bombed at night, then the 8th Army Air Force bombed during the day before the RAF returned for another night bombing.

As we disembarked at the railroad station, a crowd of townspeople came at us shaking their fists. Two guards gathered us close together. One of them dropped a bayonet on the stomach of a citizen. He backed off. And more guards came in.

All that was left of the station was the front, but our captors locked us in one of the remaining rooms. One guard stayed with us. The other guarded the door. We could hear angry voices. We couldn't understand their language but we thought they were saying: "Hang 'em!" "We'll beat them to death!" "Throw them in a fire!"

I was glad to get out of there, as another local train came in.

Ten or twelve miles later, we arrived at an Interrogation Center. Bear in mind, in four days, we hadn't had anything to eat except a bowl of porridge in Frankfurt. When a man goes without food, his mind deteriorates with his body. At the center, we were given one small slice of bread and colored water in the morning and at night.

Three days, I was escorted from my 6' x 8' cell into an interrogation room, where I would give out only my name, rank and serial number and say they were wasting their time.

The first time, the German officer, a nice-looking gentleman who had spent six years in the United States, didn't give me much trouble. The next time, he hollered and whooped, demanding to know "What was your bomb load?"

The six-foot interrogator scared me, but I just said, "You know, and I know you know. But I'm not going to confirm it."

He whooped and hollered some more and let me go.

The third day, he bore down on me. He held up a picture of me from the *Winston-Salem Journal.*

I showed no surprise, just acted dumb and happy. (I should have gotten an Oscar!)

His voice took on a threatening tone. "Is this your mother's name?" he asked, pointing to the article. "What's your bomb load?" His menace grew louder. "I'm going to do one of three things: turn you over to the Gestapo, break every bone in your body or have you shot."

I believed him. But I said, "I'm not going to tell you. You're wasting your time."

His high military boots stomped the wooden floor.

"I'm expendable," I told him, hoping he wouldn't think so. "You're not talking to a bunch of dumb bunnies, you know. In England, they probably know you're interrogating me. When they come through here, they're going to hang you to the highest tree."

"Get him out of here!" he bellowed, then looked me in the eye. "You'll know in the morning what I'm going to do with you."

I worried all night. Gestapo? Broken bones? Shot? "Dave," I said to myself, "You opened your big mouth one time too many."

Before daybreak, not one but two guards came for me. They didn't have sidearms; they had rifles. We left the building and went down a steep hill. I figured they were going to stand me in front of the hill and shoot me.

Instead, they opened the door of an old building. Inside a space a little larger than a living room was a whole bunch of bearded

POWs with body odor that would repel a rat, but they were mighty pretty looking to me.

"Thank you, Lord!"

Wildfire Bomb Crew (l to r) front: Claude Farris, pilot; Charles Ray, co-pilot; Marcus McWaters, navigator, David Helsabeck, bombardier; top: Arthur Sicliano, flight engineer; Walter Garber, radio; Bob Shultz, waist gunner; E.J. Cowan, waist gunner; Harold Lindsey, ball turret; Harold Wells, tail gunner. Blythe, California, 1943. This entire crew survived the war, a very rare feat.

Worms and Steak
by
David K. Helsabeck
Rockingham/Forsyth Counties, NC

American fliers (perhaps some of our buddies from the 96th Bomb Group) were overhead on a bombing mission to Frankfurt. About a hundred POWs were being marched to the Frankfurt train station, but our captors took us into a shallow dugout shelter for protection. A bomb dropped less than 200 feet from us. It blew our shelter doors open on both ends. We waited for the next one. Generally, we had carried sixteen 500-pounders in our bomb bays, each one of which we dropped a second or less apart.

The next bomb hit farther away. Soon, we were hustled onto one of several awaiting cattle cars. We had room to sit for the three-day trip across Germany, but there was no bucket. Somebody pulled a board from the floor, making a hole just big enough to double for a bucket.

Only once did they let us out when the train was standing at a station. We stretched awhile and dipped water from a pail. Five minutes later, we were put back into the cattle cars.

At last, we arrived at our permanent camp, Stalag Luft I, about 250 miles north of Berlin near Barth, Germany, on the Baltic Sea.

Each of the ten rooms in the barracks held double-decker bunks for 24 men. There was a low pot-bellied stove for warmth, for cooking and for heating water in a bucket, so we could take a bath in the latrine down the hall.

Our meals were mainly barley, maybe a few potatoes and some rutabagas that were too big and splintery to eat. The barley, yellowish brown, always had worms. We boiled it on our stove and ate it like oatmeal. One morning, my bowl had more worms than barley. I dipped them out with my oversize spoon. There was hardly any barley left! I dumped the worms back into the bowl, closed my eyes and ate them. At least, we were getting some fat and protein, and we never got sick from eating them.

For fifteen and a half months, we passed the time telling each other our sob stories. None of us was strong enough to do much. Sometimes, if we got a pack of cards (by then, as thick and crusty as crackers), we'd play bridge, setback or poker. But, of course we had no money to gamble with. Some of the fellows made pans out of cans from the Red Cross boxes. Amazingly, none leaked. A number of the guys started digging tunnels. The Germans found most of them.

I wasn't interested in that. I knew we were going to win the war; if we got out, the civilians would have killed us. The majority of the men felt the same way.

Stalag Luft I was on a little peninsula. We could hear the Russians fighting south of us, but we knew they wouldn't come where we were. They might get cornered.

On the morning of May 1, 1945, we looked out and there were no guards in the towers. In fact, all the German personnel had left during the night. From our Barracks #1, I could see over an open field a lone Russian soldier running and zigzagging between us and the town a mile and a half away. He approached the gate. I observed him talking with our American colonel, who had surrounded himself with men who could speak some Russian, including a Lithuanian guy from our barracks. The colonel reportedly told him, "We don't want these men out yet."

I watched the Russian, as he took his gun off his shoulder, and ordered, "Open that gate!"

The colonel complied, and a group of POWs rushed out. Most of the 10,000 of us—English, American and Canadian fliers—didn't go.

The Americans came in the next day. "We'll send planes for the sick and wounded," they told us. "The rest of you, we'll get out as quick as we can."

Soon, Russians were bringing in pigs and cows from nearby farms. We had no trouble finding POW butchers. But some of the guys ate too much of that feast and got sick.

By V-E Day, we were at Camp Lucky Strike on the coast of France, waiting to catch a ride for the next leg of our journey back home. It's a wonder those planes took off, they were all so packed.

At Le Havre, the Army fed us sweets and steaks for dinner and supper for 30 days. Our stomachs had shrunk. We couldn't eat much of what they put in front of us. I would take a couple of bites and just look at it.

On June 26, 1945, I finally got home to Rural Hall, North Carolina. Harvey Kiger, the owner of a local grocery store, had promised my mother that he would hold back some meat—steaks, bacon, sausage and ham—for whenever I came back.

My parents had saved their ration coupons for months. Proudly, they put bacon and sausage and a pile of eggs on my breakfast plate. I couldn't eat it. I begged them to share it.

After much protesting, they finally did. They ate as though they hadn't had meat in months.

I enjoyed watching them.

Some Would Say We Were Lucky
by
David C. Wylie, Jr.
Fairfield County, SC

The Germans had just launched a heavy artillery barrage on that cold morning of December 16, 1944 in the Ardennes Forest.

223

Artillery shells were exploding. Limbs of trees were falling. Dirt and snow was flying. It was the opening of what we would later call the Battle of the Bulge.

My squad from Company A of the 394th Regiment, 99th Infantry Division was on an outpost across a railroad bridge near Losheimergraben the farthest out from the front line. We were several hundred yards in front of our company.

The shelling in our direction started early that morning and continued most of the day. The telephone lines on the bridge had been cut by artillery, so we had no contact with company head-quarters. Our platoon sergeant, with no idea of the enemy's tremen-dous punch, sent a man back across the bridge to get reinforce-ments. He never made it.

Suddenly German soldiers came running down the railroad track, we assumed to blow up the bridge. We didn't know that the Americans had already placed explosives under the bridge to blow it if necessary. We fought the Germans off until late in the day. Then we were being shelled by our own mortars.

All during the day, German patrols were infiltrating our lines, coming from all sides. We were completely surrounded.

After dark, we were almost out of ammunition. The platoon sergeant gave orders for us to surrender.

The Battle of the Bulge was the second worst bloodbath in American history. Only the Meuse-Argonne battle of World War I surpassed it in casualties. From our squad, no one was killed. Some would say we were lucky. What would come next may prove otherwise.

Our captors were young boys, about 18. Most of them spoke the English language, which they had learned in school. They escorted us a short distance and asked us what outfit we were with. When they saw our patches, they pulled out a book which contained complete information: where we trained, the time of our debarka-tion, date of arrival in Belgium, and when we crossed the Belgium/German border.

They took us to a schoolhouse, where we stayed a couple of days. A lot of soldiers from our division joined us. It was freezing weather with snow, and the schoolhouse was not heated. They took some of our clothes, among them my pants and rubber boots. They intended to dress Germans in American outfits to infiltrate our lines. On the second day, an Army POW, who wore fatigues over his wool pants, gave me the fatigues to cover my longjohns.

Throughout this ordeal, we had nothing to eat.

Finally, it was time to move. We started out on foot in the snow. One of those nights we were allowed to rest in a building with a cold concrete floor. Although indoors, we were still miserable. Men were sick with colds and dysentery.

At Bonn, we ended up in freight cars packed so tight that we could sit only by pulling our legs up. There was no food, no water, no relief. The freight car had an opening up high near the roof. Some GIs were able to reach out and grab a handful of snow to moisten their lips. They passed more along to the rest of us.

Eight days after we had been captured, we arrived at the POW camp at Limburg, Germany on Christmas Eve.

We were unloaded from the train and marched to the camp gate only to be told that they couldn't accept us. The camp had been bombed by the Allies. Sent back to the train, we stood around in the snow the rest of the day.

Late that afternoon, a song broke out. Thousands of men were soon singing "Silent Night." This was the most moving and peaceful experience I have ever known. There came reports that some of the guards sang, too.

Late that night, they loaded us back on the train.

The next day was white outside, but that was the darkest Christmas I've ever experienced.

That night we arrived at Hammelburg Stalag XIII C, a big building converted to hold prisoners. We had bunks with straw mattresses but only blankets cut in half, so we doubled up to keep warm. Once a day, we got a piece of bread, two small Irish potatoes and water.

In early February, 150 enlisted men were sent on a work detail to Würzburg, a small city in Bavaria that had never been bombed. There was a lot of excitement that day. Himmler was in town because the Allies had given them an ultimatum. It would be declared an open city and not bombed, if they would remove their anti-aircraft and other armor.

Würzburg had a large hospital that served the military but also a number of big warehouses storing confiscated grain and supplies from other countries, especially France. Our job was to turn and aerate the grain, load or unload boxcars or bale hay. Farmers could bring their hay there to be baled if they left some to supply the Nazis' horses.

The guards paid us in German bills and coins (the equivalent of $18 each) one time. Soon thereafter, the guards brought in beer to sell. Our only containers were the soup bowls we had been issued, so everybody bought it by the bowl.

Almost every night, Allied planes flew over us to bomb Schweinfurt, where there was a ball bearing plant.

One night in the middle of March, an air raid siren went off, and we were rushed into the basement of a building. Then BOOM! The building we were in was set afire! Everything around us was flaming! As we evacuated the city, we kept close to each other, for sparks were burning our clothing. Our guards, men too old for active duty, took us to the outskirts of town and bedded us down in haystacks. To our surprise, they protected us; they kept angry civilians from mobbing us.

We were moved to a small town on the outskirts of Würzburg. We worked there on railroads and in warehouses.

The second week after the bombing of Würzburg, we picked up from a guard that something big would happen the Saturday before Easter. Sure enough, on Easter Eve, we had to scurry to the basement of our buildings when the air raid sirens went off. There were five warehouses in our complex. We were in the third when American planes bombed and hit the corner of our building.

They just grazed it, but everyone went running for their lives. Most of us ran into a vineyard, which was terraced up a steep hill. We stayed there most of the day, watching the bombings from our grandstand seats.

Late that day, they gathered us back down to where the warehouses were. We spent that night in a tunnel, an underground warehouse. Hurrah! It was packed with huge wheels of Swiss cheeses, assorted canned meats, and boxes of crackers! On a rail siding just outside, a wooden tank car loaded with cider had been hit by a .50 caliber machine gun bullet. A constant stream of cider drained from the car. Prisoners were lined up, catching it in everything available.

On Easter Sunday morning (April 1, 1945), we were started on a march toward Bamberg. On Easter night, we stopped in a village, where they put us in a barn. A few POWs slipped away on the march.

The next morning, two buddies and I decided to hide in the hayloft, while the others moved on. When we were left behind, we realized we had company. There were eight of us. Knowing the Americans must be close, we debated whether to take off or wait, when some Polish slave laborers from that farm found us. They indicated that we should stay and they would take care of us. They later brought us milk from the cows and some bread. We had carried some cheese and canned meats from the tunnel warehouse, so we "feasted" for ten days.

On April 12th, the Polish slaves (boys and girls in their teens) were excitedly trying to tell us something about Roosevelt. We thought the President must be having a conference with Stalin and Churchill. We did not realize he was dead.

On Friday the 13th, we could hear Allied tanks in the distance. Our Polish protectors urged us to wait until dark. They would escort us down the road to the Americans outside of Ebrach. At nightfall, we took off.

"Halt!" called a fellow on guard duty.

We didn't know the password.

The guy from Missouri looked at our tattered uniforms with various insignias and, guessing our fate, asked where we were from.

We and our Polish escorts were given K-rations, C-rations and cigarettes and invited to stay at the Bürgermeister's house. In his home, one room was a pub. Unfortunately, the kegs had already been drained before we got there.

The next morning we were put in ambulances and sent to hospitals in the rear, leaving the Polish teenagers behind. They thought we would take them to America with us. That was not to be.

What Now?
by
Gene Newton
Cleveland County, NC

We had already lost one engine before starting on the bomb run. But, being "gung ho," we were intent on inflicting our little bit of pain on Hitler. So we continued our low level flight right over the railroad marshalling yards at Eschwege, Germany and dropped all eight of our bombs.

As tail gunner, it was my job to pull the pins out. Reconnaissance pictures would tell us later how accurate we had been.

Heading home to our Army Air Corps base in North Pickingham, England, that February 22, 1945, we could not keep up with the rest of the 491st Bomb Group formation. Then it happened.

Kraut flack batteries opened up on us until we had only one propeller turning. The pilot rang the bail-out bell. I fell out backwards from the tail turret, hooked my parachute in front and clipped my walking shoes into the back of the harness. It didn't take much nerve to be the first one out, especially knowing what 100-octane gasoline can do when a B-24 blows up.

World War II parachutes were made for one purpose: to save your life. The trouble was, they did not let you down easy. When I hit the ground, it felt like my leg bones had gone clear through my collar bones. After swapping fleece-lined boots for walking brogans and hiding my parachute, I crawled toward some tall trees. When I stood up, a young sandy-haired guy in country clothes pointed a shotgun straight at my head and yelled, "Halt!"

A civilian? I wondered. But just then, five others wearing military uniforms soon had three of us assembled at a farm house. They lined Frank Ryan, "Rocky" Nawrocki and me up against the barn wall. Three of the Germans soldiers facing us were ordered to load their rifles. These guys weren't quite playing cowboys and Indians. They were going to kill us!

But they didn't. They made us climb back over the fence near the barn and, before long, we were walking through a small town.

The military had always warned us, "If you get shot down, hope and pray that German soldiers capture you, because they are disciplined enough to know about the Geneva Convention. Civilians would as soon kill you."

Well, there they were—old men, women, teenagers even children spitting on us, shaking their fists and trying to get to us. The German sergeant major and I were leading the column. Occasionally he would grin, drag his finger across his throat and say, "Kaput." He was letting us know that the people wanted to kill us.

Before nightfall, we arrived at what appeared to be an airfield with a bombed-out building. We were taken down some steps to a pitch black basement, which already held many other American fliers, known to the Germans as "terrorfliegers." We got no food. No water. A hint of things to come. To make matters worse, they had one bucket for what must have been 50 men. Even in the dark, enough people knew where it was, because they would take your hand, pull you in the right direction, then lead you back.

After a day or two, they put us on a truck, which operated from a huge charcoal burner behind the cab. We didn't know it, but they were taking us to a prison camp in Nürnberg. But first, we were smushed into a cattle car, seated knees-to-chin, for a couple of days. Ours was a "luxury" car: it had a pail.

Once on the trip, they let us out to stretch at a train station. Another time, as we were going through a little town, we heard sirens. The train stopped and they unlocked and opened the doors. We saw townspeople crossing the track and running toward a tremendous cave. A lot of us ran there, too. It was spooky being in that cave with all those Germans. When we got an "all clear," I ran like heck back to the cattle car.

In Nürnberg, we were housed in an enormous circus-like tent with pallets. The whole time I was there, I got one bath. When it was my turn, I stood in a long line for hours to jump under an outdoor shower.

Everybody was skin and bones, because about the only food available came in Red Cross packages, and that was very sporadic. Every now and then, we'd get some kind of stew made out of food from the parcels. One guy got caught by fellow prisoners going through the line a second time. He was never seen again.

Hours and days passed as a blur. The next thing we knew, we were walking 91 miles to another camp in Moosburg, two abreast on each side of the road. It was cold. It was rainy. It was miserable.

Mad at the world, we trudged on, unaware of time passage. Our comic relief was Herman, the guard with a mustache like Hitler's who rode along beside us on his bicycle. He kept saying, "Soon you be riding bicycle. I be walking."

The American colonel sent word that we would continue walking day and night. He cautioned that you'd likely die, if you lay down in the cold rain.

Gene Newton
1944

And die some did. But not from the rain. Our own P-47s strafed us, thinking we were Germans. They released bombs from underneath their wings. As they turned to come back at us, I ran under a bridge for protection. When it was all over, I damn near had a heart attack when the manhole cover next to me started slowly rising. A GI popped out.

At Moosburg, there were 110,000 POWs; 30,000 were American. We were in pens like chickens. Our food came in from Switzerland in white trucks with red crosses.

Near the end of April, we could hear the American cannons coming. To us, they sounded like bells ringing. We were "on guard" though.

On the day we were liberated, word was out that SS troops were firing through the fence into the prison camp. But General Patton's 3rd Army killed off the SS attackers and tore down our fences. They moved us out in trucks to a riverbank. At the river, gas engines were pumping water onto rectangular steel plates with gas burners underneath, heating the water to go into showers. All along the bank was shower after shower.

When we were clean, they dusted our hair and our entire bodies with DDT, gave us new clothes and burned our old ones. We were new men. We were free, liberated just in time.

After the war, orders were found that Hitler had issued immediately before he committed suicide: "Kill all the terror-fliegers."

THOSE IN JAPANESE CAMPS

The Bataan Death March: Just the Beginning
by
Earl Marshall Williams
Mecklenburg County, NC

We heard about the attack on Pearl Harbor at breakfast, six hours after the fact. By lunchtime, the Japs were bombing us on Luzon in the Philippines. We could hear them explode, but we didn't know exactly where. Clark Air Field was their main target, but they later bombed the Navy yard and other military installations.

Our 454th Ordnance Aviation Bombardment Company, which was attached to the 27th Bomb Group, was stationed outside of Manila. Since our arrival on November 1, 1941, we had bull-dozed out a landing strip near a sugar refinery at Del Carmen. We were supposed to load bombs on planes, but no planes ever came. They had gone to Australia.

We were bivouacked on the rifle range at Fort William McKinley when the bombs hit, but our forces quickly headed south to another airstrip. We drove all night. At 10:30 a.m., four or five of us climbed up into an abandoned Filipino bamboo shack on stilts to sleep. That's when they called us back. Dead tired, we headed to Bataan.

Within days, 100,000 Japanese troops landed on the Philippine islands, outnumbering our three branches of the service five to one. With a very few tanks and planes and World War I vintage rifles, we were no match, but there was a rumor that American ships were on the way to evacuate us. That never happened.

Our company furnished ammunition to the front lines, loaded ammunition on trucks and kept moving back toward Mariveles and the China Sea.

In early January 1942, we were put on short rations: two light meals per day. Until then, we had been getting about 5000 calories per day. That dropped to 2000. Some men picked green bananas and hid them in the ground covered with straw, but monkeys found them before they ripened.

Actually, the monkeys were our friends. We could tell when the Japanese planes were coming before they hit us. The jungle full of monkeys got eerily quiet.

On February 1, we were limited to less than 1500 calories per day. By March 1, that number went down to 1000 or less. Orders came down to slaughter the 26th Cavalry's horses and the mules of the Mountain Artillery Battery. We ate whatever they put before us.

Malaria was prevalent in that part of the world. We slept under mosquito nets, and I did not catch it. But once-virile men became susceptible to all kinds of illnesses as their bodies weakened.

Not only did the bombing and strafing continue, but by March, another 100,000 fresh Japanese troops moved in. We and the Filipino Army were overwhelmed.

On April 9, Lt. General Edward P. King gave orders to surrender. In my opinion, he did the only thing he could do. It was the largest surrender in US history.

Soon, Japanese tanks were coming down the road with interpreters telling us to stay where we were until they came back.

Grim as our plight was, a few of us had one stroke of good luck: we found an Army truck loaded with cans of peaches. We ate peaches all that day.

When the interpreters returned, we were told to go to the Marine base, Mariveles Field, where POWs were assembled into small groups and sent in the direction of Camp O'Donnell. We started to march in columns of four.

The Japanese were bringing in troops to fight at Corregidor, just across Manila Bay from Mariveles. Hot and sweaty, they took our canteens, drank from them and returned them empty. I didn't get mine back. It served them right! Mine was full of chlorine (to purify our water). I didn't see what happened to the guy who drank it straight.

As we trudged along, some Filipino women in the small towns we passed through tried to give us sugar. Our guards wouldn't let us take it. I grabbed a piece of sugar cane from beside the road and sucked on it awhile. In my pocket was a tin of Nescafe from our C-ration kit. It was hard like tar, but I sucked on that to keep on going.

Even when we got a break, we had to sit in the sun. Men passed out from the heat and exhaustion. I had a buddy, G. W. Eddleman from Tennessee, who fell out when he became deathly ill with malaria. Filipino civilians found him and took care of him for several days. When he was well enough, he joined another group.

The guards seemed to take pleasure in beatings, bayoneting and killing. And as prisoners marched along the highway, Japanese soldiers passing by would lean out of their trucks and strike them with rifle butts.

When we started out, each of us had a tent half, blanket, change of clothes and an extra pair of shoes, but, as we got weaker, we threw them down. I had picked up another canteen along the road, which I filled at a well.

One night, we slept on a pile of rocks in the rain; another night, on a pile of onions in a tin building. After I scratched around among the decayed ones, I found an onion that was edible. Our captors did not provide us food, so that was supper.

Six days into the Bataan Death March, exhausted, starved, beaten, filthy and almost insane with thirst, we stopped briefly at an artesian well. I did not think I could go on. Others had been shot or bayoneted when they collapsed. Sweltering from the jungle heat, I kneeled and drank faster and faster, afraid we would have to leave before I could get enough.

Aaarghhh! Severe cramps! While I was crying out in agony, a guard yelled orders in Japanese for me to get up. I braced for the pain of his bayonet. "Kill me now!" I screamed back.

Wade Carter of Gaston County and First Sergeant Mickey McGuire from Mississippi saved my life. They grabbed me up, stopped a Filipino passing by and loaded me into his two-wheel cart pulled by a Palomino pony. Two or three others who could no longer walk joined me on the journey to San Fernando, where we spent the night on the dirt in a barbed wire enclosure.

232

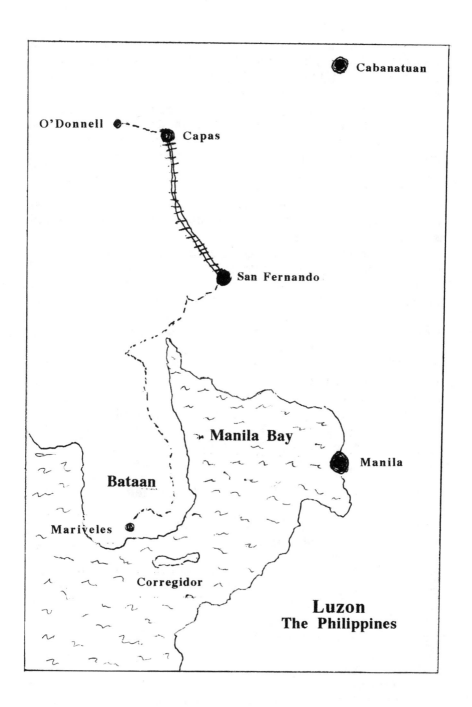

Cabanatuan

O'Donnell

Capas

San Fernando

Manila Bay

Bataan

Manila

Mariveles

Corregidor

Luzon
The Philippines

A lot of the men had dysentery, and the filth and flies were disgusting. For the first time, the Japs gave us food: sticky rice with worms, weevils and mouse droppings. We ate it anyway. The ones who couldn't didn't last long.

The next morning, we were crammed into boxcars, packed so tight that we couldn't move standing up. Tin roofs on the northern-bound train heated our cars like ovens. Men with malaria, dysentery and other tropical diseases added to our misery. As we stopped in small towns, they would open the doors a little bit. Filipino women threw us rice balls, but I never could catch one.

After more than five hours, we pulled into Capas. From there, we were marched to Camp O'Donnell, which had been built as a training camp for Filipinos.

It is estimated that 11,000 Americans and more than 60,000 Filipino soldiers were force-marched those 63 miles. (From the US, we had ground forces: the 50th and 60th Coast Artillery, 31st Infantry Regiment, 200th Coast Artillery Anti-Aircraft, 192nd and 194th Tank Battalion; from our air forces: the 19th Bomb Group, 27th Bomb Group, 24th Pursuit Group and well as naval forces including the 4th Marines and service forces.)

Some reports say that only 54,000 reached the camp. General King estimated that 650 Americans and 10,000 Filipinos died on the march. Relatively few escaped into the jungle. Many of those were later captured or died before reaching safety.

When we got to O'Donnell, we expected to get some rest and some decent food. We were fooled.

From O'Donnell to Cabanatuan, One Hell to Another
by
Earl Marshall Williams
Mecklenburg County, NC

At the end of the Bataan Death March, Camp O'Donnell's vermin welcomed us. Even our white rice was infested with fleas and worms. After surviving the march, many of our ranks quit eating and died. More contracted diseases. Brutal beatings killed the weak ones who didn't die on their own. Lt. General Edward P. King estimated that 1475 Americans and 23,000 Filipinos perished in 51 days at that camp.

Rather than giving up, and thus letting the Japs win, I volunteered for as many work details as I could, so I could get out of there. O'Donnell had no water supply, so they'd get up a detail to go to the river to fill up all the canteens. When it was my turn to go, our Japanese guard was lax on us, so a few of us moved out of sight and got a bath. We got a few licks with a rifle butt, but it was worth it. Once, when it was raining, I left my bunk of bamboo slats and stood under the eaves. Those raindrops felt like fire ants! I never knew what caused the burning, but I never tried that again.

Although a detail could include 300 men, we were divided into groups of ten. If even one from a group tried to escape, all ten would be executed. I steered clear of men known to be desperate and was fortunate, but my friend Wade Rogers from York County wasn't so lucky.

Under the guidance of Filipino and Japanese engineers, it took 200 of us six weeks to repair seven spans of a bombed-out bridge. "Now you can march across it," we were told. We did, singing "God Bless America" every step of the way.

Another time, when I went on a water detail, the Filipino constable who led us to the well said to me, "There are a couple of shirts in the bushes." As all of our clothes were worn out, patched and infested with body lice, that was a real gift.

After Corregidor fell May 6th, those prisoners of war were sent to Cabanatuan, a larger facility. In June, when we finished the bridge detail, our group moved there, too. Eventually, all prisoners from O'Donnell were sent to Cabanatuan.

The diet of watery white rice and soup made of some kind of greens, with a lack of vitamin B, caused me to develop dry beri beri. Pain started in my thighs and streaked like lightening to my toes. I sat for many a night with my feet in a bucket of water. Xerophthalmia from lack of vitamin A affected my sight. I knew had to get into the camp hospital before I went completely blind. My friends tried to talk me out of it, because most people who went in never came out.

After I walked by the Japanese guardhouse, I came to the hospital gate. On a pole near the gate, the head of a Filipino who had tried to escape stared a stern warning. What a shock!

At the first barracks inside, a fellow dishing out rice asked, "Where are you from?"

"Charlotte," I said.

"I'm from Charlotte, too," said the officer named Conrad.

That first night, I was assigned to a bay with three men. When I awoke the next morning, the man on each side of me was dead. Maybe this is not a good place for me, after all, I thought.

Dr. Samuel Bloom put me in the eye ward, gave me cod liver oil and made yeast out of rice. I drank a half canteen cup of yeast a day for nearly four months and got better. My right eye still has so much scar tissue that I can't read with it, but I can see to get around. My feet and legs kept hurting for 10 to 15 more years. Every now and then, I still have shooting pains and my feet still burn.

A patient who was next to me in the eye ward, Chaplain Cleveland from Des Moines, Iowa, shared some roasted peanuts, which helped me a whole lot. He was paralyzed.

Earl Williams
1945

I hated to see anyone get sent to Zero Ward, the last stop before death. One day, I watched them roll a Navy chief petty officer, who was already turning gray, from Zero Ward to the "cemetery," a huge hole outside. The four men were carrying him on what had been a slat shutter.

They stopped just before they were going to dump the body. Suddenly, he opened his eyes, got off the stretcher and walked back inside.

By the time I got back on work details, some Japanese interpreters decided that we should have a farm. We agreed. Prisoners planted and worked the fields of sweet potatoes, cucumbers and other vegetables. We were supposed to get some of the food, but the harvest was hauled off.

Had we tried to eat what we picked, we would have gotten a beating. If you accidently cut down a plant and they saw you, that caused a beating, too.

I was afraid that, if the food didn't get better, I was going to die. I didn't *want* to die; maybe I was just facing reality.

Thanksgiving Day, 1942, was a momentous occasion. Red Cross packages arrived at Cabanatuan. Without enough to go around, we shared one box between two men. Not all were alike, but most held some klim (powdered milk), corned beef, jelly, maybe a can of peanuts or some pork-and-beans.

Until that American holiday, a cemetery hole was dug daily. Before nightfall, it would be filled with about 45 bodies. They would cover it up and dig another. The day after Thanksgiving, only one body was put into the hole.

I changed my mind about dying. Like the others, I had hope.

Better Off—But Still Hungry!
by
Earl Marshall Williams
Mecklenburg County, NC

A bakery! We smelled bread baking as we marched into our new camp, Fukuoka POW Camp #17 in Japan. To starving prisoners of war, who had subsisted on mostly rice and soup—and not enough of either—for nearly two years, that aroma gave us hope that life would be better here.

No one had told us where we were going that July, 1943. Our Japanese captors lined up 1000 American men at the Cabanatuan POW camp in the Philippines. Five hundred would be sent on another work detail. "You go. You don't go," they had said randomly.

They took me, but not my buddy, Wade Carter from Gastonia. I tried to get out of it, but couldn't. Then I saw that eight of my company were in the group that were being put on trucks.

At Manila, they loaded all 500 of us on the Clide Maru, crowding 250 into each hold, where cattle had apparently just been hauled. It stunk! We made it stink even more, for many of the men had dysentery, and the heat made it worse. They had a trough up on deck, but they didn't let many of us go up.

We docked at Santa Cruz, but that was not our destination. Some magnesium ore was loaded on the ship, and we moved on.

After we got to Formosa, a prisoner got real sick. Dr. Thomas Hewlett, one of two POW doctors assigned to keep us healthy, tried to get him sent to a hospital. The Japs refused, so Dr. Hewlett had to operate for appendicitis. Jerry Okonski was placed on a hatch cover and held down by several men.

A dentist had a little Novocain, and the doctor talked someone into sterilizing some rags, so he could perform the appendectomy. Seven days later, August 9th, when we landed at the Japanese port of Moji, Okonski walked off the ship carrying his own bag.

From Moji, we took a train to Camp #17 that had been built for us at the Mitsui Mining Company, near the town of Omuta. The weather was much like North Carolina's, conditions were much improved, and rolls became part of our diet.

At the camp we were housed 50 men to a barracks, which had rooms with partitions and sliding doors and a bathroom at the end of the building. In the Philippines, we had only trenches.

Our new bathrooms had stools with an iron pot beneath and

a trap door to the outside. Every morning, a Japanese woman came to dip the contents of the pots into her "honey wagon," an oxcart.

Even better, we had "wash houses" (more like a shed, with racks to hang our clothes on to dry) and bathhouses, one for the camp and another outside the mine. They would give us a small bucket and a little of what they called soap. We splashed water on our bodies, soaped up and then got into the hot tub, which was large enough to hold the whole shift of workers, about 130, at one time.

After ten days of training and learning the Japanese names for tools and numbers, we were assigned to work one of three shifts and one of three jobs: extracting coal, bracing the ceiling or working in the hard rock, making tunnels bigger. We who enlarged tunnels didn't have to work as hard and came out with white dust, not coal dust. But, like the others, we were slaves. Everyone had quotas and worked nine days before getting one day off. The work force was five or six prisoners to one Japanese citizen.

The cruelty continued after we arrived at the Mitsui camp. Men got beatings for not making quotas, not saluting or bowing to a Japanese soldier or for other small infractions. For instance, at the door of our barracks was a board with names of places within the camp (mess hall, hospital, bathroom, work). We were to hang our prisoner number on a nail above the place we would be. If we were found elsewhere, we'd get a beating.

One day, G. W. Eddleman passed me and warned, "Earl, put on all the clothes you can."

I hadn't put my tag in the proper place. My overcoat softened the blows.

One guy traded some rice for a cigarette. He was put in solitary confinement, where he was left to die.

On our way to the mine one day, we saw a guy named Johnson from Texas crouched on his knees on some hard rock. They had stuck a large stick behind the bend of his knees and attached a ladder to his back. A Jap would climb up the ladder and jump up and down until Johnson passed out. They'd pour water on him until he awoke, and then do it again. He lasted three days.

Although conditions were better than in the Philippines, all of us were still malnourished and miserable. That first day, we got soup, rolls and ice water. I drank so much water that I got cramps and had to go to bed, where fleas ate me up.

Our barracks were not heated. In cold weather, two blankets and the pad to go over our straw beds were not enough. We put on overcoats and piled two-to-a-bed to have four blankets.

238

Prisoner-of War Camp #17 ABOVE: Exterior, showing typical barracks and wall. BELOW: Washing area with trench. Taken after camp was abandoned. Fukuoka, Japan. 1945.

We were issued shoes like split-toed tennis shoes and cloth leggings. I eventually tightened my GI belt to my new size: 23 inches. With bronchial pneumonia, I got down to 130 pounds from my enlistment weight of 180.

My eyes were still damaged from Xerophlthalmia, caused by a lack of vitamin A, but when *everybody's* eyes grew weak from malnutrition, they sent in truckloads of oranges. We ate every one, skin and all.

In the spring of 1945, five ton-and-a-half trucks rolled in loaded with spring onions. We got them in soup and could eat them raw anytime we wanted them until they were gone. We actually gained a little weight that month.

Whenever we got bread, we did not get rice. They gave us a good grade of rice, but there's not enough vitamins in white rice, so we later were given red rice with more vitamin B and some kind of filler that looked like cane seed. A wooden vat in the mess hall was always filled with tea.

We carried lunch into the mine in a cigar-like box. Usually it was rice and a long white radish pickle or a soybean paste. Occasionally, there was something purple we called "seaweed" that was chopped like cabbage and tasted sweet.

Dr. Hewlett calculated that we got 40% filler and 60% rice, with traces of vitamins. Five hundred calories a day were allotted to men going into the mine; 408 for those not working and 153 for the ones too sick to work.

Not only was I growing more ill, I wondered whether I'd make it. And yet, of the 821 Americans at Fukuoka Camp #17, only 49 died. (In Japan, we were better off than the ones who stayed in the Philippines.) Many Australians, British, Dutch, Chinese and Indonesian prisoners did not live to go home from Camp #17. The majority did.

More than two years had passed when an announcement was made that a "big shot" in Japan had died, so we didn't have to go into the mine that day. The next day, they had another excuse: it was the Emperor's birthday. On the third day, they admitted that the war was over and gave orders to mark "POW" on our camp.

Had they let us mark the parade grounds with lime earlier, we would not have been bombed twice. My barracks had been destroyed, but they had built more, so when we came out of the bomb shelter, we had a place to go.

When we heard about the bombings of Japan, some of the fellows remembered seeing a gigantic cloud from Nagasaki a few days before; one called it "an ice cream cone in the sky." Nagasaki was only about 35 miles away. I must have been underground in the mine.

Soon after the camp was marked "POW," planes started parachuting food in to us. A drum of sugar was first, then canned peanuts, jelly, meats, then clothing and supplies—truly manna from Heaven.

I was standing under the eaves of our barracks when I saw something overhead. I ran, and a 55-gallon drum broke through the roof where I'd been standing. A miracle saved me! And inside, fruit cocktail was everywhere!

Almost immediately, we were handed Red Cross boxes. Some POWs found them locked in a storeroom. Those packages were dated before we ever arrived!

The only contact we had had with the Red Cross was in 1944. We were told that Red Cross representatives would be inspecting our camp. The camp commander issued all of us new clothes, and we got the day off. Our food was better, too: more "goodies" in the soup and more of it. However, as soon as the representatives left, the Japs took back the clothes and the food went back to normal.

We were all "walking skeletons" and probably would not have lasted much longer without the food drops. Almost immediately, I began gaining weight. In fact, within 60 days, I gained 60 pounds.

Barracks at POW Camp #17. Fukuoka, Japan. 1945.

On September 15th, I was finally liberated. At last, I was marching to the station to take a train to the port in Nagasaki.

While on the train, we were told that we'd have plenty of food on the ship home, so we should throw everything we had left out the window to the hungry kids.

I couldn't do it. I had been hungry for 1,245 days. I ate every candy bar and peanut.

When we arrived in Nagasaki, the Red Cross had hot coffee and doughnuts for us. I couldn't eat them. I was too full.

Sadists
by
Stokes K. Shealy
Lexington County, SC

When General King ordered our surrender to the Japanese on April 9, 1942, we formed groups of 100 in a column of fours in Mariveles to begin what was later known as the Bataan Death March. I did not think we'd be prisoners very long. I thought the Americans would rescue us.

Japan had not signed the Geneva Convention, governing treatment of prisoners of war. We were not POWs, we were "guests of the Empire." The Japanese said we were traitors to our country. They called us dogs and said we would be treated as dogs. Nobody I knew treated their dogs with such cruelty; I called them sadists.

At 17, I had enlisted in the Army Air Corps and left Batesburg for basic training at Savannah in 1941. As a member of the 27th Bomb Group, I arrived on Luzon in the Philippines 20 days before the war started. My outfit never received our planes. The ships carrying them were rerouted to Australia. We were assigned to take care of all ammunition. I became company clerk at company headquarters in the San Fernando Valley, where the 27th Bomb Group was stationed.

When Japan invaded the valley, we lost six or seven men in my outfit that first day. Soon, we were out of food, medicine and ammunition. They kept telling us it was on the way. Then we got news that other islands had fallen.

By the time we had surrendered, the American and Philippine armies were sick and hungry. On that long, long march, if someone fell to the ground, a Japanese guard would prod him. If no one helped him to his feet, he would get shot or stabbed with a

242

bayonet. Filipinos would try to help us by giving us food or water. If caught, they would get shot.

Along the way, a Japanese soldier took a Filipino baby, threw it up, and he and other soldiers bayoneted it when it came down. They were sadists.

Another time, a sick man had fallen and could not get up. Some Japanese were coming down the road, a half-track ran over him.

At Camp O'Donnell, our destination, there was little or no water to drink and fleas were plentiful in our pitiful portions of rice. Disease and sanitation were serious problems. I saw a man with dysentery lying in his own bowel movement. Men were dying all around me. Some said, "Death's better than living in this Hell."

We had to bury 15 or 20 at a time in a big hole. At night, dogs would dig the bodies up. We'd have to re-bury them in the rice paddies, but sometimes the bodies would float back up.

I volunteered to do work details. Although we were expected to work all day unless we were so sick we couldn't move, we got more food. The Philippine Government later gave some of us a medal, because, even as prisoners, we were helping the Allies. While rebuilding a bridge (such as one at Capas), we'd fix it so that, when tanks hit it, the tanks would break up. On the airfields we built or repaired, we put camouflaged bubbles beneath the surface, so when aircraft hit it, the plane would wreck.

When we were transferred to Cabanatuan #1, conditions were filthy and unhealthy, and there were shortages of water and food. Normally, we would get a bowl of unpolished rice the size of a baseball once a day. Sometimes, we got a sweet potato. But, on work details, we might get fed rice three times a day with a side dish. Once in a while they would let Filipinos give us some fruit. It was not enough to kill the hunger, but it helped.

One time, we caught a dog, killed and boiled it. It was greasy but tasted real good.

While working, we were not allowed to help each other, even though we had a camaraderie like family. If someone tried to escape, all ten GIs in his group would be killed.

Most of the guards were pretty fair, if we did our work. But one we called "Bugeye" was mean as the devil. He made me stand at attention, while he hit me in the face again and again. I did not fall to the ground. Finally, he stopped, put his arm around my neck and called me the Japanese word for friend.

By then, I had resolved that I wasn't going to let those SOBs get the best of me. I was going to live and was not going to let them kill me.

I even participated in the one recreation allowed: Judo! They were very good at it, but I learned a lot, and no one tried to hurt me unfairly.

One day after I volunteered to go to Lipa, I went suddenly blind while helping build an airfield from scratch. My buddy, Jack, a lumberjack, saw me and told a guard I was blind. The guard didn't believe us, so he stuck his finger in my eye. (I still have a hole in that eye.) When I didn't blink, Jack was allowed to put me across his shoulder and carry me to the the camp we stayed in.

A captain saved my life. He stole some vitamins and hid them until the guards stopped looking for them. He gave them to me at intervals until my eyesight came back.

One of our worst experiences was at Camp Murphy near Manila. All 350 of us complained about the rationing of food. We thought that they'd have to listen to 350 of us. Instead, they called in all their officers and guards, lined them up in two rows and made us run from end to end while they beat us with ax handles. One boy got paralyzed by those sadists.

What came next was more horrible. In October, 1944, they put 250 of us in the hold of a coal transport ship, headed for Japan. We had to stand up in the hold, which had one small hole, where they lowered a bucket of rice once a day. Rice was doled out of the bucket to guys they could get to, which caused a lot of fighting. You didn't have a friend on that boat!

The only good thing about the coal dust on the bottom: we could defecate and cover it up. Men were dying daily and being thrown overboard, so that by the end of the trip, we could sit down.

What should have been a three-day boat ride from Manila to Japan took 41 days. Three ships carrying POWs started out in a convoy with Japanese destroyers and a battleship. As a defensive maneuver, we had to zig zag and go all the way around by Hong Kong, Shanghai and Formosa to a dock in the Tokyo Bay. We switched ships in Shanghai and Formosa. Other ships with prisoners joined us. Because POW was not painted on any of our ships, friendly fire strafed us, and bullets came down into the hold, killing a few men. We didn't know it then, but outside of Hong Kong, two of the POW ships were sunk. I just happened to be on one that was not hit.

We were sent to an ore mine at Sendai, 50 miles from Nagaski on Kyushu. My job was to run a jackhammer or operate a push cart underground.

One day in September, 1945, the guards unloaded their guns and put them in the guard house. They told us the war was over and gave us a radio so that MacArthur could broadcast instructions to us. MacArthur said to mark a field with an X, where they could drop food supplies, and to get a gun to protect ourselves from civilians. But, as we walked out of the camp a week or ten days later, civilians acted as though we were not there.

Had it not been for the atomic bombs, no American POW would have been left alive. That's why they were moving all of us to Japan. Those two bombs saved my life.

THE SPOUSES LEFT AT HOME

Uncertainty
A Way of Life
by
Ann Spratt Wilson
Cabarrus/Polk Counties NC

Buzz! Buzz! Buzz!
7:30 a.m., July 7, 1944.

Now who in the world could be ringing the front doorbell at this hour of the morning?

Pulling my dress over my head, I rushed to answer the insistent buzzing. There stood a young boy with a yellow envelope in his hand.

Since the cottage had no telephone, important messages had to be sent by telegraph to the train station and delivered by a boy on a bicycle.

I took the envelope, rushed inside and ripped it open.

Before me in bold type were the words I'd hoped and prayed never to receive:

Ann and Jim Wilson
Chatham Air Base
Savannah, GA, 1944

245

"THE SECRETARY OF WAR DESIRES ME TO EX-PRESS HIS DEEP REGRET THAT YOUR HUSBAND, FIRST LIEUTENANT JAMES C. WILSON, HAS BEEN REPORTED MISSING IN ACTION SINCE TWENTY-SIX JUNE OVER AUSTRIA. IF FURTHER DETAILS OR OTHER INFORMATION ARE RECEIVED YOU WILL BE PROMPTLY NOTIFIED. ULIO, THE ADJUTANT GENERAL."

Only four weeks earlier Jim had driven me, our six-month-old baby daughter, Bitsy, and my 80-year-old grandmother up to the family's 100-year-old cottage in Saluda, North Carolina. How could he possibly be missing over Austria? I thought that there must be some mistake. This couldn't be happening. I'd received a V-mail letter from him only yesterday, mailed from North Africa while he was en route to his overseas assignment. As all letters were censored, he couldn't tell me his destination; I could only guess.

I relayed the sad news to our parents, and both mothers came right away. I was still in a state of shock and disbelief.

Weeks passed with no further word from Washington. Jim's mother became convinced we'd never see him alive again, but I was certain he just couldn't be dead. I rationalized that I was much too young to be a widow. It couldn't be true. We had a child to raise together—so many dreams and plans. I prayed a lot and never gave up my belief that he'd come home.

On July 30th, a letter came from Major General Twining, Commander of the 15th Air Force, giving us little hope, but additional information about the mission. It was a B-24 raid on an oil refinery near Vienna. Shortly before target time, his plane was attacked by Nazi fighters but proceeded until after the bomb run, then made a sharp left turn and was not seen again. Obviously, his plane was forced down in enemy territory, and they did not know whether the crew was able to bail out or reach the ground alive. I was advised to "wait with patience and fortitude for the final word of his fate." Not a very cheering letter, but any news was welcome.

Finally, after another month or so, a telegram came from General Ulio with wonderful news that the Red Cross had notified him that James C. Wilson was a prisoner of war of the German government, location unknown. Information as to his place of internment would take one to three months longer.

September came, and after the worst summer of my life, we returned to Concord, North Carolina to be with my parents. The folks in the community were wonderful. It was unbelievable the way they took us in as though we'd been lifelong friends. My parents had only lived there a couple of years and I only a few months while Jim had been in flight training. Added to my anxiety for Jim was concern for my three brothers, Frank, Edward and Roy Spratt, who were also in service.

Jim's first letter to me, censored by both Germany and the US, and minus any return address, arrived later that fall. I was still unable to communicate with him. POWs were allowed to write two cards and two letters a month, but as the war progressed, there was no guarantee of delivery.

Word finally came that he was interned at Stalag Luft III, a camp for Air Force officers located near the Polish border. I could now mail the letters I had written to him daily since he'd left the States. Also, I could send a food parcel once a month. However, not one of the parcels ever arrived, and only three of my letters reached him the entire time he was interned.

Rationing was a problem here for everyone. A friendly grocer would save Ivory Soap Flakes for me for Bitsy's diapers. There were no washing machines or Pampers. Everything was washed by hand. Ration stamps were necessary for gas, meat, shoes, and many other items. New tires were non-existent and retreads almost impossible to buy.

The newspaper, radio newscasts and Pathe newsreels at the movies were our only real sources of war news. Kaltenborn was my favorite commentator. I never missed his broadcasts. The horror photos, shown in newsreels taken when Nazi death camps were liberated, gave me nightmares, as I imagined what might be happening at Stalag Luft III.

Unknown to me, in January 1945 as the Russians advanced, the entire camp of 10,000 prisoners was evacuated on foot in sub-zero snowy weather. After several days on foot, they were put in the infamous forty-and-eight boxcars* and taken to Stalag VII A in Bavaria. Stalag Luft III was a "country club" compared to this place where over 100,000 men were crowded with inadequate food, water, bathing facilities, blankets or places to sleep, etc. Jim still suffers the effects of frostbite from the forced march.

We had no news of Jim's whereabouts from January until late May when a telegram arrived from Ulio, the Adjutant General, stating:"YOUR HUSBAND 1ST LT. WILSON, JAMES C. RE-TURNED TO MILITARY CONTROL AND IS BEING RE-TURNED TO THE UNITED STATES WITHIN THE NEAR FUTURE."

* A term from that era meaning a railroad car that could hold 40 men or 8 mules.

On June 6, 1945, I received this telegram: "ARRIVED SAFELY. EXPECT TO SEE YOU SOON. DON'T ATTEMPT TO CONTACT OR WRITE ME HERE. LOVE, JCW."

He intended to surprise me and went straight to my parents' new home in Montgomery, Alabama. They informed him that I was again back in Saluda for the summer with the baby, her nursemaid and my grandmother.

Early on a beautiful Sunday morning in June, he walked in, and I hardly recognized him. He had a wonderful suntan from 21 days on a troop ship from Le Havre, France to the States.

Instead of looking like a prisoner weighing barely 125 pounds, he weighed more than ever before in his life. His shirt collar wouldn't even button! The Army had fed them special diets to fatten them up before they were sent home.

Sarah ("Bitsy") Wilson
Concord, NC. Fall, 1944

Arriving by bus in Saluda that Sunday morning, Jim had walked the mile up to the cottage.

As he approached, he saw a little girl in a stroller being pushed by her nurse.

Stopping, he asked her "Whose little girl is she?"

"She is Mrs. Wilson's," was the reply.

Jim smiled. "She's mine too!"

Wife of a POW Nursing POWs
by
Martha Pegram Mitchell
Mecklenburg County, NC

Little did I know the impact that September night in 1939 would have on my future.

As I entered the chart room of Charlotte's Presbyterian Hospital for the night duty shift, Dr. Fleming said, "Come with me to Room 129 to place a head-halter traction on my patient."

The doctor and I did this to a very unhappy young auto-accident victim. The resentful 19-year-old would not be returning with his friends to Chapel Hill to begin his sophomore year. Raymond Miller Mitchell, Jr. was his baptismal name, but everyone called him Jack.

A few days later, Jack began smiling and inviting me in to sample his mother's goodies. By the end of his three-week stay, I, a nursing student, had gotten to know the blue-eyed college man. Jack and I dated that fall, and a relationship was beginning. He returned second semester to UNC, where a civilian flying course was offered for would-be pilots. Jack enrolled and received a license.

During this time, the war in Europe was accelerating. Country after country was being invaded and taken over by Germany. England was being harassed and bombed. It seemed likely that the US would become involved. People were beginning to volunteer, and the draft was put into effect.

Jack began exploring his chances of joining the Air Corps. He put in an application, met the qualifications and, by August 1941, was off to Texas to flying school.

About the time he was receiving his wings and commission, I joined an Army evacuation hospital group. Meanwhile, Jack and I were falling in love, but marriage seemed unlikely at that time. Just as our hospital was activated and sent to Fort Bragg, North Carolina, Jack's squadron from Morris Field was sent to Panama. After August 1942, letters from one APO to the other became our way of courting.

Our tent hospital followed the front lines in North Africa and then Italy for 18 long, arduous months. Finally, I was rotated home at the end of December, 1943. Jack and I were married May 25, 1944 at Fort Benning, Georgia, and enjoyed ten glorious honeymoon days in nearby Atlanta. Still a member of the Army Nurse Corps (ANC), I returned to my assignment in Brooke Army Medical Center at Fort Sam Houston, while Jack prepared to go overseas.

Jack was keen to get into combat as a fighter pilot. In his first letter from England, he excitedly told of being in a squadron of P-51s (fast fighter planes used

Martha and Jack Mitchell
Charlotte, NC. 1945

to fly cover for big bombers) commanded by a Panama colleague.

I was so scared. My new husband had left to be in the thick of the air war. I had seen the skies over Africa and Italy filled with planes on missions, so I knew the dangers. Each morning, I grabbed a paper to read the reports of the previous day's flights. My heart would nearly stop as I read about planes lost. If they were P-51s, fear gripped me.

Then, in late September, about 11:10 p.m., a call came from his mother.

Jack had been shot down on a mission over Arnhem, The Netherlands, on September 25th.

I must have gotten hysterical, for immediately, every bedroom door on my floor opened, and friends gathered. All of us walked down two flights of stairs to the living room. After tears and laughter, reassurances, hugs and more tears, my friends gave me a sleeping pill.

During the following month, all of our patients on my TB ward daily encouraged me to think positively. Many days, I would slip into the linen closet on the pretext of straightening it out, but really to quietly cry in despair. I refused to believe Jack would not be returning to me.

On a Sunday afternoon in late October, the post operator at Fort Sam Houston called to see if I were alone on my ward. Soon, a nurse from next door came in and sat down. The phone call that followed said that Jack was alive, though a prisoner of Germany. I whooped with joy, and all my TB patients came running to give hugs and kisses.

A few weeks later, our chief nurse asked if a friend and I would consider transferring to the prisoner of war camp hospital in Roswell, New Mexico. We would run it, with help from German corpsmen. Of course, our prisoners would be German.

I jumped at the chance. I felt this was the right thing to do. I, too, should be in a POW camp, thus feeling closer in spirit and love to my new husband, to personally share his imprisonment. I needed to experience this myself, to have a better understanding. I also believed that, if I took good care of the Germans entrusted to me, then they, in turn, at Stalag Luft I would treat Jack kindly. I couldn't explain that rather far-fetched idea, but it persisted.

Soon after arriving in Roswell, Robert, my senior corpsman, told me, "Don't worry about your husband, he will be treated well." Robert assured me that airmen were respected and would not be mistreated. Hans, Fritz, Louie and Robert, my four corpsmen, all spoke good English, Robert more than the others. As a pre-med student at the University of Heidelberg, he had been drafted. Like the others, he didn't want to be in the Army any more than some of our boys did. The men were all very respectful except once in a while. One over here would say something and they would all giggle. I'd ask Robert what they said. I doubt he told me the truth.

Our camp was a compound with two rows of fences and guard towers. The prisoners lived in GI barracks. They were fed field rations (hot food, not cold C-rations) like those available to our soldiers. Each day, men were trucked out to work in farm fields. Those who were hospitalized had various common illnesses, work-related injuries, appendicitis or boils. I had a ward full of prisoners with boils and became an "ace" caretaker of boil patients.

All the guys in Jack's camp were officers, so they did not go out to work. To keep occupied, some played musical instruments, others played cards or made things out of scraps. They had a stove to cook turnips, cabbage and potatoes, brought in to them. The bread, they were convinced, was made with sawdust. German shepherd dogs ran loose in the compound in case somebody got an idea to escape.

Finally, I received a V-mail from Jack dated November 2, 1944. Brief as it was, I knew he was all right. To see his hand-writing again helped my spirits soar. Even so, reports from Europe that winter were grim and discouraging. Hard work and my friends' many prayers helped me get through those long, dreary days.

Christmas of 1944 was a sad one for me. I had sent pack-ages to Jack almost weekly and letters, too. The Red Cross assured me they were getting through, but I learned later that he never got a one. But the dearest thing happened that Christmas: one of my patients got a discarded glass saline bottle and built inside a small lake scene, complete with a sailboat tied up to a dock. He wrapped it in newspaper and presented it to me. This represented a great deal of skill and thoughtfulness, and I was truly touched.

After a few months at Roswell, I was transferred to Dallas to do nurse procurement. For that job, I had to travel down into the Texas Valley.

On May 8th, the war in Europe was over, then the waiting for Jack began. On the 2nd of June, a call came from Boston. Jack was home from the war. And so began our next 52 years of marriage.

251

Local POWs Doing Absent Men's Jobs
A
Compilation

In the Piedmont

The N. Charlie Griffin family of the Unionville community in North Carolina used POWs from nearby Camp Sutton for farm labor. In the fall of 1944, Elbert C. (Ebb) Griffin, who was 12 years old, would talk to members of the work crew while they were picking cotton. "Some spoke English very well," he said.

Ebb Griffin was impressed, because those men were from Rommel's Afrika Korps, Germany's best. "They operated on the NCO system; the German sergeants looked after their privates and other noncoms."

"We went down to Sutton to get them and we paid for them," he added. "The government got the money, but the workers were, in turn, paid by the pound of cotton picked. They were expected to pick 100 pounds a day, but they only picked 40-50."

Ebb's older brother, Frank, who had just turned 18, drove a Model A school bus to Sutton's Gate 5 to pick up 30 to 35 of them. A '37 Chevrolet truck with bench seats and a canvas top was sent to get more. The farm laborers came with guards, one to approximately every seven prisoners. They were well treated and well fed. According to Frank and Ebb's younger brother, Joe, "They were fed better than we were. They took breaks and got snacks and ate lunch at noon."

"They even had hot coffee on portable stoves," said Frank.

Joe spoke of how friendly they were. "The Germans gave us candy and showed us pictures of their wives and children." He thought that they were disillusioned, "because they had been fed a lot of propaganda about how desperate we were."

The youngest brother, who was 9 years old then, recalled the day it was raining hard, and some of the prisoners asked to come inside. Mr. Griffin was very opposed to the idea, but Mrs. Griffin had already let the men in. Joe was playing with model airplanes, when one of the men asked his mother for permission to play the piano. Joe heard music that seemed strange to his young ears, but it was done well.

Joe always had his airplanes positioned so that the American plane was behind the German one. A POW pointed out that Joe shouldn't have the swastika on but one side of the vertical stabilizer.

Whenever Joe turned his back, others would make a switch, so the German plane would be chasing the American one. Soon they'd all be snickering.

"The guards had an easy job," said Frank. "There was no place for them to go."

One day, some of the POWs turned up missing. The brothers agreed that the men were not escaping, but just lost—and were searching frantically to find their way back when they were found.

On November 14 that year, Frank was dressed better than usual, and the prisoners noticed. He was headed for the courthouse in Monroe to board a bus for Camp Croft to be inducted into the service. When the workers found out where he was going, they gave him a horse-laugh. Ebb watched them jibe his big brother, goose-stepping and saluting around him that day.

There was only one unpleasant incident: Some of the prisoners were upset over a delay in the computations of their pay. Their shaved-neck commanding officer, Sergeant Major Stock, a Nazi, complained to a guard, calling him (according to the guard) a "Jew Bastard" in German. The guard started chasing him with his canteen and then stopped after about 15 feet and drew a pistol.

"Daddy tried to get me out of the way," said Joe, "but I walked behind them, right in the line of fire."

They jabbered away in German, but no one got shot that day. Mr. Griffin asked that the guard not be sent back to the farm. He was not. Ebb recalls that Stock was put in solitary confinement for a while in a fenced-in pup tent.

The one POW who spoke impeccable English got in trouble for putting water or rock into the cotton before it was weighed. "Once we saw him in that pup-tent stockade," Joe recalled.

He was the prisoner who told the boys, "The American way of government will not stand—it's too liberal, too Democratic."

* * *

While Floyd ("Chunk") Simmons and his buddies were riding the bus home from Charlotte's Central High, they spotted German POWs getting off Army trucks and orderly marching "four by four" (four abreast) and heard the ka-rump, ka-rump, ka-rump of their high-top work shoes. They were headed for a pine forest between Beverly Drive and Myers Park Presbyterian Church.

Chunk and his friends hung out the bus windows to yell "Nazi" and other bad words at the tall blond cocky laborers with skin bronzed by the sun and bodies made brawny from workouts.

Every afternoon for a month or more, those POWs would

have to listen to teenage taunts. Some of them even laughed at the sight of the black combs on the upper lips of youngsters yelling "Heil Hitler!"

Word got around that the prisoners were from Camp Sutton and were members of the Afrika Korps, Rommel's elite desert tank troops. Their job, Simmons heard, was cutting timber for more Army camps. Despite the name-calling, the boys actually admired those "dirty Nazis."

* * *

Former Charlottean, John Darracott, saw POWs when he lived on East 7th Street. "Every night, large trucks would come by headed back to Monroe with the German prisoners, who were waving and yelling things in German."

* * *

Once in a while, Concord Canteen girls would be invited to a dance at Camp Sutton. "The Army sent a bus for us, and Italian POWs cooked for us," said Helen Arthur-Cornett, who got to know some of the military men at Concord's Canteen Community Center.

Among the soldiers Helen met were boys who had learned Italian in college and acted as interpreters. They bragged about teaching the POWs American slang such as "non saponi" ("no soap") and "Che es la buona parola?" ("What's the good word?")

* * *

Not all prison labor worked on farms. In Forsyth County, for instance, about 250 German POWs were housed on the premises and worked for R. J. Reynolds Tobacco Company making cigarettes in 1945 and part of 1946.

Other prisoners worked in peach orchards.

Jane Norris, whose father, John W. Snyder, was a pioneer peach grower in Forsyth and Davidson Counties, was working in his pack house and retail sales outlet on Old Salisbury Road the summer of 1944, when she was 9 years old.

"There was a shortage of peach pickers that summer, because all of the young men had gone off to war," says Jane. She told of the German POWs who arrived at the orchard in a large green military-style truck to do the job, describing them as "fine-looking men with blond hair and blue eyes."

Although Jane had no personal contact with them, she noticed their excitement when her father brought them tobacco and papers so they could roll their own cigarettes. "They were housed in the Armory on North Patterson in Winston-Salem," she said. "It was a boxy brick building with bars over the windows."

* * *

Louise Allen Smith, who worked at Pageland's Town Hall remarked that she sometimes saw trucks carrying German POWs to Camp Sutton's Chesterfield County rifle range, where they would do construction work and repairs.

In South Carolina, there were nearly 7,000 prisoners in 28 camps. The main one at Fort Jackson housed 1500. Another was at the Columbia Army Air Base. Secondary camps scattered around Columbia and the rest of the state provided laborers for picking cotton, peaches and potatoes, cutting timber, cleaning, handling rations and working in warehouses.

* * *

A former POW recently liberated from Stalag Luft I near Barth, Germany, Bert Connor from Cayce, South Carolina, was interested to see 200-300 German POWs at the Columbia Air Base after he returned to Lexington County. He noted that they were wearing clean clothes and seemed well fed and healthy, probably because they worked jobs in the area.

At Stalag Luft I, Connor wore the same clothes he was shot down in. His heavy coats were taken away, although the temperature got as low as zero and below. He took two baths ("like car washes") during his seven-month stay. While in that camp, he lost about 40 pounds. The best food he ever ate (and only once) was boiled horse meat, one piece the size of his thumb. His usual diet was potatoes, rutabagas, and soggy black bread made with fillers.

His only exercise was to walk around the compound, careful to stay inside the warning wire, lest he get shot.

Elsewhere in the US

While Kermit Cloniger was a senior officer at the Naval Air Station (NAS) in Hitchcock, Texas, German POWs were trucked in from nearby Camp Wallace. Cloniger, who is from the Piedmont, noted that they had been Rommel's men, the pride of Germany. From 50 to 100 worked at the NAS for 90 cents a day.

"They were artisans and smart!" he commented. "Some of the men set stones around a drainage ditch like a bridge, a beautiful piece of work."

Cloniger used some of them as cooks and was impressed by their ability—and his farewell cake topped with a meringue fox. "They called me Desert Fox, a real compliment."

The Lighter Side of the War

Okay, okay, so the War wasn't all trauma and tragedy. As in any difficult situation in life, we should try to see the lighter side. And that's what these guys and gals did.

Chosen
by
Alex R. Josephs
Mecklenburg County, NC

In late 1940, I was a Charlotte lawyer and served on the draft board that drafted me.

Just a few weeks later, other local guys and I were on our way to Ft. Bragg. After we got there, we were given assignments. They asked if anyone knew anything about bridges.

Spencer Folger, one of my Charlotte friends, spoke up. "Yeah, I painted a sign on a bridge once."

"Fine" he was told. "You go to the engineers."

When they found out I was a lawyer, they sent me to the medical corps.

That Important Question
by
Billy C. Coleman
Saluda County, SC

I resigned from the South Carolina State Senate to enter service.

Actually, I was one of five who did that. Right after the '42 session, Bryan Dorn from Greenwood (He and I were the youngest senators, age 26.), Charlie Moore of Spartanburg, Warren Derrick of Dillon and James Hugh ("Moose") McFadden from Manning and I all went down to the University of South Carolina to sign up. After filling out the papers, we awaited our assignments.

They put Bryan in the Air Corps, the other three in the Army

256

and me in the Navy.

How did they decide who would go where? I can attribute it to one question on the form. To "Can you swim?" I answered honestly. I said "No."

Sure Cure
by
Ernest Henderson, Sr.
Laurens County, SC

While in college at Hampton Institute, I was trying to get into the Army Air Corps. Good health was one of the qualifications, but I had a cold.

I was talking with a guy who was working in the kitchen and asked, "You know what's good for a cold?"

He said, "I'll tell you how to cure your cold, and you'll never have one the rest of your life."

"What's that, man?"

He looked at me seriously. "Take a bucket of water. Stick your head in three times and take it out twice."

Take Note
by
R. Mack Jones
Author of *Detours Along Life's Highway*
Guilford County, NC

In my early days in the Army Air Corps, I was at Fort Bragg, North Carolina, submitting to all the necessary shots, taking an IQ test and getting all my records up to date.

Every morning, we would go through close order drill, then march up to the headquarters of our area and stand in formation while the sergeant went inside to get a list of detail assignments.

One morning, he came out and asked, "How many of you know shorthand?"

I had taken shorthand in high school, but I didn't volunteer. I learned that real fast. Surprisingly enough, two or three fellows in the formation said they did.

"Fall out," said the sergeant. He handed them a paper with their assignment. "We're short of hands in the kitchen today."

257

Showing Respect
by
Henrietta Castlebury Auman
Orange County, NC

In 1943, my husband, a Hillsborough High math teacher and coach, was drafted about the time that they started taking younger men and those who were married. I was pregnant, but he still had to go.

At boot camp, he had to learn to call the officers by their rank. But *he* was called "Mister."

His high school students were there with him.

Patton's Eating Etiquette
by
Jim Geer
Rutherford County, NC

While we were on Tennessee maneuvers near Murfreesboro in June 1941, we enlisted men were getting accustomed to sweating out a chow line and eating from our mess kits on the ground.

Our officers had an orderly who would set up a table and chairs with plates and silverware from a suitcase-like box. He would bring food from the chow line in bowls for the officers. If they wanted refills, the orderly served them and, later, cleaned everything and packed it away until the next meal. We watched with envy and disgust.

We were eating chow one day in the field about 100 feet from the main road, when a jeep passed and then stopped. Someone said."Hey, that's the Big Boy. That's Patton!"

George S. Patton, Jr., a colonel then at Fort Benning, Georgia, was in charge of forming the 2nd Armored Division, but there he was, walking across the field demanding, "What in the Hell is going on here?"

He stepped back, and then with those boots of his, kicked that table, china, food bowls, and silverware to kingdom come. He glared at the officers. "If you don't have a mess kit, get one! Get your own food and eat on the ground with your men." He pointed to the table and debris. "Dig a hole and bury this junk!"

The officers stood there with food dripping off them.

We all clapped.

258

No Snappy Salute
by
Wallace S. Osborne
Mecklenburg County, NC

In December of '44, I was playing bridge in the Officers Club in Grottaglie, Italy when someone informed me that I had a phone call. Who could it be? A B-24 pilot with the 15th Air Force, I knew that no one makes social calls in combat. I thought, "Who in the name of God could be calling me?"

I answered the phone and heard a male voice say, "Is this Lt. Wallace Osborne?"

"Yes."

"Is your serial number 0834486?"

"Yes."

"Hold the phone. General Twining wants to speak to you."

I was a 2nd lieutenant! He was a major general and Commander of the 15th Air Force. I wondered: "What have I done now?"

The general's tone was calm. "Lieutenant?"

I stood at attention. "Yes, *sir!*"

"This is Nathan Twining. I was home on leave, and your dad called and said to tell you they love you and are praying for you."

I was stunned! He was in charge of 100,000 men. I had no idea in the world why he called me.

I knew he was from Charlotte, my hometown, but, at the time, I didn't know that a few years before, when he was a young Air Corps captain, his car had broken down on a Saturday afternoon. No one could fix it. He couldn't find any place open. Somebody had said, "Call Beech Osborne." Dad's first name was Beecher. My dad was a master mechanic in charge of maintenance of streetcars for Duke Power. Twining called him, and Dad had the car towed to the old car barn. He put on a mechanic's smock, got down in the pit and fixed it.

The captain asked, "How much do I owe you?"

"Not a thing. Not a thing," my dad had said.

Then years later, when Dad saw the general on leave, he wondered if he'd remember him. He did. That's what you call "casting your bread on the waters."

I didn't know all that as I stood with my ear on the receiver, listening to our general's voice. All I could think to say was "Thank

259

you sir!"

He said a brusk "G' bye."

When I returned to the bridge table, I casually asked, "Who wants to shake the hand that held the phone to talk to the boss?"

Hands Off Approach
by
Kate Lee Harris Adams
Durham County, NC

As WASPs, Anne Berry and I were practicing instruments flying the beam to Abilene, Texas.

I was under the hood in the front cockpit, and Anne was my observer in the back cockpit of our AT-6. When I finished my procedure, I raised the hood and my hands to indicate that I was through and for Anne to take over.

Shortly, I noticed we were circling the Abilene Air Base and slowly getting lower and lower. I turned to Anne and said, "What are you going to do, buzz the air base?"

In shocked surprise, she yelled back, "Haven't *you* got it?"

Bombs Away!
by
R. Mack Jones
Author of *Detours Along Life's Highway*
Guilford County, NC

As the pilot of a B-17 heavy bomber, I was flying at 25,000 feet over enemy territory near Bonn, when our top turret gunner, John Cunningham cried out in distress, "Lieutenant, I have the G.I.'s, and I don't know what to do!"

"G.I.'s" was the term for gastrointestinal problems, better known now as "the trots."

I told him to go back to the radio room and get one of the helmet liners and do what he had to do.

He returned, and I opened the bomb bay doors and he let it drop.

I often wondered if the Germans thought we had run out of ammunition.

My Broadcasting Debut
by
Charles Malvern Paty, Jr.
Mecklenburg County, NC

On the 22nd of January, 1943, we brought $4000 worth of beer aboard the USS North Carolina and stored it in the brig.

The Guadalcanal campaign had been going on for five months, and it had been a terribly tough fight. Now it was time for R & R in Noumea, New Caledonia. The beer was for parties ashore.

A baseball game against the USS Washington had been scheduled at "Shangri La," a fleet recreational area across the harbor. A baseball diamond had been laid out, and Bob Feller, a famous pitcher from the peacetime Cleveland Indians, was scheduled to play. Everyone wanted to see Bob play and our team beat our friendly rival.

Charles Paty
with the Radio Gang
USS North Carolina
1944

A radioman, I was encouraged to take a back pack transmitter to broadcast the play-by-play for those who had duty on the ship. The transmitter was designed for a landing force and was fairly heavy with batteries and the carrying gear. I tested it topside, and Radio One received me okay. A motor launch soon took off with beer, spectators, the team and me with my transmitter.

Since this was my first broadcast, I was a little nervous. I set up near home plate and started trying to raise the ship.

After several failed attempts, I decided that a hill was obstructing my transmission. I started climbing up a ways. In the meantime, the game had started, and I was missing a lot of it. The hill was rather steep, so I was huffing and puffing into the mike, as I kept trying to raise the ship.

261

Finally, I received a weak answer, but it was obvious that I would have to be at the top to have good communications. After nearly 45 minutes, I was at the top with a clear view of the harbor and the USS North Carolina. But we could barely hear each other. From that position, I could not see enough of the play to call it, so all I could do was transmit the latest score whenever there was a change on the scoreboard.

Dreading the razzing I would get from the Radio Gang, I scrambled down the hill just in time to make it to our boat for the return trip. I had not seen the game; I had viewed Bob Feller only from a great distance, and, worst of all, I had missed the beer!

Finally Getting Serious
by
Louise Nash Dorsett
Montgomery/Wake Counties, NC

I had been in love with Howard for a long time, but I took particular care not to let him know it for a while. I was having too much fun.

Major Howard Dorsett
Lt. Louise Dorsett
Mt. Gilead, NC
November, 1945

We had dated in high school in Mount Gilead, then when he was working his way through Duke and I was at WCUNC in Greensboro, and later, on and off for about 14 years (more off than on).

After college, I had taught in Murfreesboro and then Hoffman but decided to try the business world. I was with Carolina Power and Light in Raleigh when, in late 1942, I heard that the WAVES had been authorized. The nearest place to apply was the 6th Naval District Headquarters in Charleston. I hopped a train and hurried to Charleston.

As far as I know, I was the first WAVE sworn in at Raleigh. After five weeks training at Mount Holyoke College, I was sent to the Bureau of Ships in Washington, where I would fight what I called "The Battle of the Potomac."

Meanwhile, Army Lieutenant Howard Dorsett was on board a ship in the New York Harbor ready to go overseas with the last contingent of the 2nd Armored Division.

Suddenly, I realized that life was serious. I had to settle down. He felt the same way.

Howard couldn't leave New York, so I promised to meet him on Staten Island.

That's how I became the first WAVE at the Bureau to get married.

I had to walk my papers through the chain of command.

When I reached the Admiral, he looked at me intently. "Young lady," he said, "you haven't been here but a week and you want two days off?"

His wife, I knew, was a "battle axe," so I shouldn't have been surprised when he added, "My sympathy—and congratulations."

"Dear *Who?*"
by
Ralph H. Lawson, Sr.
Union County, SC

One of the young men in our flight crew received a "Dear John" letter from his high school sweetheart, whom he intended to marry upon getting out of the service. She requested that he send back the pictures of her that he had.

He mailed them and about 50 pictures of other young ladies gathered from his crew with a note that said, "I haven't seen you in such a long time, I've forgotten what you look like. Maybe you can find yours in this group."

Hello? Who's There?
by
Charles Malvern Paty, Jr.
Mecklenburg County, NC

When the first atomic bomb was dropped, the USS North Carolina was operating off Tokyo, supporting air raids on that area and other cities in the vicinity. Even before the official surrender

263

was signed in Tokyo Bay, we were asked to provide volunteer detachments of Marines and Navy personnel from nearby ships to occupy the main Japanese naval base at Yokosuka.

A radioman, I volunteered, along with 100 others from our ship. We formed landing detachments and were equipped for combat with rifles, packs, food, ammunition and water. We knew there were many Japanese sailors and marines in that naval base, and they could decide to die for the Emperor.

We went ashore on 30 August, 1945, from regular landing craft, arriving on a small beach on the south side of the naval base. We could see many large brick buildings and began a slow advance across open ground to the first one.

Outside, looking terrified, was a lone unarmed Japanese sentry. We proceeded on inside. The building was a two-story affair with many offices still fully equipped but apparently unoccupied. We took the stairs to see what was above, carrying, as ordered, unloaded rifles at the ready. Unloaded!

On the second floor, we found a large telephone switchboard with 30 or more positions. Several were occupied by Japanese sailors, each talking to somebody. Alerting the troops? Calling in kamikazes?

Nope. Chatting with female operators in Tokyo.

Due Respect
by
Oscar G. Penegar, Jr.
Mecklenburg/Gaston Counties, NC

While serving as an armament specialist for heavy bombers in the Army Air Corps, I was awarded a competitive appointment to the Naval Academy by Senator Clyde R. Huey. The transition from the Army to the Navy was complicated, but one autumn day in 1944, I found myself in Washington, DC, with an unassigned three days before I had to report to the Naval Academy Preparatory Unit. I had not been home for many months, so I began casting about to find a means of getting to Gastonia and back quickly.

Commercial airlines were unavailable without a high priority pass. The railroads had unusable schedules for my purposes. Buses were insufferable.

I called the Air Transport Command and was told that no flight to Charlotte Air Base was on their agenda, but that a flight to

Augusta, Georgia, was in their schedule for that day.

I told the sergeant that a flight to Augusta flew directly over Charlotte and that a flag-stop there would help me very much.

He asked, "What's your name?"

"General Penegar," I replied.

The sergeant came back to me shortly and respectfully reported that a stop in Charlotte had been authorized. We even worked out a return reservation during the same phone call.

I really didn't lie. And when I checked in for the flight, my identification papers spelled out my whole name: Oscar *General* Penegar, Jr.

The use of this unusual middle name, however, came back to haunt me two years later. Just before the Christmas break in 1946, I resigned my appointment and arranged to enter the University of North Carolina at Chapel Hill. My family sent me a Pullman ticket so that I could spend holidays at home in Gastonia. The night train from Washington to Gastonia, of course, passed through Charlotte.

It was pure luxury to be a civilian again, so I slept soundly until the train pulled into Charlotte's West Trade Street station in the wee hours of the morning. I peeked out the window to view what sounded like a raucous crowd.

There was a throng of young people, rallied on by my life-long Machiavellian friend Parker Whedon, with boisterous festivities on their minds. They had a bonfire going between the tracks and the passenger platform. Stretched between support columns on the platform was a large cloth banner which read: "Welcome Home to War Hero General Penegar."

Some of the revelers boarded and rampaged through the cars, shouting out my name and disturbing sleeping travelers. But I eluded the pranksters and continued on to Gastonia.

Victory Days and Later!

Victory, sweet victory! First came V-E Day, celebrating victory over Europe on May 8, 1945. But the war was not yet won. Japanese soldiers were expected to fight to the death rather than surrender, and Allied troops were planning an invasion of Japan's mainland, which was expected to be a bloodbath. Japan DID surrender on August 15, 1945, but only after the US dropped atomic bombs on Hiroshima (August 6) and Nagasaki (August 9). This country rejoiced wildly that August 15th. However, September 2nd (when the surrender documents were signed on the USS Missouri) was later designated the official V-J Day.

V-E DAY

Reprieve — Almost
by
Charles M. Marshall
Mecklenburg County, NC

I felt as though I had been a prisoner on death row and had received a reprieve from the governor.

The news that Germany had surrendered came over our tank radio while our 15th Tank Battalion was camped at Mittweida, Germany between Rocklitz and Chemnitz. The entire 6th Armored Division was spread out over ten miles in that area, awaiting orders.

My brother, Hunter Marshall, III, a Navy ensign, had been killed in action on June 9, 1942. The Navy had assigned him to the Merchant Marine ship, the USAT Merrimac, which was sunk by a German submarine in the Caribbean.

As of May 8, 1945, I had survived landing on Utah Beach at Normandy and four other campaigns (North France, Ardennes, Rhineland, and Central Europe). Company C suffered its first casualties in the battle for Brest. Five were killed. Approximately 30 of our closest comrades would die in the months to follow. We had many skirmishes in the summer and fall of 1944.

Then came the Big One, the Siege of Bastogne, better known as the Battle of the Bulge. Our division's job was to rescue those who had been surrounded.

Our casualties were heavy, but nothing like those of the 10th Armored Division. As we heard it, they were nearly annihilated.

On March 30, 1945, our Company C column of 15 tanks was traveling north in the pitch black dark of night. We entered a fork in the narrow road six miles south of Kassel, Germany. A column of enemy Tiger tanks entered from the other fork. Neither knew that the other was in the vicinity. The result was mayhem!

Too close for tank-to-tank firing, the only option was hand-to-hand combat, with pistols, knives and fists. Their column was destroyed. Ours suffered many casualties. Wounded in the face by shrapnel, I suffered a concussion and was evacuated to our medical battalion's tent hospital about 35 miles behind us. I was back in action within ten days.

Charlie Marshall
Mittweida, Germany
V-E Day, 1945

The V-E Day news was a huge relief, and I was counting my points (days served, medals won, etc.) to be eligible for discharge.

But the war was not over. We still had to live with the dread of being shipped to the Pacific Theater.

On August 15, we got word from headquarters that Japan had surrendered. The dawn of the nuclear age saved many thousands of American lives—perhaps mine.

And yet, despite the normal nagging fear of death, we of the 3rd Army took to heart what General George Patton told us when we assembled at a tent camp in the Midlands of England before being deployed to Normandy: "Don't you even *think* of dying for your country. You make that son-of-a-bitch die for his!"

267

Home via Reims
by
Jack Mitchell*
Mecklenburg County, NC

On May 8, 1945, we came into Reims, France, and milled around the military until we hitched a ride to Paris, never knowing that the Armistice was being signed in a building only a few blocks from us.

On May 2, three of my friends and I had been able to get out the front gate (of Stalag Luft 1 in Barth, Germany) and into the woods, when Goebbels and his entourage came up from Berlin to establish headquarters for the 3rd Reich at Barth.

The Germans heard that the Russians were on their way north. The guards had left on May 1, and we walked out on May 2 and just started toward France.

We walked in the woods and hitched rides. When our ragged little group got to Rostock, the Burgermeister came out of City Hall and surrendered to us, so the Russians wouldn't take over.

Jack Mitchell on his "liberated" motorcycle with his German sword, gun and three fellow "escapees." Germany. May, 1945.

268

One day, we came across a German airfield and off in a corner revetment, I found a perfectly good FW 190, but I never could get it started and finally gave up and moved on.

We found a place to sleep with a German family and the next day, we gratefully received a horse and buggy from a Russian major. That took us about a third of the way—then we met some Belgians who gave us a tractor. I'd never run a tractor before, but it wasn't hard learning.

No one in Paris was too concerned about a 120 pound ragged POW, and I really didn't know what to do next. Finally, someone told me that a boat with POWs was leaving Le Havre the next day and I could get on it. I scrounged up some money and bought a train ticket to Le Havre and got on the boat with no orders, no nothing but the clothes on my back—and landed in Boston a couple of weeks later.

Just to show you that I ain't too smart: years later, I ran into another POW who was in Paris. He went into the first military headquarters he could find and asked if he could borrow a typewriter to write a letter home. He then sneaked some stationery out of the drawer and wrote up some orders to send him home by the first available means and signed it with some phony name and rank. Within a couple of hours, he was on a C-54 on his way home.

* Editor's note: Jack Mitchell died in 1997. His story was taken from his own typed account for Jim Starnes, historian for the 339th Fighter Group, and an interview by Martha Azer of *The Charlotte News*.

Sorting People and Sending Them Off
by
James J. Cardo, Sr.
Mecklenburg County, NC

We may have had the quietest celebration of V-E Day around!

My unit was in the German village of Idar-Oberstein, a large rail yard, to oversee the movement of displaced persons (DPs). We had commandeered a hotel there for our headquarters, so we officers (six of us) sat out on a terrace overlooking a stream which had ducks and swans on it, very picturesque. I broke out a bottle of champagne from my footlocker. We already had some gin from the British, Scotch from Scotland as well as Rhine wine, schnapps, and beers with tags that read "Reserved for the Wehrmacht." As we enjoyed the spoils of war, we noticed that there was no traffic. No horses. No people out on the streets celebrating. All was quiet.

Since late April, 1945, trains had been bringing displaced persons (mostly Poles, Latvians, and Estonians that the Allies were freeing) and German POWs in by the carload.

Our battery was not assigned to a division. We were corps troops, which meant that we were a reserve unit assigned to give help wherever needed. At that time, we were herding the displaced into an encampment area, feeding them, sorting them out and preparing them to go back home. These were men, women and children who had been doing slave labor in factories and on farms.

We housed them in an old school. Our men put straw on the floors of classrooms and fed them twice a day from big pots. We would commandeer cows from dairy farmers, butcher them and add some vegetables which we had scrounged or the Army furnished. When we finished feeding all of them, it was time to start over again.

After we sorted them and prepared to put them on trains, some of the people didn't want to go. It was tragic.

James Cardo on "liberated" bike
(bell is for gas alarm)
Idar-Oberstein, Germany.
Spring, 1945

About a dozen Russian officers and a couple dozen Soviet soldiers were supposed to be working with us. The officers sat in the German house where they were headquartered, drinking vodka and playing chess. They did very little to help us maintain the DPs, but they tried to usher those pathetic people into the freight cars with the hammer and sickle on them. The people were, apparently, afraid that they would end up in Russia.

They probably did.

The German soldiers, POWs, were taken to a separate enclosure. As they marched down the main street of the village, women were hanging out the windows of the houses, crying and throwing pillows and blankets to them. The women knew where the men were going. Although it was spring, it was cold and rainy.

Our troops had just put up a barbed wire fence along a road for a quarter mile, made a 90 degree turn, continued another quarter mile, made another 90 degree turn and so on until they completed the enclosure, which had a gate at each end.

As they entered the entrance, the prisoners were handed a can (sausage, meat stew, or perhaps one with a biscuit, candy, cigarette, gum, and bathroom tissue). All C-ration cans looked alike. We didn't care who got which can.

Officers slept in a barn or other farm building within the barbed wired area. The soldiers had to sleep on the ground wherever they stood, but that was for only two or three days.

All the gray-uniformed Krauts wanted to do was go home. Soon, they were put on trains to their home towns.

Our MPs were looking for the "black shirts." Some of those Germans had shed their black clothes for gray, so the MPs were checking for their tattoos. The few storm troopers caught were put on trains to a special prison.

On one occasion, two of us happened to be at the edge of the village, leaning on a fender of my jeep, watching a column go by toward the enclosure. A guard was about every 50 feet. Near the end were stragglers, some crippled, using tree limbs as walking sticks.

Among the last ones was a German lieutenant, about 6'2" in a dress uniform (medals, iron cross, and a cape). Whenever he took a step, he would dip and hobble. Right behind him was an American guard.

That guy was so short that he fitted a Bill Mauldin "Willie and Joe" cartoon from the *Stars and Stripes* newspaper. His overcoat went right to his ankles. His M-1 rifle had a bayonet on it.

Every time the lieutenant went down, the MP would jab him with his bayonet on the south end.

As he passed, he grinned over at us, stabbed the German saying, "G. D. Superman."

To us, this was a caricature of what the Allies had done to Hitler's vaunted storm troopers.

The Russian Factor
by
Steven Epps
York County, SC

When the 505th Parachute Infantry Regiment (PIR) crossed the Elbe River in May of 1945, we sensed that the war was grinding down. The German soldiers we encountered were older men and Hitler Youth, just boys. Those youngsters were well-trained to fight to the bitter end, but when they were finally surrounded, they reverted to their childhood and began crying. I couldn't shoot a child crying.

Meanwhile, while we were driving inland to meet the Russians, we looked up one morning at daylight to see hundreds of German soldiers walking or riding bicycles and cars, all with their hands up. They didn't want to give up to the Russians, who had burned their homes and raped their mothers and daughters. The whole 21st German Army Group gave up to the 505th, as many as 5,000 at a time. We herded them into an open field, shaking them down to get weapons, grenades, and ammunition. We also took watches, swastika patches, iron crosses, some liquor, cigars and cigarettes for souvenirs. I took home a knife, some medals, and a patch. Generally we left them their pictures, rings and other personal items.

One strand of barbed wire was strung around the field. Those guys didn't want to go anywhere. The officers didn't want to mix with the enlisted men, so we segregated them as best we could.

One day, during all the confusion, our company commander called a group of us together. "I forgot to tell you," he said, "the war in Europe was over yesterday."

Soon, the older guys in our 505th and other regiments got to go home. We younger ones (I was 20) stayed for the Berlin occupation to relieve the 2nd Armored Division.

General Eisenhower had stopped outside the city limits to let the Russians take the German capital. Although the city was divided into four sections (the British sector, the French, Russian and American), the Russians thought they owned it.

All of our weapons were taken up, but they kept theirs. The German citizens left there were no threat. Most of their buildings were flattened, and they were weary from six years of war. I don't know of any skirmishes with Germans, only Russians.

Even though we weren't supposed to fraternize with the

Germans, my buddy Mooney Clay, like any 19 or 20-year-old, was naturally attracted to a particular one. He was walking across a bridge when a Russian soldier stopped them and mumbled something.

The girl, who could speak both languages and a little English, told Mooney that the soldier wanted her to go with him.

"No! You tell him no!" Mooney instructed.

All my buddy could understand was "Wha? Wha?" before the Red Army guy demanded again to take the girl, and she translated.

"You tell him you're not going anywhere with a Russian SOB!" Mooney shouted and threw the guy over the railing and into the water.

It was typical for a Russian to come into a nightclub and motion for a girl to come to him, which would start a big fight. They found out you couldn't push paratroopers and their girls around.

Personally, I had two encounters.

I'd never seen a Russian soldier before the day I walked up to a column of them. A kid, about 14, jumped down from a tank with a bottle of vodka and a water glass. He poured the glass half full and handed it to me. I took a drink and it burnt me all the way down to my stomach. He took that glass and chug-a-lugged the rest, while I was spitting up.

One day, a fellow paratrooper and I decided to check out the Russian sector. It seemed that there were more fine structures still standing in that area. We took a trolley that made a turnaround a short distance into the sector. We got off at the turnaround and began walking alone near a brick building. Suddenly, a sniper's bullets were hitting the building, showering brick dust on us. We got back on that trolley real quick.

It was "tough duty" in Berlin. We were issued white gloves and shoelaces. Our main duty was entertaining politicians. We held a parade every other day. About all we combat veterans did was play sports: football, basketball and baseball.

The black market was flourishing. The currency was Allied Invasion Marks, backed by the US Government. We could sell cartons of cigarettes for the equivalent of $125; a chocolate bar, $5; soap, $5 and a single cigar for $2, maybe $3.

The government got wise and said we could only send home the amount of our monthly pay. Some guys lost at gambling, so we would get them to send to our mothers the money we had earned on the black market.

Army officials then issued the warning, "If you get caught, we're going to ship you home."

Hell, that's what we wanted!

Easy Ducks
by
J. Marshall Burrows
Forsyth County, NC

On board a tanker, we got the word May 8th that the War in Europe was over. The ship's whistle blew, but there was no one but us to hear it, and that was about all the celebrating we did. At sea, we were headed for London with gasoline to supply our planes.

Some ships and subs didn't get the word as soon as we did. Three days later, when we entered the port, we saw a German sub in tow behind a small British Naval vessel.

A signalman in the Navy Armed Guard, I was assigned to the SS Chadd's Ford.

To protect merchant ships supplying our troops, the Navy generally put 20 to 25 men, including a crew of gunners, two signalmen and one officer per ship and installed armament, usually a 3" gun on the bow, a 5" on the stern and as many as four to eight 20 mm guns on each side.

Merchant ships, carrying vital supplies, were easy ducks for air or sub attacks. 1942 had been a horrible year before many of these ships were armed. More than a hundred had been sunk off the East Coast, where U-boats preyed on them.

Early on, some merchant ships had only "Quaker guns," telephone poles.

In the spring of '43, I was 20, married with a child on the way, and my number had come up. I chose the Navy because I didn't want to go in the Army. I was a "selective volunteer," and after boot camp at Bainbridge and signalman training in Connecticut, I reported at the Armed Guard Center in New York City, where I was assigned to an old rust pot freighter built in 1918, a Hog Island vessel.

The SS Beauregard carried general freight such as ammunition, foodstuffs and 55-gallon drums of gasoline in the hold, tanks and trucks on deck. The fastest it could go was nine knots.

We picked up our first load in Boston and joined the main convoy, about 80 ships, which formed in Halifax, Nova Scotia.

From there, we headed for the UK on the northern route. That trip was horrendous. My first time at sea, we were engulfed in dense fog close to three weeks.

To keep in the convoy and avoid collisions during the daytime, the ship sounded its whistle every two minutes. A paravane was dragged about 500 feet behind the stern, causing water to spray up. At night, we burned a cargo cluster of lights on our stern.

Our next trip was to Scotland, then, a few days after D-Day, across the English Channel toward Omaha Beach, where we would anchor while the supplies were unloaded onto little crafts that hurried to shore and back again like bees.

As we approached the anchorage, the shore station routinely signaled by flashing light, "What ship?" I replied appropriately. The next question was, "Are you MT?"

From the signal bridge, I yelled the message down to the Captain, who said, "Hell, no. Tell him we are loaded."

I signaled back, "We are loaded."

The station replied, "Are you Military Transport?"

I don't know about the Skipper, but was my face ever red!

A third of the way back to the States, we had an engine breakdown and had to drop out of the convoy and head for the Azores, where we waited 30 days for an engine part to be flown in.

From there, we went alone to Cuba to pick up a load of raw sugar for Philadelphia.

I'd had enough, so I went to the Armed Guard Center to get another assignment.

The SS Chadd's Ford, named for a town in

Marshall Burrows aboard the SS Beauregard. January, 1944.

275

eastern Pennsylvania made famous during the Revolutionary War, was a brand new T-2 tanker which cruised at 15 knots.

On the shakedown cruise, we went to Texas to get aviation gasoline and deck cargo before picking up a convoy to Southampton.

As we prepared to dock, we saw that a submarine had been working in that area. Two ships had been sunk right outside the harbor. Their masts were sticking up in the shallow water, and destroyer escorts were trying to "do in" the sub.

Gasoline transports were a favorite target of German subs. We were all aware of that, as we made six more trips within six months. The crew joked that we should have parachutes instead of life vests.

A shipmate had survived the Murmansk Run to supply Russian troops by going around the northern tip of Norway, where German ships were in control.

The Murmansk Run was considered an assignment to death. If ten ships were sent, usually only three got through. If a freighter got torpedoed, a seaman might last 30 minutes in the frigid water, even in his rubber suit.

My friend's ship was sunk on the way back, but he was one of the fortunate few.

After V-E Day, we were immediately sent to Texas for more aviation fuel to be delivered to the Pacific by way of the Panama Canal.

As our ship was approaching anchorage off Okinawa, she headed toward another vessel which had a small craft tied alongside. I watched, waiting for the crash.

Our bow smashed into the little boat, breaking it in two. Both ends slipped into the water. The other tanker was nudged but not damaged. The Chadd's Ford was unscathed.

Without a good merchant fleet supplying our troops, we may not have won the war.

During those four years, 144,970 Armed Guards served on 6,236 ships of which 710 were sunk. We lost 1,810 men. The 280,000 merchant seamen lost approximately 6,850.

On V-J Day, we were in the middle of the Pacific, headed toward the States. Once again, we blew the whistle in celebration, but no one was around to hear it.

A few days after that, we dumped our ammunition. It was no longer needed.

Beginning at the End of the War
by
Katherine Lowe Haynes
Gaston County, NC

As our troop ship was docking in Le Havre, France, French civilians and US military personnel were going crazy—screaming and hollering and shouting! The war was over the very day we were arriving for overseas duty!

Fifty of us WACs (Women's Army Corps) along with the sailors and Merchant Marines on the ship were happy, too, but we women got rushed off and into trucks headed for our camp, so we couldn't celebrate much.

Katherine Lowe on a ship en route to Germany via France. August, 1945.

Actually, we didn't know where we were headed until we got there. We had been issued summer clothing and mosquito netting, but two days before sailing from Norfolk, we were reissued winter uniforms. France, however, was not our ultimate destination.

During our two-week crossing, we had had a few scares of possible submarine sightings.

We had fire drills all the time, but once we got as far as lining up for the lifeboats. I knew how to scramble down rope ladders over the side and kick hard to get away, but I was glad the emergency was only a fire somewhere below deck that was quickly contained.

At the camp of nothing but pup tents and cots, just about everybody was drinking. Even the guys on guard duty had tin cups of beer. I didn't drink, but after a guard showed me the latrine, guarded me while I was there and loaned me his quilt, I got my cup filled and took it to him. The officers in charge just looked the other way.

Until another ship came in, most of the guys there were in communications. All of us ladies were sent to Frankfurt about two weeks later, but I was the only CB (Cooks and Bakers). The others were nurses or clerks, except my superior officer, Capt. Murphy.

The captain, who was in charge of all the WAC clerks and CBs, was an old Southern lady. She loved to hear me play "Down in the Valley" on my guitar. Whenever I was supposed to do KP duty, she'd say, "Lowe's got to play her guitar." She gave me a pass whenever I asked for one, but I returned the favor. Whenever she had a date, I'd cook a meal and deliver it to her and then she'd serve it like she was the one who prepared it.

At Frankfurt, we were in a compound, surrounded by barbed wire, almost like a town. Of course, there were barracks and a mess hall (where I worked 24-hour shifts), and a barber shop, dry cleaners and service club. At the PX, we could get a carton of cigarettes and a bottle of liquor once a month. I did not drink or smoke, but my dates liked the liquor, and when we WACs traveled, I got a lot of things done (like getting someone to carry my luggage) with those cigarettes.

Although I was trained as a CB, I only cooked as a volunteer. Middle-aged German women, who spoke English, did all the cooking. They were grateful, not hateful, and seemed glad to have the job and food to take home. Not only were they good cooks, they were clean as pins.

The German people were pitiful. Their homes were destroyed and they had no work, no money, no nothing. Sometimes, when we had extra food, they would line up with pans to get it. I saw some crawl back under the debris when they were finished.

At night, after everyone had been fed, some of us hung around the mess hall, played music, danced and partied with some "regulars." A piano and accordion were there, and I had my guitar.

Periodically, I had to go to a warehouse outside the compound to get the rations. Usually, an Army driver took me in his truck. One time, though, a German civilian was my driver. He started to take a different route. I couldn't speak his language, but I said "No!"

He didn't stop or change, so I pulled the gun I carried in my pocket and pointed it at him. "No," I said again and showed him the right way. After that, I insisted on a military driver.

When I worked as a waitress in Gastonia, a friend and I had gone over to the post office on a whim. "I want to join the Army to get to travel, have some fun," I told her. While I was filling out the

Army application, a WAVE kept hollering at me, so I filled out her forms, too, but the Army got me first.

Well, travel I did, when we had time off, to Paris and Switzerland, where my friends and I tried the clubs and did some shopping. Most of the people were friendly, but I couldn't get over how people, men and women, "messed" or "peed" in the street, just right on the curb!

As for having fun—when we got passes, we did! One night, I had on my "whites" when a big truck drove up, and two GIs said, "Let's go to a dance."

I told them I had worked 24 hours and was tired, but they kept saying "please" and telling me about the opening of a new club. I agreed, but only if I could go to my place and take a shower. They waited while I put on my only civilian clothes, a dress I had dyed red. What I didn't know was that there were 15 GIs in the back of the truck, and the club was nearly 100 miles away! Other girls, Germans and Americans, had been invited, but none came. So they nearly danced me to death! They were all getting high, and they put me up on the bar and tried to get me to drink.

About that time, their captain came over and said, "I'm sending you home in my staff car."

He did, and when I got back to the compound gate, the MP wanted to know why I had no pass. I told him it was a spur-of-the-moment thing, and that he'd better not wake up Capt. Murphy at that hour in the morning. It worked.

While in Europe, I saw a few celebrities, as USO people ate in our mess hall. Carol Lombard and John Payne were there to do a show. I jitterbugged with Mickey Rooney, and I kissed General Dwight Eisenhower's bald head. I was sitting right behind him at a football game, when someone said it was his birthday. When Ike ran for President, I wished I had a picture of me kissing him.

I was really enjoying dating, but I took a ring from a guy named David. He was a lieutenant, and we weren't supposed to fraternize. David was overseeing a prison camp in another town outside of Frankfurt, so I was at a dance with somebody else, when he came over to see me. When I tried to give the ring back, he wouldn't take it and said he wanted me to write him. I never did. Not long after that, I was en route to the States in a hospital ship.

My overseas experience began and ended with a celebration. Soon after arriving in New York Harbor, we were invited to march in New York's Easter Parade.

"The Lucky Herndon"
by
A.L. Blackwood
Cherokee County, SC

Our ship, the USS Herndon, was anchored outside of Manila when an alarm sounded, and the captain made an announcement that the war was over. Joyous ourselves, we could hear sirens, church bells, firecrackers and people shouting from the capital of the Philippines.

We knew after the bomb exploded at Nagasaki that the Japanese were seeking some honorable way out. They had radioed a message to Manila to arrange for peace and asked for surrender terms. I was one of the fortunate ones to know this, because my daily work station was on the bridge near the quartermaster hut. I was in audible contact with the captain and other officers on the bridge, as I relayed whatever obstacles the lookouts in charge of that watch would report.

I saw the Japanese diplomats' plane similar to a DC-3, painted white and escorted by two of our P-38s, come in over the harbor. The diplomats were transferred to helicopters, which took them to the the USS Missouri, where the negotiating team signed surrender documents on September 2.

I had been in the Navy since November 30, 1943, after a deferment to play football at Gaffney High. Following stateside duty, I was attached to the USS Raymon W. Herndon, a new ship named for a Walterboro, South Carolina, Marine, who had been mortally wounded in the Solomon Islands. He had asked the others to pack enough ammunition around him so that he could keep shooting, while his fellow Marines escaped. The Herndon was a high speed transport converted to carry additional troops.

She soon was known as the "The Lucky Herndon." While escorting a convoy near the Philippines, we fired on ten low-flying Japanese planes with no losses. Approaching Wake Island while the Marines were battling to control it, we took care of the subs until the Air Corps brought in blimps. Our ship was in the first convoy, and all the ships escaped casualties.

During our next mission at the island of Kerama Retto, held by the Japanese, the Navy bombarded the island while the Marines took it over. We were patrolling the area.

We got to Okinawa on March 26, 1945 to prepare for the invasion on April 1. The Herndon dropped off Underwater Demolition Team #16 to set underwater charges near the coast. Two to three hours later, I watched how those expert swimmers lined up, 15 to 20 feet apart and locked hands. A man on a rubber life raft from our ship stuck his arm out and rolled them one-by-one into the raft, a fascinating feat.

On the day before the invasion, when they set off the charges, the entire island looked as though it was coming out of the water with explosions everywhere.

It took 82 days to secure Okinawa. The Herndon was on station 70 of those 82 days, with only a brief R & R on the tiny island Mog Mog across from Ulithi in the Caroline Islands. The rest of the time, we were being attacked by planes and subs.

Several days, we were at our battle stations 20 to 23 hours a day. The Herndon was dropping "ash cans" (depth charges) to destroy submarines. We sank two. The Navy had set up a perimeter of ships encircling the island. We would stay in the outer ring for a certain amount of time and then switch positions. Ships were being damaged or sunk all around us.

The Japanese were so desperate that they sent families out in small boats to gain sympathy and access by feigning hunger. They would beg sailors to throw food scraps overboard for them. Meanwhile, one would be attaching plastic explosives to the hull, which they would set off later by remote control.

Richard Hansel, radioman, and Larry Blackwood, operator of gun 42, on the USS Herndon. Spring, 1945.

We had been forewarned, so when a little boat came alongside the Herndon, we were not fooled. The "family" was a man and a woman holding a small baby. They were rubbing their stomachs. We warned them not to come near, then our 20 mm. machine gun ripped their boat apart. On April 6, between 300 and 400 kamikazes zoomed in on our perimeter. One headed straight for us bow to stern. I was the director operator of gun 42, which had a twin 40 mm cannon. When my radioman said the kamikaze was in range, I commenced firing until it exploded and crashed into the ocean instead of the Herndon. Once again, we were lucky.

But our luck, we knew, would run out. After more convoy duty, we were sent to the Philippines for reassignment to a mission devised by the commandant of underwater demolition teams (UDT). The OSS had acquired information from an engineer from Great Britain who had designed a tunnel for the Japanese in 1939. The tunnel was used to transport ammunition under the bay from Honshu to nearby Kyushu. Bombing could not stop the flow of supplies, so we were expected to go into a submarine base to transport UDT #15 to blow it up. When our captain recognized it as a suicide mission, he was told that we could get our medals posthumously.

Our V-J Day joy was indescribable.

As soon as the treaty was signed, we were sent to Jensen, a small town in the south of Korea off the China Sea, to be their contact with the outside world through our radio system. They had no way to communicate, and they needed everything, especially food. The Japs had wiped them out. We stayed until the Army Quartermasters could build a radio tower.

Then we were sent back to the Philippines to start a shuttle service. We received orders to pick up four LSTs in Manila and escort them to the Subic Bay area, where we would pick up six more LSTs. Those round-bottomed boats normally carried a crew of 50 to 60 each. On this mission, 1000 Japanese POWs were to be transported to Sasebo, Japan. When we arrived at that destination, two LSTs would tie up to a dock and disembark the prisoners. The men would enter a long barracks as POWs and come out as civilians, then the next two LSTs would do the same until all the prisoners were unloaded. We made more pick ups in the Lingayen Gulf and at Pusan, escorting a total of 30,000 POWs to Sasebo.

Next, we went to Tsingtao. While there, work crews came aboard. Chinese men would offer to clean the bilge, scrub decks, whatever. As a boatswain mate 2nd class, my duty, along with others on the deck force, was to keep the ship clean. We figured for a couple of dollars, we could get the ship clean from top to bottom, so we could goof off. Our pay, by the way, after the allotment was taken out, was what we called "$21 a day once a month."

By the end of March, 1946, I was released from the Herndon in Shanghai, China, and hitched a ride on a returning ship.

Because of the lasting friendships established on "The Lucky Herndon," *I was the lucky one.*

Flying from Tinian
by
Howard T. Gilchrist
Durham County, NC

Even just before V-J Day, those of us at Tinian Island did not realize that the war would soon be over.

The government had built what looked like a mile of hospital buildings on Tinian and brought in 500 nurses to staff them. Our thoughts were toward an invasion of Japan, which would have resulted in terrible loss of life and injuries —hence, the hospitals.

We had seen the Bockscar and Enola Gay B-29 planes down in a segregated area on the North Field and noticed other elite crews and planes. But no one else from the island could socialize with them. We thought them to be a special photographic outfit with stripped down B-29s to take our strike photos.

The radar man on our crew had been down at the field and came back to the quonset hut to say he had seen "the damnest bomb" being loaded into what must have been the Enola Gay. A pit had been dug, the bomb lowered into the pit, then the plane backed over the pit so that the bomb could be hoisted into the bomb bay.

Our B-29s had two bomb bays, so I think the Enola Gay had been specially renovated to take the huge bomb.

We soon heard about the dropping of the atomic bombs, but that was the first time we knew that anything like that existed. It did give the Japanese a reason to save face and surrender. Thousands and thousands of lives, both American and Japanese, were saved by this action.

After I enlisted in the Army Air Corps in Durham during my junior year at Duke University in 1942, I took my flight training at Bennettsville and Sumter, South Carolina and my advanced training in Albany, Georgia. At Maxwell Field in Montgomery, I learned to fly B-24s and then B-29s. Finally, in June, 1945, my buddy Bill Chatlos and I were sent on a B-29 replacement crew to Tinian in the Mariana Islands.

We flew six regular 3000-mile missions before the war was declared over.

Undoubtedly our worst flight was our 4th bombing mission which began August 1, 1945. Nagaoka, Japan was our target.

We went in at 9,000 feet and were approaching a violent up-draft and smoke column from the already-burning city. When our incendiary bombs were dropped, the plane was sucked into the smoke column like a leaf in a tornado. Some of the unbuckled crew bounced against the walls, painfully hitting the metal edges of the fuselage. We were blown out at about 12,000 feet, and I took a heading out to sea. The bomb bays were stuck open, and several bombs were hung up in the racks. Though cut and bleeding, the navigator and bombardier pried out the bombs with screwdrivers. Two Japanese fighters circled us but never fired a shot. As five of our crew were injured, we elected to bypass a gas stop at Iwo Jima. About 100 miles out from Tinian,

1st Lt. Howard Gilchrist in front of quonset hut. Tinian. Summer, 1945.

though, fuel was at a premium. Despite transferring fuel from one tank to another, the engines began to quit as we nosed down near our destination.

As co-pilot, I noted that the outboard engine on my side was at full power, the only one pulling us toward the island. It made the wing come up, and full opposite controls would not bring it down. The whole crew was praying. I watched as we flew over the cliff and chopped the engine. The wings leveled, and we hit the runway, bouncing as high as a barn. All engines were out, but there wasn't an atheist in the entire crew!

After the atomic bombs were dropped, we flew two more missions: one to Yawata and one to the Marafu Railroad Yards, which I believe was the last official US bombing mission.

On V-J Day, we killed a few drinks in celebration at our homemade officers club. But we immediately began flying missions to Japan. This time, the bomb bays were full of supplies for prisoners of war. We dropped food, clothing, medicines and more on pallets with parachutes attached. But first, we had to find the camps. Most were like old wild-West log stockades in mountain valleys far from towns. After our drops, we did some sightseeing.

Once, we flew over Hiroshima at a very low level. It looked like a hayfield, with one structure of steel and concrete that no longer resembled a building.

My final overseas flight was in a B-29 with a new engine and extra bomb bay gas tanks—a 19-hour sunset mission to return 14 battle-weary men to the place where it all started: Pearl Harbor.

Subdued Celebration
by
Velma Eller Washington
Wilkes/Mecklenburg Counties, NC

On V-J Day, there was no jumping or hugging in my ward at Atlanta's Lawson General Hospital—just a sigh of relief. An Army nurse, I was assigned to a paraplegic ward.

My experience showed the uselessness of war and made me wonder, why can't mankind live in peace?

From a Wilkes County farm family, I had trained at Presbyterian Hospital in Charlotte, home of the 38th Evac Group. It took the death of my brother, Jacob A. Eller of the 29th Infantry Division, who was killed on November 19, 1944, to urge me to join the Army Nurse Corps.

My first day on ward duty at Lawson was somewhat trying. I saw at least 30 men who had lost a part or all of both legs. There was not a whole leg in that group. Then I was hit with a dilemma —how was I going to bathe the black men in beds three and four? I was not a racist—in fact, the few blacks I knew in Wilkes County were neighbors and some were friends.

As a child, I could never understand why mothers allowed black women to tend their children and yet would not sit with them anywhere. Even so, I had never bathed a black man, and I was uncomfortable at first.

That day, I also visited other parts of this sprawling temporary hospital, built hurriedly as the war wore on. I saw arm amputees in a dining room, learning to use their new prostheses. They were doing pretty well, too.

Lawson General was a rehabilitation hospital, so most of the men had been transferred there for therapy. Sincere efforts were made to get these fellows back to the real world. Wards were built with wide doors and ramps on the sunny side, making any outside activity welcome and really a part of their therapy.

Soon, I became oriented to Army nursing and the need for rehabilitating those who had lost so much. One of the wards I served had all officers with various impairments. I learned very quickly that, no matter how many colonels were there, I, a second lieutenant, was still boss. I made my authority known when I walked into their bathroom one day, and under the old bathtub with feet was a bunch of liquor bottles. I returned and called them to attention. "I am disappointed in you as officers," I said. "I want those bottles gone, and I mean gone by today."

They complied, but I never saw where they put them.

Early in October, 1945, my boyfriend, Willis Washington, called me when he arrived in Newport News. He said he would spend a couple of days with me before returning to his family at Honea Path, South Carolina.

And so my happiest day was not V-J Day, but my wedding day: November 15, 1945. We were married at a friend's home in Atlanta. Before I left, some of my patients presented me with what appeared to be a pair of old bloomers. In one leg was an International Sterling Prelude plate; in the other, a beautiful silver fruit bowl with my new initial—still treasures.

A Sweet Reaction
by
Jean Beaty Settle
Iredell County, NC

I wore my "Remember Pearl Harbor" scarf and sang songs like "Anchors Aweigh" and the Marine hymn. At school, I bought stamps for war bonds, even though my grandmother, who gave us money, didn't want me to spend it that way.

An elementary student at Cool Spring School, I watched the guys on maneuvers outside the school yard throw slips of paper with their addresses on them, but I wasn't one of the girls who raced to pick them up. Only the senior high girls did that.

I did collect old pots and pans, had a Victory garden and used to point out a rock near the road that had a natural "V" on it.

Our family was self-sufficient, except for sugar, which was also rationed. We tried saccharin tablets, a poor substitute. I bit into one and, to this day, I'll never try another.

On August 15, 1945, I was walking on Highway 64 when a car slowed down and somebody yelled out the window, "The war is over!" I went right home and ate some brown sugar.

Too Much Celebrating!
by
D. Kermit Cloniger
Lincoln/Guilford Counties, NC

When we received the V-J Day dispatch at the Naval Air Station in Hitchcock, Texas, we sent word that there would be open bars in the service clubs. Officers got whatever they wanted. Enlisted men couldn't get liquor, but they had very strong beer. Nearly everyone was drinking.

As I was the Executive Officer, I wasn't and the chaplain wasn't. We went to the chapel to give thanks but were the only ones to show up. Later, a man whom I have never seen take a drink had become so intoxicated that he fell and got a bad head injury.

I could not find a sober corpsman to help him!

Finally, I had to send the guy to a Marine hospital in Galveston to get him sewn up.

Wounded in the Heart
by
Willie A. Neal
Mecklenburg County, NC

Victory over Japan! That meant I would see my mother, my family again. But my 375th Engineer Regiment was headed for the Philippines on the USS Gordon.

We had seen plenty of action, the first in 1943 in St. Austell, England, before we ever confronted the Germans. A race riot! The military and the townspeople had established a dance hall with a black night and a white night.

The 29th Division wanted to horn in on our night.

After training and then temporary duty unloading ammunition from ships, we headed for Normandy, a month and a half past D-Day. Guides kept us out of the Omaha Beach mine fields, and we got to St. Lô in time to see it blow. Our Air Force had dropped leaflets, telling people to leave, but the Germans machine-gunned anyone who tried. When the bombs dropped, the smell of burning flesh was more horrible than anything I've ever experienced.

Though trained as a demolitions expert, I became a messenger between my outfit and Army headquarters, with a truck to pick up mail and supplies. A T/5 (technician), I also became a dispatcher for trucks, mail clerk, and bugler, when I wasn't setting mines, deactivating them or dealing with booby traps. The 375th Engineer Regiment served as support for the 85th "Rail Splitters" Division.

Much of the time in Europe, it was the same thing over and over. We got bombed and strafed. Those 88s were vicious guns. As long as we could hear them, we could try to get out of the way. Near the Ruhr River, there was so much shelling that, if we were still alive, we knew God was in our corner. Those Germans knew how to make good guns. And their Tiger tanks far surpassed our Sherman tanks with little guns.

At Linden, Germany, we got strafed before sunrise and after sunset. The German equivalent of a .50 caliber bullet shot the heel off my boot. It could have been my head! We were trying to keep lines of communication open so the 85th could get supplies. Before we could cross the Ruhr, Von Rundstedt broke through our lines, and we were ordered to go to Belgium. Some personnel had to be picked up and taken to Gembloux, our rendezvous point. I was always the one sent for that kind of job, because, as dispatcher, I could read a terrain map.

Soon after Christmas, 1944, we were in Liège, Belgium, known as "buzz bomb alley." At least we could hear and see those V1 rockets as they were coming in on us. Back in Linden on the way to Wegberg, the explosive pressure from a buzz bomb picked me up and threw me 50 feet. I landed on my head.

Next, we were at Aachen, Germany, where our artillery blew it off the map. In Kohlscheid, the strafing was as bad as it could be, but I didn't get hurt. That's where I saw the new German jets chasing after P-47s. They were twice as fast as our planes but couldn't maneuver as well. A P-38 out-maneuvered one and drove it into the ground. It completely disappeared!

At Rheinhausen, we built a bridge across the Rhine and went

to Duisburg. We were supposed to go on to Berlin, when we were told to back off so the Russians could go in first. Soon after that, we were sent to Saint-Victoret, France, a staging area. The war in Europe had ended.

What hurt me the most over there was to see little children and old people walking on ice with bags on their feet coming through our lines trying to get away from hostilities. They had walked out of their homes in Krefeld, leaving almost everything. Some of the elderly people were pulling carts like donkeys. All this suffering and misery—and ours—caused by power-hungry people, who didn't care who they hurt, as long as they got power.

Around Rheinhausen, we saw children, ages 3 to 5, using open tin cans to dig in the garbage for food. I was supposed to get court-martialed for what I did, but I still had food in my mess kit, so I put it into their cans. Others saw me, but no one turned me in.

Racism was always a problem, although we were treated better by people from other countries than our own. General Eisenhower helped quite a bit. He authorized the formation of a black infantry division, the 88th "Bearcats." Captain Matthew J. Pacifico from Al Capone's Cicero, Illinois, (who, like all officers except one then, was white) wouldn't let me join it. I was his conscience. Before he tried something on the troops, he'd sound me out. I never was proactive, but I gave an answer. I never would take rank because I knew he'd bust me. I'd insult him sometimes.

Even after all we had experienced, I was surprised by what happened after we got to the Philippines. We were bivouacked at St. Angeles (now known as Angeles, although a recent volcano covered it up). We had duties, but there were no hostilities until I heard someone yell "Get down! Get down!" Bullets were sailing over our heads and our pup tents. Another race riot!

I don't know how it started. There were always smart alecks on both sides, but hostilities had never reached that level. All of us were trained killers. When the colonel tried to stop them by persuasion and couldn't, he opened up his .30 caliber machine gun. Bullets are democratic, but everyone hit the ground. End of riot.

In late December, 1945, we arrived at Angel Island, California. For the first time in two years we had decent food: steaks, pork chops, fresh eggs, milk, pies. A sign over the door of the mess hall said "Take all you want. Eat all you take."

From California, many of us rode a troop train through Texas to the Southeast. When we got into Louisiana, they stopped the train and made us change cars until we were all segregated. In

Mississippi, they made us pull the shades down and keep them down through Alabama. Not until Georgia could we raise them.

Back at Fort Bragg, I couldn't get discharged until two days after Christmas. I had earned four campaign ribbons, but never got the fourth one. It didn't matter. The happiest day in my life was when I saw my mother and my family again.

But disappointment followed. Within a week after I got home to Charlotte, reality set in: the same old prejudices as when I left. Jobs weren't available, even if you were well qualified. No one wanted to deal with you if you were black. Nothing was available except in freight, landscaping or automotive repairs. I finally got a job at Speas, a vinegar plant, and later at Sykes on South Mint and on the loading dock of Central Motor Lines at 65 cents an hour.

After six months of frustration, I moved to New York to live with my sister, marry my high school sweetheart and work for Con Edison.

I tried not to be bitter.

Standing:
Itolia Cowan
Willie A. Neal
Victor Mardenborough

Seated:
Floyd Griffin
of the 375th Engineer
Regiment. England.
Spring, 1944.

How That War Changed Us Forever

Personal lives and family life were drastically affected, of course, by the physical and psychological injuries as well as the deaths of those who served in the military.

Speedy war marriages did not always work out, causing more divorces than the country had ever seen. Many men suffered from epidemics of VD; many women were devastated by the love'em-and-leave'em syndrome. On the other hand, people met wonderfully compatible spouses they never would have known were it not for the massive movement of men and women at home and abroad.

Despite all the efforts of the New Deal, the Great Depression finally ended when the war started, as males and females were needed for defense jobs and the military. Salaries soared to meet demands.

Women who, in the past, had been expected to stay home or were accepted only for certain types of jobs, suddenly were proving to themselves and the world that they were capable of many untried tasks.

African-Americans and the disabled (derided as "cripples") also got unexpected opportunities to display their capabilities.

Food production required new machinery and techniques, when farm laborers went to war. The unsatisfactory share-cropping system made worse by the Depression virtually disappeared after worldly soldiers returned with better skills for employment. Most of those who left the farms never returned. Cities and towns grew rapidly.

Probably the most dramatic changes in lifestyle came about because of the GI Bill. Men and women who had never aspired to get a higher education could attend college, compliments of the US Government.

Patriotism was at an all-time peak during the war, but love of God, country and high moral values caused many Americans to declare the '50s "the best of times."

New Horizons and a New Opportunity
by
Leroy ("Pop") Miller
Rowan County, NC

World War II was one of the highlights of my 83 years. My tour of duty made a man out of me. I felt I could do anything anyone else could do.

My grandparents on both sides were slaves. I knew my father's father. He couldn't read or write. My daddy got to the 4th or 5th grade; my mother, about the same. Daddy was a blacksmith's helper for the Southern Railroad in the Spencer Shops. We (four boys and six girls) were also sharecroppers for Mr. Link, who owned a Salisbury store and had 40 acres of cotton.

I plowed and hoed and picked cotton, when we were getting eight and nine cents per pound for a bale and our family got only one third of the profit.

Our cotton field was next to Livingstone College's farm. The college president, Dr. Trent, sometimes came out to exercise his horse. He'd put a harness on him, hop into a two-wheeled sulky and get him to do some high-step trotting up and down the road. President Trent was always dressed up in what we thought were Sunday clothes.

Sometimes, he's stop and tell Daddy, "Brother Miller, you're raising them right. You're teaching them how to work."

But Daddy told us, "When you get an education, you can wear Sunday clothes every day."

Education became our goal. Out of the ten of us, five were math majors. I was the dumbest. I was the only Miller who didn't lead his class at Salisbury's J. C. Price High School.

I finished NC A&T with a BS on a Friday in 1942 and was sworn into service on Saturday.

The war experience took me to places I never would have gone: London, Paris, Versailles, Leeds and Charleroi. In fact, I never would have been to Europe—and I also got to see a lot of the United States: Florida, Georgia, Kansas City, Seattle. It taught me to be methodical, and I learned how to meet people—and get along.

I cried when I got discharged. We were supposed to have R & R in Switzerland, and I was going to have to leave my "brothers." But then, I was happy to get home.

When I got out of service, I was offered one of two teaching jobs in Charlotte: at Second Ward or West Charlotte High School, but Assistant Superintendent Elmer Garinger told me, "You've got the GI Bill. You can get your advanced degree."

I told him I'd like to go to Carolina or NC State, but they didn't take blacks there then. So he called Dr. Fretwell, at NYU, where he had gotten his doctorate. Dr. Fretwell suggested the University of Minnesota or Pennsylvania State.

I chose Penn State to study under Dr. John Freese, the father of industrial education. It was the right place for me. They even had left-handed desks right in front of the professor.

When I returned to North Carolina, I went to West Charlotte, where I taught for 18 years and was assistant principal for eight. After that, I was named principal at Carmel Junior High School for a year and a half before I became principal of East High School.

God has been good to me.

A Bail-Out
by
Lester (Les) Roark
Cleveland County, NC

Since military conflict seemed inevitable, World War II came at a good time for our family.

The four youngest of eight Roark boys "scratched and grabbled" through the Great Depression, then struggled for survival through the readjustment years.

I was the youngest, born in 1924, when our family moved to a cotton farm near Grover in south Cleveland County. My next three brothers, in age, were Sidney, born in 1918, Hubert, 1916 and Broadus, 1914.

Economic conditions throughout my first 18 years were stressful. An older brother, Reece (1910), had died in infancy; my oldest brother, Glenn (1906), died in a Model T wreck in 1931. In 1933, my father, Alex (1882), died. In 1936, the Federal Land Bank foreclosed on our farm loan. Two older brothers, Coley (1912) and Wayne (1909), then found jobs in cotton mills and left the farm, got married and started families. Broadus—we called him Broad—oldest of the four remaining, entered the Army at age 22.

We three youngest then moved to Grover with our mother in late 1936. Hubert and Sid got jobs in the mill. I worked at odd jobs and finished high school in 1942. Smack in the middle of all this,

Uncle Sam was providing relief. Broad, home on furlough, showed good health and a happy disposition.

The military, at around $50 a month, plus room and board, clothing and medical care, showed a brighter future. Hubert enlisted in the Army in 1940; Sid went in 1942, both serving in the infantry.

After several months at Glenn L. Martin, a defense plant in Baltimore, I got the President's greeting and entered the US Army Air Corps in February of 1943. (At the end of World War II, this became the US Air Force.) As the only adult male at home with a widowed mother, I could have gotten a deferment, if requested. With three brothers in service, I chose to follow.

Growing up on a farm with no electricity or plumbing, we lived pretty much as primitives. Health care was limited to childhood vaccinations at school and patent medicines for minor ailments. We had no dental check-ups and no brushing of teeth. The Army's care and attention changed all of that, in a very positive way.

The four of us went in different directions, all overseas at one time or another. Our widowed mother was home alone, wondering, hoping, praying and without financial resources. Each of us sent a small pittance home as available. Community churches, neighbors and relatives pitched in to assist in such circumstances. I have never known the level of patriotic zeal in this nation to be higher.

On March 6, 1945, just before I left for overseas, I got word that my brother, Broad, was killed in combat. Sid had just arrived home from Europe, where he served in 1944 and early 1945 in the Battle of the Bulge. He was the only one at home to comfort and provide for our mother.

After serving as a gunner and gunnery instructor with the 8th Air Force in England in early 1945, I returned home in late June of that year. Following a 30-day furlough, I ended up in Clovis, New Mexico, en route to the Pacific Theater for duty with another bomber group there. The Big Bombs were dropped, our troop movements were halted and I was discharged in February of 1946.

By that time Sid and Hubert were out of the service. Hubert was married and Sid was "courting." After trying their hands at civilian life for a few months, both re-enlisted and were assigned to the US Air Force, each with the rank and credits previously held. Neither had graduated from high school, but, with government assistance, and special courses, earned their diplomas. They both advanced in rank and pay and retired with a combined total of 52 years of active service.

The last "get together" of the Roark family. Front (l to r): Broadus, Coley, Wayne. Second row: Hubert, Lester, Sidney. Back: Margaret Earle Roark, their mother. Grover, NC. Summer, 1940.

My three brothers had all been in close quarters combat situations. I only flew some photographic and surveillance missions. The only time I thought of myself "in harm's way" was flying home in an old war-weary B-17 Flying Fortress over the big Atlantic with one engine gone and no land in sight. With 20 men on board and a bomb bay filled with luggage and equipment, we were literally "coming in on a wing and a prayer." We made it.

Yes, my life was changed forever and for the good—things like dental care. The government authorized and paid for extensive dental work started, but not finished, when I was discharged.

Although four years of college tuition was available, I was unable to take it. I was the only one at home, and my mother was, in reality, penniless and unable to work. I had $20 a week from the government as "mustering out" money for awhile, but found employment, instead, to support the household. I got the GI assistance I needed to take a correspondence course in creative writing. With those modest credentials, I obtained a job as a reporter for a small hometown bi-weekly paper. Two years later, I was managing editor.

With that, I gained an interest in public affairs and political activities. From there, I was elected to a seat on the Shelby City Council and served 22 years, the last four as Mayor of our city.

I can truthfully say, that the Great Depression "wiped us out," but that Uncle Sam's military "bailed us out."

As we mourned the loss of a brother, who left behind a wife and a four-month-old son, we survivors felt an abiding love for country and a deep commitment to it—at home or abroad.

From Farm to Furniture
by
Fred C. Agner
Edgefield County, SC

At the end of the war in 1945, I was glad to come home to Modoc, South Carolina, and my dad was thrilled to death to see me. When I left, I was close to my family, but when I came back, I couldn't stay on the farm. It was too quiet.

I had no education. The only things I knew how to do was grow corn, pick cotton, plow with mules and raise hogs, chickens and cows. My father, a widower who had been gassed during World War I, and my grandfather were both farmers. If they expected me to continue the tradition, I wouldn't have.

When I left to go into the military in 1940, the Depression was still affecting farmers. When I returned, farm life was not much better. We had no electricity and no running water.

My uncle from Greenwood was tuning pianos in Concord, North Carolina, so I went to see him. While I was visiting, he got me to help clean piano keys.

After a couple of weeks, the owners of Sprott Brothers talked me into delivering furniture and pianos. That began my career in the furniture business, from delivering to sales to management: from Sprott Brothers to Woodlawn, Bridges, Maxwell and Heilig-Meyers, as one company bought out another. With promotions, we moved to Charlotte, Winston-Salem and back to Charlotte.

Did I miss farming? Not at all. The furniture industry educated me, provided a good income and, as incentives, gave me trips overseas. I'm glad I made the change.

Oh, yes, and I met my wife on a mattress.

She bought it, and I started calling her for a date. Louise finally accepted, but she's still mad at me for not giving her a discount on that mattress.

Another Direction
by
Ralph H. Lawson, Sr.
Union County, SC

Upon my discharge from the Naval Service, I returned to college to complete my education. My intentions were to get a BS degree from Newberry College and then attend law school at the University of South Carolina.

During my studies at Newberry College, I began to have doubts about becoming a lawyer. I was also having nightmares more frequently about fighting the war. I had come close to death on three separate occasions and began questioning why God spared me.

After many talks with my pastor, E. P. Bell of Buffalo Methodist Church in Buffalo, South Carolina, I was convinced to enter the ministry of the Methodist Church. But I had taken only six hours in religion at Newberry.

The GI Bill paid for my classes at Newberry, but when I enrolled in Wofford College, a Methodist school, I had to work at Excelsior Mill in Union (28 miles from Spartanburg) from 3 to 11 p.m. My junior year, I was invited to supply preach at Pacolet Methodist Church, although I still worked at Excelsior and went to school full time. During my senior year, the church asked me to be their full time pastor. When I received my BA degree in religion and philosophy, I graduated fifth in my class. My church allowed me to attend Emory University, where I received a BD degree, and later, a Masters in sociology.

I never really had peace of mind until I accepted the call to the ministry. After 35 years, I retired.

A Teacher? Not Me!
by
Wilson V. Eagleson
Durham County, NC

My grandmother was a teacher. Both of my parents were college professors. My sister was a math teacher at Hampton Institute. I was destined to be one, too. But that's not what I wanted to do. I have loved aircraft all my life. My wife said I loved flying more than I loved her. This is something I would never admit.

However, aircraft was a very close second.

During World War II, I lived out my dream, even though combat was no fun. I was a member of the Tuskegee Airmen, sometimes called "Red Tail Angels." When I got back to the States, I helped close down the air base, then went through RIF (reduction in force). I tried working for the Veterans Administration. I tried the US Post Office, but I didn't like paperwork, so I went down to Maxwell Field and re-enlisted and was soon back in the pilot's seat.

After serving in Korea and Vietnam, I continued flying for most of my 30 years in service. I logged more "bootleg time" than official time (8000 civilian hours vs. 1200 military)

I was also a member of the "three-minute egg club." That's when you land with less than three minutes worth of fuel. Once, I landed with just enough to get off the runway and into the taxiway before the motor died.

But my last eight years, I ended up teaching aircraft systems at Seymour Johnson Air Force Base in Goldsboro, North Carolina, and at Plattsburgh Air Force Base in New York.

After all, I *did* enjoy it.

Unlikely Friendships
by
Alex Patterson
Cabarrus County, NC

Before and immediately after the attack on Pearl Harbor, the US Army was having maneuvers in our area, and, on weekends, many of the soldiers stationed at Camp Sutton in Monroe would come to Concord.

One Saturday evening in December, St. James Lutheran Church was entertaining the 180th Field Artillery Band with supper, after which the host asked for volunteers who could put up a soldier that night. "First, we will start with a group of eight boys who pal around together. Is there anyone here who could sleep eight?"

There was a chuckle or two, but then Mother and Dad held up their hands. Wow! This caused a good-humored commotion. What they didn't know was that our home had three bedrooms for our family of six and a sleeping porch with four double beds that the eight soldiers could use.

Professional musicians, they played a variety of instruments (accordion, violin, piano, saxophone, trombone). That night in our living room, they gathered with our family for a music session. Mother and Russell Buchanan took turns playing the piano, Daddy played the flute and Dominic Magazzu (a burly Italian) picked up our violin and joined in. A high school student then, I played the trumpet, while the other band members and my siblings Betsy, Mary Kay and Jimmy sang Christmas carols.

At breakfast the next morning, we ate in two shifts, soldiers first. An excellent cook, Mother had resources from her former home in Mount Pleasant, Green Hills Dairy Farm. The menu was country ham and eggs, with plenty of hot biscuits, butter, jelly, jam and coffee. Since all of these boys were from Massachusetts, they had to be introduced to grits, Southern style, with "red eye" gravy. It was a hit.

This was the beginning of many new friendships. They were invited back "any time." Dad and Dominic Magazzu corresponded during the war, while Dominic was in Australia, New Caledonia, Guadalcanal and the Fiji Islands.

Dominic suffered an attack of jaundice, was sent to a hospital on the American West Coast, and, upon his recovery, was given a medical discharge. On his way home to Boston, he first stopped by Concord to see his new-found friends at a home away from home.

After the war in Europe was over, our church became involved with a relief program established by the Lutheran World Action Committee for countries which had suffered extreme hardships.

Mother and Dad packed a box of clothing, including an outgrown heavy wool suit, like new. Dad didn't tell us that he had stuffed a note with his return address into a coat pocket. It found a new friend in Finland: Esko Lipponen.

Time passed, then Dad received a letter from Finland, plus Christmas cards and photographs of Esko's family. Later on, Christmas presents were exchanged.

We followed Esko's life through high school and the University of Helsinki, where he learned to speak five foreign languages and received an MA in political science.

Our friend joined Finland's Foreign Service after graduating and had been assigned to the Embassy of Finland in several world capitals: China, Switzerland, Germany. He even had cocktails with Khrushehev in Russia. In 1966, he was sent to New York on a special mission for his country to the United Nations.

When he arrived in New York, he called Dad, and

arrangements were made for a visit to Concord. I was married by then, so Jane and I would show him around town and take him to the country club to introduce him to friends. My sisters and our children would help entertain him, too.

On a Friday, a pen pal friendship of almost 20 years became a *personal* friendship when Finish Foreign Service Representative Esko Lipponen stepped off the plane at Douglas Municipal Airport.

A Wounded Future
by
Ralph S. Ross
Union /Mecklenburg Counties NC

In the fall of '46, when I was released from the Veterans Hospital in Columbia, you couldn't buy a job. The boys who earned their 65 points and got out before the war was over got the first jobs. The ones who came home at the end of the war got their old jobs back. But by the fall of 1946, there was no work available, not for someone disabled.

After being wounded in the left knee in Okinawa, I had spent time in many a hospital, but, when I got to Columbia and saw all those Spanish-American and World War I vets, I knew that the medical help was next to nothing.

I would have used the GI Bill to get into an agricultural college, but although I was one of 17 graduates from Bain School in Mint Hill, I had none of the prerequisites for college.

A fellow I played basketball against at Sharon School saw me getting off a bus with crutches and got me into the 52-20 Club. All I had to do was sign a paper saying that I would work if I could get a job and I could draw $20 a week for 52 weeks if I didn't get employment. I got it for 27 weeks.

Had it not been for Public Law #16, I would not have found employment. The law was passed to help the disabled. A company would get a subsidy to train and employ someone with a disability. Many corporations took advantage of that to get cheap labor. By the time I got into the program, the fields I was most interested in were filled up. I really wanted to be an electrician.

At first, I was making $80 a month and had bought a diamond on credit for my girl, Betty Forbis. Then I broke my leg again and had to go back into a hospital. I was afraid I wouldn't be able to finish paying for the diamond. I did, but it was tough.

300

And I told Betty, "I want our children to have all the love you can give. I'll work day and night."

First I was a sales rep for Ticket-a-Graph, a payroll system for textile mills. My boss had a heart attack and they went to another system, so I was out of a job. Next, I went into the printing and advertising business, but I couldn't stand on my feet all day, so I became a sales rep for Johnson's Wax and then for the Janitor Supply and Service Corporation. I had a management position there when it was bought out by a national conglomerate.

I was also a supervisor for a building maintenance service, which cleaned offices at night. I trained other sales reps, and I became the state commander for the Veterans of Foreign Wars (VFW).

By the time I developed a heart condition in 1989 and had to slow down, I was an independent manufacturer's rep.

Until then, I always stayed employed, and we raised a family. Betty and I had four kids and got them educated. We were never called by a teacher and they all went to college.

How was my life affected by the war? I lost faith in my ability. It set me back, but there's no way to value how much.

Yet, by the grace of God, we survived the turmoil. We enjoyed the fulfillment of living long and useful lives with our families, thanks to the sacrifices of the teenagers who gave *their* lives for our freedoms.

A Hand-Picked Substitute
by
Mozell Page Cobb
Caswell/Alamance Counties, NC

While my husband, Melvin, was overseas, our one-year-old daughter, Carol, and I were staying with my brother and sister-in-law in the Pagetown community of Caswell County. Our cute little brown-haired baby was just beginning to walk.

One day in December, 1944, I noticed that the mailman had stopped at our mailbox on the road. He just stood there until he saw me coming out the door, and then he climbed back in his car and pulled off.

When I got the mail, I opened a telegram for me from the Army. Pvt. Melvin Wilson Baker—my Melvin—had been killed in action on December 2 in Germany! I started screaming, and Minnie Mae Wilson, a neighbor, came running outside. That telegram, not even hand-delivered, was telling me that my life would never be the same!

How can I stand this? I wondered. Left alone with a little baby. I felt like my world had come to an end that day.

Both my parents were already gone. My father had died when I was 10; my mother, when I was 17. As soon as I turned 18, I went to work at the McEwen Mill in Burlington. Melvin worked in another mill in town, but I met him because his uncle had married my cousin, and he was living with them. He was neat and good looking with dark eyes—a really likeable man.

We had courted awhile and then, in August, 1942, were married in a preacher's home in Burlington. At first, we got a room in a boarding house in Burlington. When I got pregnant, we moved to my brother's home in Pagetown. Melvin went into the service April 24, 1944.

Melvin came home one time after that, and my cousin Lila Baker and I took Carol on an old dirty train down to Fort McClellan, Alabama to visit him once at the base where he was training.

My husband had only six weeks training before they sent him to the front line. Almost all the soldiers from his infantry unit got killed. He must have assumed that would happen. I didn't know it at the time, but, on his last trip home, he told my cousin's husband, "I want y'all to look after Mozell, because I won't be back." He told a neighbor, Charlie Cobb, who was his best friend, the same thing.

The telegram said a letter would follow. His commanding officer from B Company the 26th Infantry Division soon wrote that, although he was prohibited from discussing details of Melvin's death, he wanted to assure me that my husband had "died as a soldier, in the manner he would wish, fighting on the field of battle against the enemies of our country." Then he added something comforting: "He was killed immediately with no suffering or lingering pain."

Much later, near the end of August, the War Department notified me that he had been buried in a military cemetery in Henri Chapelle, Belgium, seven miles southwest of Aachen, Germany.

I knew I had to put aside all those sad and bad feelings and think of the good times we had had together. I was lucky to have Carol, a part of him. We both loved her so much. Death can take away your loved ones. But, thank the Lord, it can't take away your memories.

My brother, Roy Page, told me not to move away. "We will

302

help you build a house," he said.

But I didn't have any land.

Roy added, "I'll give you the land to build on."

He ordered the lumber and asked Jim Massey (a local fellow who used to live with us when I was young) to do the carpentry work. Roy's wife, Lucy, kept Carol so I could help Jim. One day, the neighbors all came to assist us.

I only had $100 from the sale of Melvin's old car. My checks had stopped when Melvin got killed. I didn't get any money until all the papers were finished, which was about July. Jim only charged me $100 for what he had done. Roy signed the note for the lumber, and I paid it when I got my money. My new house had only two rooms and a front porch, but boy was I happy! I had a home of my own.

Charlie Cobb was kind before and after Melvin's death. He treated Carol just like his own child. He would take her to the store and buy her candy. She liked him a lot and was real happy to be with him.

I re-read one of Melvin's last letters. He had said, "You are young, and if I don't make it back home, I know you will marry again. I want you to marry someone who will love you and Carol both. I hope you will marry Charlie."

And so I got to going with the man Melvin asked to "look after" me. He would take me and Carol to the movies and other places. Within two or three years, I married my tall, blue-eyed friend, Charlie.

Later, he and I had another daughter, Joann, and as soon as she was old enough, she and Carol were always playing together and with their dad.

Carol says that, "If he ever showed partiality to either of us, it was to me."

Melvin chose a good man, husband and daddy.

WAR DEPARTMENT

I Married a Kraut
by
Robert Brownlee Welsh
Author of *Two Foes to Fight*
Mecklenburg County, NC

In 1999, I was at an "I" Company convention at Myrtle Beach, giving a short resume of my book, *Two Foes To Fight*, with the wrap-up being the statement, "After killing all those Krauts, I ended up marrying one, and there is the result sitting right over there." I pointed to George, our third child, who had driven over from Orangeburg for the reunion.

It's true. Katherine, Robert, Jr. and George would not be here, if it weren't for Adolph Hitler. Each one is special in his or her own way to Marlis and me, and we wouldn't want finer children.

Marlis was bombed out of Hamburg to live in Bavaria, and at war's end I was with the Cavalry Squadron of the 4th Armored Division stationed in Regensberg. Marie-Luise (Marlis) Osmers, and her sister, Karla, could speak excellent English, so the German employment board had assigned them to work in the American Library of Special Services there.

Being the avid reader that I am, I, of course, was checking out library books, but it didn't take long for me to begin checking out Marlis, a cute culmination of both Nancy and Estelle, my former American girlfriends. Blonde and blue-eyed like Nancy, with a figure like Estelle's, Marlis had the best attributes of all my other dates and girlfriends—and she wasn't 5000 miles away. Those other two never had to write any "Dear John" letters to me, since I never became either of their "Johns."

As soon as I met Marlis I asked her for a date, and she said she got off at eight. She must have had some misgivings about me, for at 7:59 as I was approaching the library, there she was coming down the broad staircase on the other side, leaving early and not looking around.

I intercepted her to walk her home just as huge lazy snow-flakes started filtering through the lamplight. I kissed her on the church steps.

Later that month, she refused to see me and locked herself in the apartment she shared with her sister. I don't remember what the lack of chemistry was all about, but I just broke that heavy oak door down. Just to prove a point: that she would never get along without me.

We did date a few more times before our squadron was deployed to Cham, near Czechoslovakia. We were to conduct constabulary operations, patrolling the border to prevent sabotage. Coincidentally, the library was also moved there and sent a bookmobile to troops stationed in outlying villages. Karla Osmers, who, at 17, was two years younger than Marlis, came with the bookmobile. Marlis was conveniently in the library.

There was a ski slope along the border where we were patrolling, and all the units convened every weekend for snow fun. Our ski lift was the four-wheel-drive Jeep, and our instructors were some of the GIs' girls, who tried to tell us what to do.

Marlis already knew how to ski. I "acquired" the equipment from each village by ordering the mayors to assemble it for us.

We ended up using the skis like sleds, just speeding straight down the hill, rolling over to stop. (Later, we became ski bums in America, being on the Charlotte Ski Bees race team. Marlis won top prize in the nine-state USA Ski Association's giant slalom event.)

My mother sent my ice skates, and we enjoyed ice skating on a pond. Marlis was very musical, too. She could play a violin and a recorder, but I never heard her play them. Through Marlis, I later acquired an interest in the culture of Old World philosophy and symphonic music.

Around Thanksgiving of 1945, my Aunt Aleta came in to visit from the United Nations Relief & Rehabilitation Administration (UNRRA), stationed in Yugoslavia. Aleta Brownlee was the first in my family to meet my Hitler Youth girlfriend.

As Troop Commander, I'd go on patrol every day. As a Special Court Martial Defense Counsel, I also had to travel around to collect depositions, but I saw Marlis every night.

Marriage to German Nationals was finally permitted in 1946, and, by that time, I was in Landshut with Operation Paper Clip, the unit responsible for secretly obtaining scientists for the US rocket program.

I had met Vater Osmers at his apartment in Hamburg on one of my trips all over Germany. I had a bottle of bourbon, and he had a loaf of grain-speckled black bread. In a few minutes, we were able to converse, and I supposed he gave me permission to marry Marlis.

I heard later he had told me that he was "paying no other reparations." He had been a cavalry officer in both world wars.

We were married in the Landshut Lutheran Church with Marlis's father giving her away. Her mother and Karla, the bridesmaid, my aunt Aleta representing my family, and Major Becker, my

305

best man, were present.

Only local servicemen were invited (if they could get off duty), so I was really surprised to see the whole church packed with townspeople when Major Becker and I walked in. Marlis came down the aisle on her father's arm, wearing a gown of parachute silk and carrying a bouquet of chrysanthemums.

MPs kept the crowd back as we came out to get into a flower-bedecked truck and parade through the streets before going to the reception at the officers club.

Bob and Marlis Welsh on their wedding day. Landshut, Germany. June 14, 1947.

War is strange for soldiers of both sides. We are brainwashed to kill, and then when it's over we get along fine.

Is the fact that I wanted to marry Marlis because I loved her and she was not 5000 miles away? Or is there a human side, forgiving each other in spite of the folly of our leaders?

I didn't marry a German to prove a point, unless it was that we needed each other.

Index

Betsy Ann Shepherd (now Ancrum) fastens a Red Cross pin on the lapel of US Senator, James F. Byrnes, assisted by another member of the Junior Red Cross, Jan Norman (now Stedman). The Byrnes' home, Spartanburg, SC. Circa 1942. A *Spartanburg Herald* photo.

ORDER NOW FROM ABB!

True-experience stories and anecdotes, autographed:

__copies *World War II - Hometown and Home Front Heroes*
    Life-experience stories from the Carolina's Piedmont
    77 authors and 23 contributors Vintage photos and Index
    2003. 131 stories. 320 pp. ISBN:1-893597-06-7
    Paperback @ $17.95 $_____

__copies *The Great Depression: How We Coped, Worked and*
    Played Life-experience stories from the Carolina's Piedmont
    65 authors Illustrated by Lexie Little Hill. Vintage photos and Index
    2001. 131 stories. 288 pp. ISBN:1-893597-04-0
    3rd printing 2002. Paperback @ $15.95 $_____

__copies *Gray-Haired Grins & Giggles*
    Guess what - Grandy & Grammy have a sense of humor, too!
    True tales from 45 authors. Cartoons by Loyd Dillon
    1995. 160 tales. 128 pp. ISBN:0-9640606-3-9
    4th printing 1996. Paperback @ $12.95 $_____

__copies *Gray-Haired Grins & Giggles* LARGE PRINT
    With the seal of approval of N.A.V.H.:
    1998. ISBN:0-9640606-7-1 Paperback @ $13.95 $_____

__copies *World War II: It Changed Us Forever*
    From the battlefront to the homefront and places in between
    33 authors tell it like it was! Vintage photos and Index
    1994. 93 stories. 140 pp. ISBN:0-9640606-0-4
    3rd printing 2001. Paperback @ $12.95 $_____

Bigger's guide to recording memoirs:

__copies *Recalling Your Memories on Paper, Tape or Videotape*
    Self-help guide to preserving memoirs & photos. Also, how
    to assist relatives. Excerpts from seniors' family booklets.
    1996. Vintage photos 160 pp. ISBN:0-9640606-4-7
    2nd printing 2002 (revised). Paperback @ $13.95 $_____

Bigger's humor books of regional one-liners:

__copies *You Can Tell You're a Charlottean If...*
    244 ways that people from Charlotte, NC differ from the
    rest of the world. Margaret Bigger & Betsy Webb
    1998. 96 pp. ISBN:0-9640606-6-3
    Cartoons by Loyd Dillon Paperback @ $7.95 $_____

__copies *You Know You're In Charlotte If...*
    90 contributors show the uniqueness of Charlotte
    + cute & clever business names & license plates
    Charlotte celebrities & Local Sports History Quiz.
    2000. 96 pp. ISBN 1-893597-03-2
    Cartoons by Loyd Dillon Paperback @ $7.95 $_____

Please complete the other side of this order form.